This book is about the role that psychological impairment
should play in a theory of criminal liability. Criminal guilt in
the Anglo-American legal tradition requires both that the
defendant committed some proscribed act and that he did
so with a certain attitude such as intent, knowledge, or recklessness. The second requirement corresponds to the intuitive idea that people should not be punished for something
they did not do "on purpose" or if they "did not realize what
they were doing." Although intuitive, this underlying idea
can be highly controversial in theory and in practice, espe-
cially in cases involving the insanity defense.

This important new book addresses the conceptual and
moral foundations of these issues. Unlike many previous
works in this area, it addresses the automatism and insanity
defenses by examining the types of functional impairment
that typical candidates for these defenses actually suffer.
What emerges is a much wider conceptual framework that
allows us to understand the significance of psychological
states and processes for the attribution of criminal responsibility in a manner that is logically coherent, morally defensible, and consistent with research in psychopathology.

The book will be of particular interest to legal theorists and
practicing lawyers, philosophers of law, psychologists, and
criminologists.

Automatism, insanity, and the psychology of criminal responsibility

Cambridge Studies in Philosophy and Law

GENERAL EDITOR: JULES COLEMAN (YALE LAW SCHOOL)

ADVISORY BOARD

David Gauthier (University of Pittsburgh)
David Lyons (Cornell University)
Richard Posner (Judge in the Seventh Circuit Court of Appeals, Chicago)
Martin Shapiro (University of California, Berkeley)

This exciting new series will reflect and foster the most original research currently taking place in the study of law and legal theory by publishing the most adventurous monographs in the field as well as rigorously edited collections of essays. It will be a specific aim of the series to traverse the boundaries between disciplines and to form bridges between traditional studies of law and many other areas of the human sciences. Books in the series will be of interest not only to philosophers and legal theorists but also to political scientists, sociologists, economists, psychologists, and criminologists.

Other books in the series

Jeffrie G. Murphy and Jean Hampton: *Forgiveness and mercy*
Stephen R. Munzer: *A theory of property*
R.G. Frey and Christopher W. Morris (eds.): *Liability and responsibility: Essays in law and morals*

Automatism, insanity, and the psychology of criminal responsibility

A philosophical inquiry

ROBERT F. SCHOPP

COLLEGE OF LAW, UNIVERSITY OF NEBRASKA-LINCOLN

The right of the
University of Cambridge
to print and sell
all manner of books
was granted by
Henry VIII in 1534.
The University has printed
and published continuously
since 1584.

CAMBRIDGE UNIVERSITY PRESS

CAMBRIDGE

NEW YORK   PORT CHESTER   MELBOURNE   SYDNEY

CAMBRIDGE UNIVERSITY PRESS
Cambridge, New York, Melbourne, Madrid, Cape Town, Singapore, São Paulo

Cambridge University Press
The Edinburgh Building, Cambridge CB2 8RU, UK

Published in the United States of America by Cambridge University Press, New York

www.cambridge.org
Information on this title: www.cambridge.org/9780521401500

First published 1991
This digitally printed version 2008

A catalogue record for this publication is available from the British Library

Library of Congress Cataloguing in Publication data
Schopp, Robert F.
Automatism, insanity, and the psychology of criminal
responsibility: a philosophical inquiry / Robert F. Schopp.
p.   cm.–(Cambridge studies in philosophy and law)
Includes index.
ISBN 0-521-40150-X
1. Insanity–Jurisprudence. 2. Criminal liability–Psychological
aspects. 3. Automatism. I. Title. II. Series.
K5077.S36   1991
345′.04 – dc20
[342.54]   90–27604
                                                                CIP

ISBN 978-0-521-40150-0 hardback
ISBN 978-0-521-06133-9 paperback

For those who show us how to live:
Frank C. Schopp
Winifred Schopp

Contents

Contents

Preface and acknowledgments

In the Anglo-American tradition of criminal law, the state cannot convict and punish people for serious offenses merely because they have performed proscribed conduct. Legal guilt requires both that the defendant engaged in illegal behavior and that certain psychological requirements were fulfilled. Traditionally, these requirements have been very difficult to describe and justify. Consequently, they have been highly controversial, both in theory and in application.

This book clarifies and justifies the psychological components of criminal responsibility. It adopts two methodological premises that differentiate it from many prior investigations of these issues. First, it directs primary attention toward the structure of offenses. Historically, many writers have concentrated on the insanity defense, either as an independent concern or as the central piece of the larger puzzle involving criminal responsibility. The book treats the structure of offense elements as the core of the problem, addressing the insanity defense as an ancillary aspect of the broader system of offense elements and defenses. Second, to the extent that psychopathology undermines attributions of criminal responsibility, the book looks to the available information regarding the nature of the dysfunction involved in that pathology in order to advance the analysis of responsibility.

This book is based on a doctoral dissertation submitted to the Department of Philosophy at The University of Arizona. Several individuals made diverse and valuable contributions

ix

to that dissertation. I am particularly indebted to Joel Feinberg, who contributed both to the dissertation itself and to the educational preparation that preceded it through his direction, teaching, writing, and guidance. David Wexler helped me appreciate the complexities of the law, the myriad of interactions that occur both within the law and at its intersection with other fields, and the importance of approaching interdisciplinary studies with careful attention to the potential contributions and limitations of each discipline. Allen Buchanan, Bruce Sales, and Holly Smith each contributed substantially both to this project and to my preparation for it.

I am also grateful to Jules Coleman, who introduced me to the formal study of moral and legal philosophy and reassured me through example that one can do serious work without taking it too seriously. Michael Quattrocchi accompanied me in our first tentative attempts to explore what I now think of as the philosophy of law and clinical psychology, although neither of us realized at the time that this was what we were doing. Perhaps the greatest credit should go to Mary, Bill, and those they represent for providing the impetus sufficient to move even Mike and me. Unfortunately, it seems unlikely that they will recognize their contributions or benefit from them. Ed O'Dowd has participated in a seemingly endless series of prolonged conversations about many topics relevant to this book. Let us hope that it draws primarily on the conversations during which we made some progress. I am also grateful for helpful comments made by two anonymous reviewers from Cambridge University Press and for Ronald Cohen's editorial skills.

Finally, Joel Feinberg's prominent influence on this undertaking requires one kind word for Josiah S. Carberry. Although he contributed nothing to this project, neither did he detract from it. For some, perhaps, this is the kindest word that honesty will allow or history will record.

ROBERT F. SCHOPP
Lincoln, Nebraska

Note to the reader on language

Previous drafts of this book were written in gender-neutral language. Unfortunately, the results were awkward, distracting, and sometimes confusing because the book contains numerous real or hypothetical actors illustrating a variety of concepts and situations. In order to avoid detracting from the substantive argument, I have reverted to the traditional practice of using male pronouns and possessive adjectives when making general statements. Identifiable actors are referred to according to their proper gender. My aim is to present the arguments clearly to readers without offending them.

Chapter 1

Introduction

The Anglo-American law has traditionally defined criminal offenses as requiring both an *actus reus* and a *mens rea*. The state must prove both types of elements in order to secure a conviction. The *actus reus* is usually described as the criminal act or the physical part of the offense, whereas the *mens rea* defines the required state of mind or the mental part. Various offenses have required mental states such as intent, recklessness, negligence, depraved mind, malice aforethought, and many others. Unfortunately, it has proven extremely difficult to establish either the precise meaning of these terms or the relationships among them. Additionally, many offenses are not easily divisible into physical and mental parts.

The American Law Institute's Model Penal Code (MPC) avoids some of the traditional problems by substituting a relatively simplified set of terms and requirements for offense definitions.[1] The MPC eschews the traditional terminology of *actus reus* and *mens rea* in favor of a system of objective offense elements and culpability requirements.[2] The basic

1 American Law Institute, Model Penal Code, and Commentaries sec. 2.01, 2.02 (official draft and revised comments, 1985).
2 *Id.* at sec. 1.13(9). The MPC includes the absence of excuse or justification in the list of offense elements. Paul Robinson makes the distinction between objective criteria and culpability requirements, and he argues that the absence of justification and excuse should not be included among the offense elements. I will adopt Robinson's approach on these issues throughout this book. *See* P.H. Robinson, Criminal Law Defenses sec. 11(a) (St. Paul, MN: West Pub. Co., 1984).

principles of the MPC are widely accepted as representative of dominant trends in mainstream American law. Many states have incorporated these principles into their criminal codes since the MPC was officially recommended by the American Law Institute in 1962.[3]

In order to secure a conviction in a criminal trial under the MPC, the prosecution must prove all elements in the definition of the offense.[4] The objective elements include the conduct required for the offense as well as the circumstances and results of that conduct.[5] That conduct must include a voluntary act as that phrase is defined in the MPC.[6] With the exception of a few strict liability offenses, the MPC includes a culpability requirement for each material element of the offense. The state satisfies its burden to prove this culpability requirement only if it establishes that the defendant acted purposely, knowingly, recklessly, or negligently regarding each material element of the offense.[7]

When the state satisfies the burden of proving all offense elements including both the voluntary act and culpability requirements, the defendant may avoid liability by establishing a general defense. Some general defenses are based on extrinsic policy considerations, whereas others demonstrate that the defendant was not morally responsible for his actions and hence not appropriately subject to criminal liability.[8]

---

3 Greenawalt, *The Perplexing Borders of Justification and Excuse*, 84 Colum. L. Rev. 1897, 1897n2 (1984); W. LaFave and A.W. Scott, Jr., Substantive Criminal Law sec. 1.1(b) (St. Paul, MN: West Pub. Co., 1986). I will treat the MPC as representative of American law throughout this book. General terms such as "law" or "legal" will refer to the MPC and to criminal codes patterned after the MPC unless otherwise specified.

4 MPC, *supra* note 1, at sec. 1.12(1).

5 *Id.* at sec. 1.13(9); Robinson, *supra* note 2, at sec. 11(a).

6 *Id.* at sec. 2.01.

7 *Id.* at sec. 2.02. According to section 1.13(10) of the MPC, material elements of an offense are those elements that do not relate exclusively to the statute of limitations, jurisdiction, venue, or other matters unconnected to the harm or evil of the offense or the existence of a justification. This book will address only material offense elements.

8 Robinson, *supra* note 2, at sec. 21, 25 (1984). *See infra*, chapter 1.2 for further discussion of defenses.

Introduction

The psychological states and processes of the defendant are relevant to the voluntary act and culpability requirements, as well as to certain general defenses. Although these provisions directly address the psychological states and processes of the defendant, the exact nature of these offense requirements and defenses, the relationships among them, and the significance of various forms of psychopathology for them remain unclear. Certain defenses, such as the insanity defense and automatism, are relevant to criminal liability, yet the theoretical foundation of these defenses in the conceptual structure of offense elements and general defenses remains controversial. For example, automatism has been accepted as a defense in the United States and Britain, but it has been interpreted in various cases as relevant to the voluntary act provision, the culpability requirement, or the insanity defense.[9] One commentator has rejected all three of these options, recommending a separate general defense of "impaired consciousness."[10]

The history of the insanity defense reveals a similar picture of theoretical uncertainty. Although the defense is long established, the courts and legislatures continue the search for a satisfactory standard of exculpation.[11] Theorists also continue to debate the status of the insanity defense in the broader system of criminal liability. Some interpret it as a special defense, based on considerations uniquely appropriate to the mentally ill, whereas others argue that it is merely a special application of the common excusing conditions such as ignorance or coercion.[12]

9   LaFave and Scott, *supra* note 3, at sec. 4.9. *See infra*, chapter 3.
10 Robinson, *supra* note 2, at sec. 172.
11 S.J. Brakel, J. Parry, and B.A. Weiner, The Mentally Disabled and the Law 707–19 (Chicago, American Bar Foundation, 3d ed. 1985); Callahan, Mayer, and Steadman, *Insanity Defense Reforms in the United States – Post-Hinckley*, 11 Mental and Physical Disabilities L. Rep. 54 (1987); LaFave and Scott, *supra* note 3, at sec. 4.2, 4.3. *See infra*, chapter 2.1.
12 For examples of writers who have the taken former position see: H. Fingarette, The Meaning of Criminal Insanity (Berkeley: Univ. of Calif. Press, 1972); M. Moore, Law and Psychiatry 217–45 (1984); Morse, *Excusing the Crazy: The Insanity Defense Reconsidered*, 58 S. Cal. L. Rev.

This book will examine the offense elements and general defenses that directly address the psychological states and processes of the defendant. It will advance a conceptual framework for the structure of these offense elements, and it will contend that this framework clarifies the nature of these requirements, the appropriate interpretation of certain general defenses, and the relationships among these provisions. This framework supports the contention that these provisions can be understood in a manner that is internally consistent and morally defensible. As an initial step in this process, the remainder of this chapter will examine the MPC's system of offense elements and describe a framework for categorizing defenses that involve the psychological processes of the defendant.

1.1 MPC OFFENSE ELEMENTS

The conduct that renders an actor liable for a criminal offense must include either a voluntary act, or a voluntary omission of an act that the defendant has a legal duty to perform and is physically capable of performing.[13] The MPC defines an act as a bodily movement without regard for the circumstances, consequences, or internal processes related to that movement.[14]

The MPC follows in the tradition of Aristotle in that it initially defines voluntariness by exclusion.[15] According to the MPC, bodily movements that occur as a result of reflex or convulsion, or during sleep, unconsciousness, or hypnosis are not voluntary. Generally, acts are not voluntary unless they are the product of the effort or determination of the

---

777 (1985). The latter position has been defended by Goldstein and Katz, *Abolish the Insanity Defense – Why Not?*, 72 Yale L. J. 853 (1963) and, initially, by J. Feinberg, Doing and Deserving 272–92 (Princeton: Princeton Univ. Press, 1970).

13 MPC, *supra* note 1, at 2.01.

14 *Id.* at sec. 1.13(2); LaFave and Scott, *supra* note 3, at sec. 3.2(a).

15 Aristotle, Nichomachean Ethics 53–59, 1109b L.30–1111b L.4 (T. Irwin trans., Indianapolis: Hackett Pub. Co., 1985).

4

actor.[16] Commentators have described the voluntariness requirement as one that excludes acts that are not the product
of the actor's will or conscious volition.[17] This conception of
voluntariness reflects the traditional notion of voluntary conduct as an "external manifestation of the actor's will." It is
intended to differentiate movement due to reflex or convulsion from conduct that is within the actor's control in the
sense that ordinary human conduct is under control. The
voluntary act provision requires an inquiry into the mental
states of the actor, and constitutes a preliminary requirement
of culpability.[18]

The phrase "ordinary human conduct" bears closer examination. As used in the comments to the MPC, such conduct is contrasted with reflexes or convulsion. If the term
"ordinary" is interpreted broadly, seizures, reflexes, or convulsions are ordinary human movements. Eye blinks and
heart beats, for example, are perfectly ordinary bodily movements in the statistical sense of "ordinary." Yet the MPC
conception of a voluntary act apparently should not be interpreted to include either eye blinks or heart beats as they
occur under usual conditions. In order to be useful and consistent with the examples given in the MPC, "ordinary human conduct" must be understood as activity that is subject
to direction by the actor's effort, determination, or will in the
manner that conscious, intentional movement is related to
these faculties in the unimpaired person.

On this interpretation, the term "ordinary" is in some manner a normative one and not merely statistical. An act that is
voluntary in the sense that ordinary human activity is voluntary must be the kind of action that we would usually consider
as appropriate grounds for evaluating the blameworthiness
or praiseworthiness of the actor. This cannot be the criterion

16 MPC, *supra* note 1, at sec. 2.01.
17 H.L.A. Hart, Punishment and Responsibility 105 (1968); H. Packer,
    The Limits of the Criminal Sanction 76 (Stanford: Stanford Univ. Press,
    1968).
18 MPC, *supra* note 1, at sec. 2.01 and comments at 215–21. This inter-
    pretation will be examined more closely in chapter 4.

of voluntariness, however, because voluntariness serves as one necessary condition for culpability. If acts were categorized as voluntary on the basis of their being of the type for which the actor is appropriately held liable, then voluntariness would be rendered vacuous as a necessary condition for liability. That is, the voluntary act requirement would reduce to the claim that an actor can be held liable only if his conduct includes an act of the type for which he can be held liable. In order to avoid rendering the voluntary act requirement trivial, one needs a conception of voluntariness that takes the form of a descriptive account of the appropriate relationship between bodily movements and mental processes and that does not appeal to considerations of culpability. This issue will be addressed again in Chapters 4 and 5.

It is important to recognize that this voluntary act requirement applies a rather narrow conception of voluntariness. Joel Feinberg has advanced a much more comprehensive account of voluntariness as a relationship among an individual's rational capacities, his action, and his environment. According to this conception of voluntariness, an act is fully voluntary when it is a product of the actor's rational capacities without undue ignorance or impairment on the part of the actor or excessive pressure from the environment. Voluntariness, on this account, is a matter of degree, and it is important to determine whether a particular act was voluntary enough for specific purposes.[19]

The conception of voluntariness contained in the MPC's voluntary act requirement, in contrast to Feinberg's account, is a threshold concept. The conduct that constitutes the offense must include a voluntary act. If it does, the requirement is met, and if it does not, there is no offense (putting omissions aside). Voluntariness, on Feinberg's comprehensive account, is reduced by undue ignorance, impairment, or pressure because it describes a relationship among the actor's act, his psychological processes and his environment.[20]

19   J. Feinberg, Harm to Self 117–24 (New York: Oxford Univ. Press, 1986).
20   *See generally, id.* at 143–374.

The limited MPC conception of a voluntary act addresses a much more narrow relationship between the actor's physical movements and a rather vaguely defined subset of his psychological processes. Although it is not clear exactly what this relationship involves, many factors that would impair voluntariness on Feinberg's account are not relevant to the MPC's voluntary act requirement. For example, an individual who acted in response to a threat from another person or on the basis of an important mistake of fact would not have acted in a fully voluntary manner on Feinberg's interpretation, although he would clearly satisfy the MPC's voluntary act requirement. Chapter 4 will include an account of the relationship between bodily movement and the actor's psychological processes that is required by the MPC's voluntary act provision. Throughout this book, the term "voluntary" will be used in the narrow sense in which it is employed by the MPC unless the more comprehensive use is specified.

A voluntary act is necessary but not sufficient for criminal liability. In addition, the actor must meet the culpability requirement by acting with the specified psychological attitude (purposely, knowingly, recklessly or negligently) regarding each material offense element.[21] Although the culpability requirement is expressed in terms of specified psychological states and labeled "culpability," both the culpability and voluntary act requirements involve examination of the psychological processes of the actor and evaluation of the relationship between those processes and other offense elements. In addition, both requirements are relevant to the blameworthiness of the actor. Yet, these two provisions do not merely restate the same requirements, as the following example illustrates.

A person commits murder if he purposely or knowingly causes the death of another human being.[22] By virtue of the voluntary act requirement, the conduct that caused the death must include a voluntary act. If A were driving a car in the

---

21 MPC, *supra* note 1, at sec. 2.02.
22 *Id.* at sec. 210.1, 210.2.

ordinary sense of "driving" when he hit and killed B, this requirement would be met, but if A were unconscious behind the wheel due to an unanticipated convulsion, there would be no voluntary act. The culpability requirement would be met if A hit and killed B purposely (for the conscious object of killing B) or knowingly (aware that it is practically certain that B's death will result whether A wants B's death to occur or not).

Although the MPC requires both a voluntary act and the appropriate level of culpability in order to establish criminal liability for an offense, the relationship between the two requirements is not clear. One can argue with some confidence that voluntariness does not entail culpability. A may be driving carefully and competently when B darts out from between two cars in such a way that A is not even aware of B until A hits B. In such a case, A would have engaged in voluntary conduct (driving) that caused the death of B, but the conduct would not constitute homicide because A did not act with any culpable mental state toward B's death. That is, A drove voluntarily, but A did not kill purposely, knowingly, recklessly, or negligently. Thus, A did not kill voluntarily in Feinberg's more comprehensive sense in which voluntariness is defeated by ignorance or mistake. In the terms employed by the MPC, however, A's killing B met the voluntary act requirement, but it did not satisfy the culpability provision.

The converse relationship is more troublesome. H.L.A. Hart suggests that satisfaction of the culpability requirement entails voluntariness. Hart argues that only severe psychopathology can render an act involuntary, and such pathology will prevent culpability. Hence, any condition that negates the voluntariness requirement will also negate the culpability condition.[23]

Hart's claim may be accurate when one uses "voluntary"

23 Hart, *supra* note 17, at 107. I use the term "suggests" here because Hart speaks of most cases, not all. The context indicates, however, that he intends his claim to apply to all cases except strict liability ones.

8

in the broad sense in which Feinberg uses the term, but it does not hold for the narrow MPC sense of "voluntary." If Hart's claim were accurate, then voluntariness would be a necessary condition for fulfilling the culpability requirement, and therefore, fulfilling the culpability requirement would be a sufficient condition for voluntariness. On this account, inquiry into the voluntariness condition is superfluous in all but strict liability cases. The court can simply address the culpability element. If it is satisfied – and satisfaction of culpability entails voluntariness – then the voluntariness requirement must be met. If the culpability element is not present, then the defendant is not guilty regardless of voluntariness.

This analysis is problematic, however, in that voluntariness and culpability are presented in the MPC as separate requirements that must each be proven by the state. Furthermore, defenses that defeat an ascription of voluntariness are sometimes allowed by the courts in cases in which the defendants have acted in an organized, and apparently goal-directed, manner that would usually indicate that they acted purposefully. In one case, for example, the defendant called the victim to the window, hit him with a mallet, and threw him from a window.[24] The defendant apparently performed this series of actions for the purpose of injuring the victim, yet the defendant was acquitted on the grounds that he had not acted consciously. In cases such as these, the defendant satisfies the most stringent culpability requirement without meeting the voluntary act criterion. It seems, therefore, that as applied by the courts, culpability cannot entail voluntariness.

24 Regina v. Charlson, [1955] 1 All E.R. 859; *see also* People v. Newton, 8 Cal. App. 3d 359, 87 Cal. Rptr. 394 (1970); Fain v. Commonwealth, 78 Ky. 183 (1879). The English courts retain the older terminology regarding *actus reus;* hence, the *Charlson* court does not directly address the voluntary act requirement. The relationship between the voluntary act and culpability requirements is discussed more fully in chapter 4.2. Chapters 5.1 and 5.2 will address Hart's entailment thesis more completely and present an alternate account of the automatism defense.

Wayne LaFave and Austin Scott, Jr., argue that the mental fault (intent, knowledge, recklessness, or negligence) must actuate the act that fulfills the act requirement. They argue that A must not only form the intent to kill B, and engage in voluntary behavior that causes the death of B, but in addition, A must engage in that behavior in order to kill B. A would not have committed an offense, therefore, if he formed the intent to kill B, but then ran over B accidentally while engaged in driving that was neither negligent, reckless, nor related to his intent to kill B.[25]

To actuate is to "render active . . . stir into activity . . . communicate motion to . . . act upon, or move the will, as motives do."[26] This interpretation seems to work well when applied to cases, such as the one just described, in which the offense definition requires that the defendant purposely caused the results that constitute the objective element of the offense. The analysis encounters difficulty, however, when applied to the other fault elements such as knowledge. Consider a case in which A decides to rob a bank by blowing a hole in the wall in order to gain access to the vault. A knows that a guard station is located on the other side of the wall directly adjacent to the spot where A intends to blast, that the guard station is constantly occupied, and that the guard is virtually certain to be killed. A does not want to kill the guard; he even hopes against all odds that the guard will survive. When A sets off the blast, the guard is killed, exactly as A expected. A has clearly "knowingly caused the death of another," yet the mental fault of knowledge did not actuate his act. Rather, his desire for the money and his expectation that he could get it in this way actuated his act *despite* his knowledge that the guard would die.

The actuation hypothesis also fails to accommodate satis-

---

25 LaFave and Scott, *supra* note 3, at sec. 3.11(a). This work uses the term "mental fault" to refer to the four culpability levels collectively. Throughout this book, I will use the terms "culpability level," "culpability requirement," and "mental fault" interchangeably.

26 Oxford English Dictionary (compact ed., Oxford: Oxford Univ. Press, 1971).

factorily offenses that require reckless or negligent conduct. Suppose that B suddenly realizes that he is late for a potentially profitable business engagement. B drives well above the safe speed limit through a residential neighborhood despite his conscious awareness that he is creating a substantial and unjustifiable risk to the residents. B makes a turn at excessive speed, skids into the bicycle lane, and kills a bicyclist.

A person who recklessly causes the death of another human being commits manslaughter.[27] According to the MPC, "A person acts recklessly with respect to a material element of an offense when he consciously disregards a substantial and unjustifiable risk that the material element exists or will result from his conduct." This risk must be such that "its disregard involves a gross deviation from the standard of conduct that a law-abiding person would observe in the actor's situation."[28] In order to meet the culpability requirement for manslaughter, then, a person must meet the following three conditions: (1) The actor's conduct must create a substantial and unjustifiable risk of death to another human being, (2) the actor must consciously disregard that risk, and (3) that disregard must constitute a gross deviation from the law-abiding person's standard of conduct.

By hypothesis, B's conduct fulfilled these conditions and constituted manslaughter, but did his recklessness actuate the voluntary act that fulfills the act requirement? B met the voluntary act requirement by driving his car. B's decision to drive his car was motivated by his desire to attend the meeting and his belief that he could do so most quickly by driving his car to the meeting.

The first of the three conditions listed is not strictly a part of the psychological attitude that constitutes the culpability level, but rather a normative description of the risk created by the actor's conduct. It is descriptive in that it describes the nature of the risk that must be created – the risk of death

---

27 MPC, *supra* note 1, at sec. 210.1, 210.3.
28 *Id.* at sec. 2.02(2) (c).

to another human being. It is normative in that it requires that the risk meet certain valuative criteria; it must be substantial and unjustifiable.

B's conscious disregard of the risk is the second condition listed and the only component of the culpability requirement that directly addresses the actor's psychological processes. In order to consciously disregard the risk, B must both perceive the risk and decide not to alter his behavior in light of that perception. At first glance, it seems plausible to argue that this decision not to modify his manner of driving actuated his voluntary act. It would be more accurate to say, however, that his desire to get to the meeting quickly motivated both his voluntary act of driving and his decision to disregard the risk. Had he not perceived the risk, he would not have decided to disregard it, yet he would still have driven in the same manner for the same reasons.

B's decision to disregard the risk was a necessary condition for his continuing to drive in a reckless manner. The psychological state that actuates a voluntary act must be more, however, than merely a necessary condition for that act. B's belief that there was gas in his car and many other background beliefs were necessary conditions for his action and affected the type of action that he took, but his desire to get to the meeting as quickly as possible moved him to act.

Psychological states that move an actor to voluntary action are usually desires or purposes for which the actor acts. Hence the actuation hypothesis works seductively well when applied to crimes committed purposefully. This should not be surprising because it is actually written into LaFave and Scott's formulation of the actuation hypothesis. They contend that the actor must engage in the voluntary action that constitutes the offense *in order to* achieve the effect specified by the offense definition.[29] An actor who performs an act in order to promote a consequence performs the act as a means to achieving the consequence; that is, the actor acts for the purpose of promoting the consequence. Hence, his mental

29 LaFave and Scott, *supra* note 3, at sec. 3.11(a) (emphasis added).

state that meets the culpability requirement activates his act just because he commits the offense purposely.

The third condition listed in the analysis of recklessness for manslaughter is a normative comparison of the actor's disregard with the law-abiding citizen's standard of conduct. As such, it is not the kind of factor that could move the actor to act. It is not a state or process of the actor at all, but rather an evaluation of the actor's psychological state according to a criteria defined by a hypothetical law-abiding person. In short, recklessness involves certain psychological processes and normative standards, but the psychological processes do not involve the desires and purposes that move the reckless actor to act.

The actuation hypothesis encounters difficulty in cases of criminal negligence that are quite similar to those encountered with recklessness. The story of C is identical to that of B except that C is so preoccupied with his business strategy that he fails to notice that he is creating an unreasonable risk to others. A person commits negligent homicide when he negligently causes the death of another human being.[30] According to the MPC, "A person acts negligently with respect to a material element of an offense when he should be aware of a substantial and unjustifiable risk that the material element exists or will result from his conduct."[31]

The analysis of the culpability requirements for negligent homicide parallels the three-part analysis provided earlier for manslaughter. The only substantial difference occurs in the second component, which requires that the defendant should have been aware of the substantial and unjustifiable risk that his conduct created, though he was not. It seems clear that C was moved to perform the voluntary act of driving his car by his desire to attend the meeting, and not by his failure to notice the risk that his driving created. As with B's conscious disregard, C's failure to notice the risk may have been a necessary condition for his continuing to speed,

---

30 MPC, *supra* note 1, sec. 210.1, 210.4.
31 *Id.* at sec. 2.02(2) (d).

but this is not sufficient to say that his negligence actuated the act of driving for the reasons provided.

In summary, the actuation hypothesis works well when the actor commits the offense purposely. This appears to be an artifact, however, of the fact that voluntary actions are ordinarily motivated by the purposes of the actor. The analysis does not accommodate offenses that require that the actor acted knowingly, recklessly, or negligently. Hart's entailment suggestion would lead us to deny that some acts met the culpability requirement despite the fact that by all usual indications, those acts were performed purposely. Both the voluntary act and culpability requirements involve the psychological processes of the defendant, and there appears to be some relationship between them. Yet, the exact nature of the requirements, and of the relationship between them, remains unclear.

1.2 DEFENSES

Whereas the state must prove all offense elements, the defendant may put forward defenses in order to avoid criminal liability. Robinson classifies defenses into five general categories: failure-of-proof defenses, offense modifications, justifications, excuses, and nonexculpatory defenses. The defendant who advances a failure-of-proof claim does not raise an affirmative defense; rather, he argues that the state has failed to carry its burden to prove the elements of the offense with which he is charged.[32] Technically, a taxonomy of defenses would not have to include failure-of-proof defenses because these provisions merely recognize that the state must prove the case in chief, including all material elements of the offense. However, Robinson and other theorists include these failure-of-proof claims in their systems of defenses.

The defendant can avoid conviction through a failure-of-

32 Robinson, *supra* note 2, at 70.

proof claim by showing that the state has not proven all offense elements. For example, the defendant can demonstrate that he acted under mistake of fact or law that negates a required element of the offense charged.[33] A defendant might establish such a mistake by showing that he shot the victim while rehearsing for a play under the honest and reasonable belief that the gun was only a prop. Under those conditions, the defendant engaged in voluntary behavior that caused the death of another, but he did not fulfill the culpability requirements of any homicide offense. He would not have caused the victim's death purposely, knowingly, or recklessly because he honestly did not believe that there was any risk of injury. In addition, he did not cause the death negligently because, by hypothesis, his belief was reasonable under the circumstances.

As demonstrated here, the psychological processes of the defendant are directly involved in both the voluntary act and culpability requirements. Therefore, evidence regarding these processes, or impairment of them, is directly relevant to failure-of-proof defenses that address either of these requirements.

Offense modifications, Robinson's second category of defenses, are not failure-of-proof defenses because they operate in cases in which all offense elements are satisfied. These claims modify offense definitions in the sense that they specify certain conditions under which an act will not be considered an offense despite the fact that all offense elements have been met. Robinson contends that the following principle underlies all offense modifications: "While the actor has apparently satisfied all elements of the offense charged, he has not in fact caused the harm or evil sought to be prevented by the statute defining the offense."[34] Many offense modifications apply only to a single offense or to a limited group of offenses. For example, "Wharton's rule" bars conviction for conspiracy when the underlying offense, such as dueling,

---

33 *Id*. at sec. 21, 62.
34 *Id*. at sec. 23(a), 77.

necessarily requires more than one participant. In this way, the same individuals are not convicted of both dueling and conspiracy to duel for the same set of acts.[35]

Different rationales support various offense modifications. Some modifications are supported by public policy considerations independent of culpability, whereas others reflect specific factors that mitigate the actor's culpability.[36] Generally, however, the offense modifications can be understood as limited scope variations of other categories of defenses described next, including nonexculpatory defenses and excuses. For this reason, offense modifications will not be treated as a separate category in this book.

Robinson's three remaining categories are general defenses that, in contrast to failure-of-proof defenses, are based on principles that operate independently of particular offense elements. These defenses can prevent conviction in cases in which all offense elements are satisfied. The nonexculpatory defenses, such as the statute of limitations and possibly entrapment, further extrinsic policy considerations by preventing conviction of blameworthy defendants. The defendant's psychological processes are not a central concern in these defenses because culpability is not at issue. Other general defenses exculpate defendants who have met all offense elements but who are not appropriate subjects of legal condemnation for other reasons. This latter category includes both justifications and excuses.[37]

When a defendant raises a justificatory defense, he claims that although his conduct fulfilled all offense elements, the societal benefits outweighed the harm under the circumstances. The law encourages, or at least refuses to condemn, justified behavior.[38] The defense of necessity or lesser evils

35 *Id.* at sec. 23(a).
36 *Id.* at sec. 23(a).
37 *Id.* at sec. 21.
38 *Id.* at sec. 21, 25(d); Hart, *supra* note 17, at 13. This account oversimplifies the theory of justification, but it will suffice for the purpose of this book, which does not directly address justificatory defenses.

has been called a model for justification defenses generally.[39] Justifications exculpate the actor, but they do not do so primarily on the basis of his psychological processes or impairment. Justifications exculpate because the action was socially acceptable under the circumstances, rather than because the actor was not responsible for his action.

Suppose, for example, that X is walking home late on an icy night in January. He slips on the ice, breaks his leg, and is unable to walk. He is unable to move to safety, and there are no passers-by to help him. In order to avoid hypothermia or frostbite, he drags himself to a fire alarm and pulls it despite the fact that there is no hint of a fire. He would have fulfilled the offense elements for the misdemeanor of creating a false public alarm.[40] His behavior would have been justified, however, under the justificatory defense of "choice of evils," which exculpates an actor who believed that the behavior in question was necessary to prevent some more serious harm or evil.[41]

Whereas justification emphasizes the circumstances of the action, the focus of an excuse is on the responsibility of the actor. A defendant is excused when he fulfills all the offense elements, but lacks personal culpability due to his psychological state at the time of the offense.[42] For example, the insanity defense serves to excuse a defendant who, by virtue of mental illness, is unable to appreciate the wrongfulness of his act. Although mental illness can also prevent a defendant from meeting all offense elements, the insanity defense excuses those who have fulfilled all offense elements.[43]

Robinson presents his five-part taxonomy of defenses as

39   MPC, *supra* note 1, at sec. 3.02; Robinson, *supra* note 2, at sec. 124(a).
40   MPC, *supra* note 1, at sec. 250.5.
41   *Id.* at sec. 3.02. Note that the MPC justifies action on the basis of the actor's beliefs about justifying conditions, whereas other formulations require reasonable beliefs. Thus the distinction between justification and excuse may not be so clear as one would like. *See, for example,* Greenawalt, *supra* note 3.
42   Hart, *supra* note 17, at 14; Robinson, *supra* note 2, at sec. 21, 25(d).
43   MPC, *supra* note 1, at sec. 4.01; Robinson, *supra* note 2, at 173.

exhaustive, and he argues that all excuses share a common structure. Each excuse involves a disability that causes an excusing condition. The disability is some condition of the actor that can be confirmed on the basis of some observable indicators apart from the conduct to be excused.[44] The disability serves to clearly distinguish the defendant from the population at large, and it supports the contention that the excusing condition genuinely exists.[45] Robinson contends that the disability is important because it produces the excusing condition that is some effect in the actor that renders him blameless for the specific conduct that constitutes the offense. The excusing condition, rather than the disability, provides the primary justification for exempting the defendant from punishment.

Robinson lists four socially accepted types of excusing conditions: (1) The conduct constituting the offense is not a product of a voluntary act by the actor, (2) the actor does not perceive the physical characteristics or consequences of his act, (3) the actor does not know that his act is illegal or wrong, and (4) the actor is unable to control his conduct. According to Robinson, a disability provides an excuse for otherwise criminal conduct when, but only when, it causes one of these four excusing conditions for the specific conduct that constitutes the offense.[46]

Robinson categorizes insanity, mental subnormality, and immaturity as excuses. The actor is excused for otherwise criminal conduct if, at the time of the offense, he suffered one of these disabilities, and his disability produced one of

44 Robinson, *supra* note 2, at sec. 25(b).
45 *Id*. at sec. 25(c).
46 *Id*. at sec. 25(b). Note that the first two conditions overlap with the failure-of-proof defenses in that excuses established on the basis of these excusing conditions would also constitute failure-of-proof defenses in many cases. Robinson acknowledges this overlap and contends that there might be theoretical advantages in conceptualizing certain offense elements, particularly voluntariness, in terms of defenses rather than as offense elements. For example, the standard view includes voluntariness in the voluntary act requirement, but an alternative approach would treat lack of voluntariness as an affirmative defense.

the four excusing conditions regarding the specific conduct that constitutes the offense.[47] He proposes, for example, an immaturity defense that establishes a conclusive presumption of immaturity for children below a minimum age, a rebuttable presumption of maturity for any defendant above a certain age, and a rebuttable presumption of immaturity for those between the two ages. The presumption of immaturity would be rebutted by evidence showing that the actor lacked the excusing condition regarding the particular conduct in question. A fifteen-year-old defendant, for example, could be held responsible for his behavior if the evidence demonstrated that at the time of the offense he had the experience and education necessary to appreciate the illegality and wrongfulness of his conduct. Similarly, the presumption of maturity would be rebutted by showing that the actor's lack of education or experience produced the excusing condition regarding the specific conduct at issue.[48]

Although Robinson's proposal is consistent with his model of excuses, it is not the majority approach. Currently, most states either establish a fixed age under which criminal capacity is conclusively presumed to be lacking, or the issue is addressed as a jurisdictional one that is resolved by specifying an age below which the defendant is directed to the juvenile courts.[49] These approaches treat immaturity as a status defense rather than as an excuse as Robinson defines excuses. The status approach differs from Robinson's model in that it exculpates some actors on the basis of their membership in some defined class rather than on the basis of a demonstrated disability and resulting excusing condition regarding the specific conduct that constitutes the offense.

Michael Moore distinguishes "status excuses" from "true excuses" and classifies both infancy and insanity as status excuses. Moore agrees that excuses prevent attribution of responsibility to the actor, particularly in light of that actor's

---

47   *Id.* at sec. 173, 174, 175.
48   *Id.* at sec. 175.
49   LaFave and Scott, *supra* note 3, at sec. 4.11(b).

mental states. True excuses, in Moore's view, are those that exculpate on the classic grounds of mistake or compulsion regarding the particular action that constitutes the offense with which the actor is charged. The actor is excused because he performed the proscribed conduct under compulsion or as a result of relevant mistakes.[50]

Moore's two grounds for true excuse are roughly comparable to Robinson's excusing conditions, which involve specific types of ignorance, mistake, or impaired volitional control. Moore's true excuses, like Robinson's excuses, are directed toward the specific action for which the actor is charged; that is, the defendant is excused for this particular action due to the presence of identifiable excusing conditions that take the form of impaired knowledge or control regarding this action. Although Moore's true excuses exculpate the actor by virtue of states or events that constitute excusing conditions regarding the offense charged, he does not specifically require an independently verifiable disability that causes these excusing conditions.[51] Robinson agrees, however, that the excusing condition is the actual reason for exculpation, with the disability playing a largely evidentiary role.[52] Moore not only provides a category of true excuses that is roughly comparable to Robinson's category of excuses, he also includes an account of "excuses negating the case in chief" that generally corresponds to Robinson's failure of proof defenses.[53]

Moore parts company with Robinson, however, in his treatment of infancy and insanity. Whereas Moore's category of true excuses corresponds generally to Robinson's excuse category, Moore does not classify infancy and insanity as true excuses. Rather, he identifies a separate class of defenses that he labels "status excuses" that exculpate by virtue of the defendant's general status without regard to his specific state of mind regarding the act that constitutes the offense with

50 Moore, *Causation and the Excuses*, 73 Calif. L. Rev. 1091, 1096–97 (1985).
51 *Id.* at 1097.
52 *See supra*, notes 44–48 and accompanying text.
53 Moore, *supra* note 50, at 1097–98.

which he is charged. Juveniles, for example, are excused because they are young, not because they lack some particular capacity or state of mind at the time of the offense.[54]

Robinson has no category comparable to Moore's status excuse. He claims that infancy and insanity are excuses and that as such, they must conform to his structure of excuses, according to which a disability produces an excusing condition regarding the particular offense in question. Moore's account of infancy as a status excuse seems to reflect the currently predominant practice. As indicated earlier, most states either address age as a jurisdictional issue by channeling defendants below a specified age to juvenile court, or they set a fixed age for the age of responsibility. These practices sort defendants by class membership without regard for excusing condition or disability.

One is tempted to ask, however, how these status categories are selected. If they are defined by some external policy considerations – for example, that it would not promote society's preventative goals to imprison juveniles – then these status excuses would be categorized appropriately as a subset of Robinson's nonexculpatory defenses. If, however, the status categories are selected because there is a strong presumption that the usual excusing conditions will apply to any action by any actor in these categories, then the underlying rationale of the status excuse is the same as that of the true excuse (in Moore's terms). Finally, if there is some separate justification for precluding punishment of these classes of actors that differs from the rationales for true excuses and for nonexculpatory policy defenses, then status excuses would most accurately be identified as a separate category.

The primary purpose of this book is to examine and clarify the role of psychological processes and impairment in the contemporary system of criminal offenses and defenses. This discrepancy between Robinson and Moore regarding the nature of excuses is central to that purpose because it reflects a dispute about the form and rationale of defenses such as

54 *Id*. at 1098.

insanity and infancy that directly involve the psychological processes of the accused. In order to effectively pursue the aims of the book, the following classification of defenses that directly involve the psychological processes or impairment of the defendant will be adopted. It is primarily drawn from Robinson's system, with Moore's category of status excuses maintained as a possible variation on Robinson's taxonomy in order to avoid prejudging the analysis of automatism and insanity in Chapters 5 and 6.

The psychological processes of the defendant, and impairment of those processes, are directly relevant to criminal liability when the following issues are addressed:

1. Failure of proof defenses:
   a. Lack of voluntary act
   b. Lack of culpability requirement
2. General defenses:
   a. Specific excuses (involving an excusing condition regarding particular conduct)
   b. Status excuses (provisional)

The exact nature and role of status excuses will be left open for now. If status excuses are appropriately understood as a category of exculpatory provisions that stands apart from the specific excuses as Robinson describes them, there are at least four plausible accounts of their appropriate place in the larger taxonomy of defenses. First, they may be nonexculpatory policy exemptions from punishment. Second, they may identify groups for whom there is a strong presumption of one of the standard excusing conditions. In this case, treating certain categories of defendants according to class membership may be appropriate if we are unable to reliably identify the few who are responsible for their behavior, or if identifying those few would require disproportionate investment of judicial resources.

Third, they may be subsumed under the category of specific excuses when suitable additional excusing conditions are added to the four listed by Robinson. Finally, status excuses may constitute a separate type of defense based on class membership without reference to particular actions or excusing conditions. In this last case, the grounds for identifying the appropriate classes becomes the central issue. The psychological processes of the defendant would be directly involved in status excuses on the second, third, and possibly the fourth interpretations.

In order to promote consistency, I will generally adhere to Robinson's terminology. Failure-of-proof defenses will be referred to by that term rather than as "excuses negating the case in-chief." The term "excuse" will refer to specific excuses unless "status excuses" are specified.

One further clarification may avoid confusion in later chapters. Sanford Kadish has distinguished two senses of the term *mens rea* in the literature of the criminal law. In the special sense, *mens rea* refers to "the mental state which is required by the definition of the offense to accompany the act which produces or threatens the harm."[55] *Mens rea* is also used in a broader sense in which it encompasses all of the mental capacities and states required for legal responsibility. The law absolves a person due to lack of *mens rea* in this broader sense "because his deficiencies of temperament, personality or maturity distinguish him so utterly from the rest of us to whom the law's threats are addressed that we do not expect him to comply."[56]

Both the automatism and insanity defenses have been interpreted by some writers and jurists as claims that defeat an ascription of *mens rea*, whereas others have characterized these defenses as general defenses that may exculpate independently of the *mens rea* requirement. When *mens rea* is used in the narrower special sense, it corresponds to the culpability requirement of the MPC. When it is used in the broader general sense in which it encompasses all of the mental aspects of criminal responsibility, however, it would be negated by any defense that challenges the mental aspects

---

55 Kadish, *The Decline of Innocence*, 26 Cambridge L.J. 273, 274 (1968).
56 *Id*. at 275.

of responsibility. That is, in the general sense, any failure-of-proof defense or general defense that addresses the psychological functioning of the defendant challenges *mens rea.* In order to interpret the debate regarding whether the automatism and insanity defenses defeat an ascription of *mens rea* as a substantive dispute, therefore, it must be understood as a debate about the relationship of these defenses to *mens rea* in the special sense in which the term corresponds to the MPC culpability requirement. Interpreted in this manner, the question is whether these defenses are most accurately understood as failure-of-proof defenses regarding the culpability requirement or as some alternative category of defense. Throughout this book I will employ the MPC terminology whenever possible. When the term *mens rea* is used, it should be understood in the special sense unless the general sense is specified.

1.3 CONCLUSIONS AND PLAN

In summary, criminal liability requires that the defendant fulfill all objective offense elements, that he do so through conduct that includes a voluntary act, that he act with the specified culpability state toward each material element of the offense, and finally that there be no general defenses that would preclude conviction. The defendant's psychological states and processes are directly relevant to his criminal liability at three different points in the analysis. Evidence regarding psychological factors can support a failure-of-proof defense regarding either the voluntary act or culpability requirements, or it can provide an excuse. Unfortunately, neither the nature of the psychological processes contemplated by the voluntary act and culpability requirements nor the relationship between these two types of offense elements is clearly explicated. Similarly, the type of psychological dysfunction that will establish the various excuses has not been satisfactorily described.

The automatism and insanity defenses illustrate this lack of clarity regarding the role of psychological dysfunction in

criminal liability and exculpation. Automatism has been interpreted as a form of the insanity defense, as a separate
general defense, and as a failure-of-proof defense going to
either the voluntary act requirement or the culpability element. The history of the insanity defense reveals a constant
search for a satisfactory formulation, with little evidence to
suggest progress across time. There has also been an ongoing
debate regarding the basic classification of the defense, with
some writers arguing that it is a *sui generis* form of excuse
reflecting the unique status of certain mentally disordered
offenders, and other theorists contending that it is merely
an application of the more general ignorance and coercion
excuses or one way to establish a failure-of-proof defense.

To some degree, this pervasive lack of clarity regarding
these defenses reflects our unsatisfactory understanding of
the clinical syndromes that give rise to these defenses. Our
difficulty in classifying and formulating these defenses also
reveals, however, the deficiencies of our current conceptual
framework of offense elements and defenses. These deficiencies are both analytic and normative. They are analytic
insofar as the nature of the various offense elements and
defenses, and the relationships among them, have not been
clarified. They are normative insofar as we are unsure about
the moral foundations for culpability and exculpation.

The primary purpose of this book is to examine and clarify
the significance of psychological processes and dysfunction
for matters of criminal responsibility and exculpation. I will
argue that when the system of offense elements, failure-of-
proof defenses, and excuses outlined is examined more
closely and explicated more fully, it reveals a pattern of exculpation that corresponds roughly to the conception of personal responsibility that we need, and intuitively apply, for
legal and moral purposes. The argument will proceed in the
following manner.

Chapters 2 and 3 will examine more closely the insanity
and automatism defenses, demonstrating that the current
approaches to these defenses are inadequate and attributing
part of the difficulty regarding both defenses to the poorly

articulated voluntary act and culpability requirements. Chapter 4 will advance a conceptual structure, based on philosophical action theory, that is intended to clarify the role of psychological processes in the structure of offense elements and to explicate the nature of the voluntary act and culpability requirements and the relationship between the two.

Chapter 5 will apply this structure to the automatism defense in order to clarify the appropriate interpretation of automatism as a failure-of-proof defense that defeats an ascription of voluntary action as that phrase is currently understood in the MPC. Chapter 6 will examine the insanity defense in light of this conceptual structure, and argue that this defense is most accurately understood as a separate type of excuse that reflects the particular form of psychological dysfunction that constitutes an important part of certain types of psychopathology. Automatism and insanity do not exhaust the set of problematic defenses that involve psychological process. Space limitations prevent me from pursuing other relevant defenses such as infancy and duress. I hope, however, to demonstrate through the analysis of the automatism and insanity defenses that the conceptual framework proposed in Chapter 4 can provide a useful approach to defenses that address the psychological processes of the defendant.

Finally, Chapter 7 will advance a conception of free will that is grounded in current psychological theory, consistent with widely held intuitions, and illuminating for legal and moral purposes. I will argue that this conception of free will grounds an approach to personal responsibility that corresponds to the conceptual structure for offense elements advanced in Chapter 4 and provides a normative foundation for this structure, as well as for the system of failure-of-proof defenses and excuses discussed in this book.

Chapter 2

Problematic defenses: Insanity

The psychological dysfunction of the defendant plays a central role both in the automatism defense and in the defense of not guilty by reason of insanity (NGRI). The unsettled state of the law regarding these two defenses illustrates the uncertainty regarding the current system of offense elements and defenses discussed in Chapter 1. Courts and legislatures have encountered difficulties in formulating and applying these defenses, but more fundamentally, the theoretical justifications for these defenses and their place in the larger system of offense elements and defenses remain unclear. Familiarity with the primary controversies regarding the NGRI defense will provide helpful background for the discussion of automatism; for that reason, Chapter 2 will examine the NGRI defense and Chapter 3 will address automatism. Two recurring issues regarding the NGRI defense warrant attention for the purposes of the book. The first is the constant search for a satisfactory NGRI formulation, and the second is the status of the defense in the structure of offense elements and defenses.

2.1 THE SEARCH FOR A SATISFACTORY STANDARD

The historical pattern of development of the NGRI defense has been discussed repetitively elsewhere.[1] That discussion

---

1   S.J. Brakel, J. Parry, and B.A. Weiner, The Mentally Disabled and the Law 708–12 (Chicago: American Bar Foundation, 3d ed. 1985); H. Fin-

will not be repeated here. Rather, I will sketch briefly the four common NGRI tests in American law, and then examine more closely the most recent developments in the ongoing search for a satisfactory formulation of the NGRI defense.

Four NGRI standards have dominated the history of the defense in the American Law. The first and most common test is the *M'Naghten* standard and its variations. *M'Naghten*-type standards are often described as ignorance tests because they exculpate psychologically disturbed defendants who were ignorant of the nature, quality, or wrongfulness of their acts. The second type of standard addresses volitional impairment by exculpating psychologically disturbed defendants whose acts, which would otherwise have been criminal, were the result of irresistible impulses. The third general type of standard combines the first and second in that it includes both ignorance and volitional clauses. The most popular test of this type is the one put forward by the MPC, which exculpates those psychologically disturbed defendants who were unable to appreciate the criminality of their acts or to conform their conduct to the law. Finally, some courts have instructed juries to exculpate defendants whose acts were the product of mental disorder. These jurisdictions are usually said to employ product tests.[2]

garette, The Meaning of Criminal Insanity 11–15 (Berkeley: Univ. of Calif. Press, 1972); D. Hermann, The Insanity Defense 18–59 (Springfield, IL: C.C. Thomas, 1983); W. LaFave and A.W. Scott, Jr., Substantive Criminal Law sec. 4.2, 4.3 (St. Paul, MN: West Pub. Co., 1986).

2 For a brief summary of these four types of tests, see M. Moore, Law and Psychiatry 218–20 (Cambridge: Cambridge Univ. Press, 1984); See LaFave and Scott, *supra* note 1, at sec. 4.2, 4.3 for a more complete account of the nature, criticisms, and development of these four approaches. For a more detailed discussion of the *M'Naghten* and MPC tests, *see infra*, notes 3–13 and accompanying text.

  The text of the statutes or court rules often refer to a "disease of the mind" or to a "mental disease or defect." These phrases, as well as the term "mental illness," raise perplexing problems about the nature of illnesses and diseases. In order to avoid prejudicing such issues I will use relatively neutral terms such as "psychological disorder," unless I am directly discussing issues such as the nature or significance of a mental disease or illness. My arguments presented in section 2.1 draw on those made in Schopp, *Returning to M'Naghten to Avoid Moral*

Although all four standards have had some popularity during various periods of American law, the major dispute for approximately the last quarter of a century has been between those who favor the historically predominant *M'Naghten* test and those who advocate the MPC standard. The pattern of shifting back and forth between these two standards during the last quarter of a century illustrates the frustrating search for a satisfactory test, and introduces the relationship between this process of standard selection and the broader issue introduced in Chapter 1 regarding the general system of offense elements and defenses.

Historically, the predominant standard for the NGRI defense has been the *M'Naghten* test.[3] According to this test, the defendant is exculpated if he committed the offense while he "was labouring under such a defect of reason, from disease of the mind, as not to know the nature and quality of the act he was doing; or, if he did know it, that he did not know he was doing what was wrong."[4]

This test has been widely criticized by those who think that it overemphasizes the cognitive aspect of personality at the expense of emotional and volitional factors, and that it unduly limits the scope of expert testimony to these narrow cognitive issues.[5] When "know" is interpreted to mean simply that the defendant was aware of certain facts, this test seems to apply only to a limited set of delusions – those that deprive the defendant of awareness of facts that would inform him about the nature, quality, or wrongfulness of his behavior. The nature and quality requirement has usually been interpreted narrowly to require only awareness of the

Mistakes: One Step Forward or Two Steps Backward for the Insanity Defense?, 30 Ariz. L. Rev. 135 (1988).

3 Brakel, Parry, and Weiner, *supra* note 1, at 709; LaFave and Scott, *supra* note 1, at sec. 4.2(a).
4 M'Naghten's Case, 8 Eng. Rep. 718, 722 (1843).
5 People v. Drew, 22 Cal. 3d 333, 341–42, 583 P.2d 1318, 1322, 149 Cal. Rptr. 275, 278 (1978); Brakel, Parry, and Weiner, *supra* note 1, at 710; Fingarette, *supra* note 1, at 144; A. Goldstein, The Insanity Defense 46–49 (1967); Hermann, *supra* note 1, at 37, 138; LaFave and Scott, *supra* note 1, at sec. 4.2(c).

physical characteristics of the act and awareness that the act is harmful.[6] Given this narrow interpretation of the nature and quality disjunct, most plausible candidates for the NGRI defense will qualify for exculpation under the wrongfulness disjunct, if at all.[7]

When the *M'Naghten* test is understood in this manner, two problems arise. First, it seems to misconstrue the nature and significance of psychological disturbance in that psychopathology appears to be viewed merely as a source of false beliefs, and only those false beliefs that mislead the defendant about the wrongfulness of his behavior are treated as exculpatory. Second, even if one accepts this view of the nature and significance of psychopathology, the courts have found it extremely difficult to develop a satisfactory interpretation of "wrongfulness."[8] In short, this restrictive approach to the *M'Naghten* test attributes significance only to a very limited set of delusions, and no one can state clearly the criteria for inclusion in that category.

The MPC test provides an alternative standard that appears to remedy these perceived deficiencies in the *M'Naghten* test. The MPC test provides that "[a] person is not responsible for criminal conduct if at the time of such conduct as a result of mental disease or defect he lacks substantial capacity either to appreciate the criminality [wrongfulness] of his conduct or to conform his conduct to the requirements of the law."[9]

Many prefer this standard to the *M'Naghten* test because it substitutes "appreciate" for "know," suggesting a broader and more personalized evaluation of the defendant's understanding. In addition, it is often preferred because it explicitly addresses volitional impairment, and requires only that the

6 State v. Brosie, 113 Ariz. 329, 331, 553 P.2d 1203, 1205 (1976), *overruled on other grounds*; State v. Chavez, 143 Ariz. 238, 693 P.2d 893 (1984); LaFave and Scott, *supra* note 1, at sec. 4.2(b) (3); P.H. Robinson, Criminal Law Defenses sec. 173(c) (3) (St. Paul, MN: West Pub. Co., 1984).
7 H. Fingarette and A. Hasse, Mental Disabilities and Criminal Responsibility 29 (Berkeley: Univ. of Calif. Press, 1979).
8 *See infra*, chapter 2.1.2.
9 American Law Institute, Model Penal Code and Commentaries sec. 4.01 (official draft and revised commentaries, 1985).

defendant lack substantial, not complete capacity.[10] Since the MPC test was officially adopted in 1962, there has been a general trend toward it from *M'Naghten*. In 1961, *M'Naghten* was applied, alone or in combination with other tests, in federal jurisdictions, the armed forces, and all but three states.[11] Only one state had a standard similar to the MPC test.[12] By 1985, only about one-third of the states used *M'Naghten* in its original form, and a few more employed variations of it. Approximately one-half of the states used the MPC test, either verbatim or with slight modifications.[13] Apparently, many courts and legislatures found the widespread criticisms of *M'Naghten* to be persuasive, and they moved to the MPC standard in order to accommodate more accurately the exculpatory force of psychological disorder.

2.1.1 Recent developments. A series of recent developments suggest a reversal of this general trend toward the more inclusive MPC standard. Major indicators of this reversal of the older trend include recommendations of professional organizations as well as changes in statutory law and case law. During the late 1970s, twenty-four states altered their NGRI defenses in order to make them less inclusive.[14] Since the 1982 *Hinckley*[15] verdict, seven jurisdictions have restricted the

---

10   *Drew,* 22 Cal. 3d at 346, 583 P.2d at 1325, 149 Cal. Rptr. at 282; Brakel, Parry, and Weiner, *supra* note 1, at 711–12; Goldstein, *supra* note 5, at 87; LaFave and Scott, *supra* note 1, at sec. 4.3(d), (e).

11   F. Lindman and D. McIntyre Jr., The Mentally Disabled and the Law 332–35 (Chicago: Univ. of Chicago Press, 1961).

12   Vermont had adopted by statute a test very similar to that proposed by the American Law Institute. The Vermont statute required that the defendant "lacks adequate capacity either to appreciate the criminality of his conduct or to conform his conduct to the requirements of law." Vt. Stat. Ann. tit. 13, sec. 4801 (1959).

13   Brakel, Parry, and Weiner, *supra* note 1, at 712; Robinson, *supra* note 6, at sec. 173(a).

14   Slovenko, *The Insanity Defense in the Wake of the Hinckley Trial,* 14 Rutgers L.J. 373, 374 (1983).

15   United States v. Hinckley, Crim. No. 81–306 (D.D.C. June 21, 1982). Hinckley was found NGRI for the attempted assassination of President Reagan. His acquittal was followed by publicity and controversy regarding the NGRI defense. Many calls for abolition or restriction of

definition and use of the insanity defense – four changed to the less inclusive *M'Naghten* standard from the more inclusive MPC test or a supplemented form of *M'Naghten,* two restricted use of the insanity defense by barring its use to negate *mens rea* or its use as a defense to certain offenses, and one repealed the plea entirely. Only two jurisdictions expanded the test from *M'Naghten* to the MPC standard.[16]

The federal government has recently adopted its first NGRI statute that authorizes the NGRI finding only when "the defendant, as a result of severe mental disease or defect, was unable to appreciate the nature and quality or the wrongfulness of his acts."[17] This standard is similar to *M'Naghten* in that it directs attention to the defendant's capacity to understand the nature, quality, and wrongfulness of the act, and provides no direct volitional test.

On its face, this federal statute differs from *M'Naghten* in that it refers to the defendant's ability to "appreciate" rather than to "know." Critics of *M'Naghten* have argued that the use of "know" limits the defense to a superficial and narrowly cognitive sort of intellectual awareness.[18] The term "appreciate" is sometimes seen as a remedy for this limitation. Unfortunately, it is not clear what "appreciate" means in this context.[19]

"Appreciate" is sometimes thought to suggest a broader sense of understanding, including affective or emotional as-

the defense resulted. For discussion, *see, for example,* Callahan, Mayer, and Steadman, *Insanity Defense Reforms in the United States-Post-Hinckley,* 11 Mental and Physical Disabilities Law Reporter 54 (1987); Wexler, *Redefining the Insanity Problem,* 53 Geo. Wash. L. Rev. 528, 537–40 (1985); W. Winslade and J. Ross, The Insanity Plea 181–97 (New York: Scribner's, 1983).

16   Callahan, Mayer, and Steadman, *Id.* The authors tabulate state by state changes as summarized in this paragraph and describe the pattern of changes that occurred before, during, and after the *Hinckley* trial.

17   18 U.S.C. sec. 17(a) (1986).

18   Goldstein, *supra* note 5, at 49; Hermann, *supra* note 1, at 37, 44; LaFave and Scott, *supra* note 1, at sec. 4.2(c).

19   Robinson, *supra* note 6, at sec. 173(d) (3). The author reviews several suggested interpretations, finding none satisfactory.

pects of the defendant's personality.[20] Some writers have interpreted "appreciate" as "affective understanding" or "knowledge fused with affect." This interpretation requires that the defendant not only have cognitive awareness that the act is wrong, but also that the defendant experience the usual or normal affective responses associated with the act.[21] This requirement, however, would seem to exculpate the cold or vicious criminal who victimizes innocent people without experiencing sympathy or remorse. Yet, the insanity defense certainly is not intended to exculpate such criminals. Rather, these are just the people that the criminal law – and the prison system – are designed to deter.

One might respond that these criminals would not meet the psychopathology requirement. This response raises the issue of the relationship between the psychopathology and excusing clauses in an NGRI standard. The NGRI defense is usually thought to excuse certain persons, not merely because they are mentally disturbed, but because their mental disorder causes certain excusing conditions such as impairment of capacity to comprehend or to reason.[22] When the condition caused would not excuse a person who was not mentally disturbed, and the mental disturbance itself is not grounds for excuse, it is difficult to understand why that condition would excuse the mentally disturbed offender.

The mere fact that neither the psychopathology nor the lack of usual affective responses would exculpate independently does not establish that the conjunction of the two factors should not excuse. Simple ignorance of wrongfulness is not usually sufficient grounds for excuse, but such igno-

---

20 Brakel, Parry, and Weiner, *supra* note 1, at 711–12; LaFave and Scott, *supra* note 1, at sec. 4.3(d); American Bar Association Standing Committee on Association Standards for Criminal Justice Proposed Criminal Justice Mental Health Standards 332–33 (Official Draft 1984) [hereinafter ABA Standards].

21 Fingarette, *supra* note 1, at 151; Goldstein, *supra* note 5, at 87.

22 U.S. v. Brawner, 471 F.2d 969, 991 (D.C. Cir. 1972) ("The second component . . . [the excusing condition] . . . defines the ultimate issue."); Fingarette and Hasse, *supra* note 7, at 17; Goldstein, *supra* note 5, at 89; Robinson, *supra* note 6, at sec. 161(a) (2).

rance as a product of mental disease or defect can excuse under *M'Naghten*, the MPC test, or the federal statute. One could argue that mental illness excuses in certain cases just because it is a nonculpable source of ignorance. Even if one accepts this interpretation of the role of mental illness in the NGRI defense, however, the lack of usual affective response does not occupy a position in the law of excuse analogous to that occupied by ignorance. Ignorance of fact, and in certain circumstances ignorance of law, can excuse independently of mental illness. There is no comparable excuse of "nonculpable lack of usual affective response."[23]

It is not surprising that the law does not include such an excuse based on the lack of usual affective response. Not only would such an excuse exculpate the cold, hardened criminal described earlier, it would also apply to many average citizens in just those situations in which the criminal law might reasonably be expected to provide some deterrent effect.

Consider the case of A, who was late for work this morning because her children were fighting and her spouse provided no assistance. When she arrived at work, her boss complained about her tardiness and continued to criticize her throughout the day for a series of mishaps over which A had no control. While driving home, A becomes preoccupied with the injustices of the day, and as a result, she runs into the back of a car that has stopped in front of her. The driver, who bears a striking resemblance to her boss, gets out of his car, calls her names, and criticizes her driving skills. A feels a strong desire to run over him with her car, and the knowledge that this would probably kill him is not accompanied by the feelings of revulsion that A would usually experience at the idea of killing someone. Rather, A is positively gleeful at the prospect of flattening her tormentor along the road.

---

23 For a more complete account of ignorance excuses, see MPC, *supra* note 9, at sec. 2.04; LaFave and Scott, *supra* note 1, at sec. 5.1; Robinson, *supra* note 6, at sec. 62.

A restrains herself only by repeating to herself, "Don't do it A; you're in enough trouble already."

Most average citizens probably conform to the major dictates of the criminal law without giving a thought to the penalties for violations. They probably do so because the criminal law generally reflects the conventional social morality, and most citizens would probably feel guilty or ashamed if they seriously considered committing homicide or assault under ordinary circumstances.

The deterrent effect of criminal penalties is intended to serve as a behavior-guiding influence for the average citizen in just those unusual circumstances in which that person does *not* experience the usual emotional responses to the prospect of harming others. Under these conditions, the average citizen, like the cold or vicious criminal, needs the deterrent effect of criminal penalties. A system of criminal law that recognized the lack of usual emotional responsiveness to one's own criminal behavior as an excusing condition would remove the threat of punishment in just those circumstances in which it is needed.

Contrary to the claims of those who have criticized the traditional *M'Naghten* standard, there appears to be no good reason to think that the "know" of *M'Naghten* is necessarily more narrow than the unspecified "appreciate." Many jurisdictions present the *M'Naghten* standard to the jury without any interpretation of "know," and of those that have interpreted the term, the majority have favored the broader interpretation that is consistent with the vague "appreciate" used in the NGRI defense.[24]

---

24 Goldstein, *supra* note 5, at 49–50; LaFave and Scott, *supra* note 1, at sec. 4.2(b) (2); People v. Wolff, 61 Cal. 2d 795, 800–01, 394 P.2d 959, 961–62, 40 Cal. Rptr. 271, 273–74 (1964) (noting that California trial courts give a commendably broad interpretation to the M'Naghten "knowledge" test); State v. Davies, 146 Conn. 137, 144, 148 A.2d 251, 255 (1959) (responsibility requires the capacity to judge the act wrong and criminal); State v. Esser, 16 Wis. 2d 567, 598, 145 N.W.2d 505, 521–22 (1962) (requiring the capacity to make normal moral judgments about the act).

Although it is not clear what "appreciate" means in this context, there is no apparent reason to think that it differs substantially from the broad sense of "know." Thus, the mere fact that the federal statute employs the term "appreciate" whereas the *M'Naghten* test uses "know" does not establish a substantial difference between the two standards.

According to the legislative history, the federal statute was intended to replace the MPC test in the federal jurisdiction because it was thought that the statute would provide a clear standard that would avoid moral mistakes. Although the term "moral mistakes" is not very clearly explicated, it apparently refers to erroneous decisions based on guesses regarding who is morally blameworthy. Some critics have identified the volitional standard as a likely source of such mistakes.[25]

Some who favor the abolition of volitional tests have described such standards, and accompanying expert testimony, as confusing to the jury because the tests have no clear meaning. They argue that such tests preclude rational deliberation because it is often impossible to distinguish between those who are unable to conform to the law and those who merely fail to conform.[26] *M'Naghten*-type standards, including the new federal statute, that emphasize cognition are presented as workable tests with clear and definite meaning that will prevent these moral mistakes.[27]

---

25 ABA Standards, *supra* note 20, at 329–32; 1984 U.S. Code Cong. and Ad. News 3408–9 (reporting the testimony of professors Bonnie and Robinson at the hearings on the insanity defense before the Committee on the Judiciary, and the Subcommittee on the Criminal Law of the Committee on the Judiciary, U.S. Senate, 97th Congress, 2d session (1982)). By "moral guesses" these writers seem to mean guesses regarding whether or not the defendant had the capacity to conform his behavior to the law. For a further discussion of moral mistakes, *see infra* chapter 2.1.2.

26 1984 U.S. Code Cong. and ad. News, *id.* at 3405, 3408 (reporting the testimony representing the Department of Justice at the Crime Control Act Hearings, and the testimony of professors Bonnie and Robinson); *see also*, American Psychiatric Association, *Statement on the Insanity Defense*, 140 American J. of Psychiatry 681, 685 (1983) [hereinafter APA Statement].

27 ABA Standards, *supra* note 20, at 329–32 (claiming that the standard is in concert with current clinical expertise and theoretical possibility),

The American Bar Association (ABA) and the American Psychiatric Association (APA) have issued statements on the insanity defense. Both organizations have supported standards that focus on the defendant's capacity to appreciate the wrongfulness of his conduct and that do *not* include volitional tests. The ABA recommended that the defendant be exculpated only when "as a result of mental disease or defect, that person was unable to appreciate the wrongfulness of such conduct." The APA did not formally recommend a test, but it indicated approval of a standard that would declare a person NGRI when "as a result of mental disease or mental retardation he was unable to appreciate the wrongfulness of his conduct at the time of the offense."[28]

Both organizations opted for primarily cognitive tests without volitional prongs because they held experts to lack the capacity to distinguish irresistible from merely unresisted impulses. In addition, they considered the phrase "appreciate the wrongfulness" to be sufficiently broad to accommodate appropriate expert testimony regarding the relevant aspects of mental disorder. They endorsed their respective standards as tests that would not confuse the jury and would avoid moral mistakes based on moral guesses.[29]

The federal statute, the ABA recommendation, and the APA endorsement are all similar to *M'Naghten* in that they are ignorance standards that focus primarily on the defendant's lack of capacity to understand the wrongfulness of his act.[30] All three reject volitional prongs on the ground that such standards are not amenable to precise clarification, and thus are likely to confuse the jury and lead to moral mistakes.

see also, 1984 U.S. Code Cong. and Ad. News 3404–11; Wexler, *supra* note 15, at 532.

28 *See, respectively,* ABA Standards, *supra* note 20, at 323; APA Statement, *supra* note 26, at 685.

29 ABA Standards, *supra* note 20, at 339–44; APA Standards, *supra* note 26, at 684–85.

30 18 U.S.C. 17 (a) (1986) also exculpates those who, by virtue of severe mental disorder, are ignorant of the nature or quality of their act. It is rare, however, for a defendant in an actual case to meet this requirement. Fingarette and Hasse, *supra* note 7, at 29.

This common rejection of volitional tests in favor of ignorance standards represents a reversal of the prior trend from *M'Naghten* to the MPC formulation. All three of these recent provisions present *M'Naghten*-type standards as sufficient to accommodate the relevant aspects of mental disorder, while they avoid more inclusive tests as likely to be over-inclusive.

In 1984, the California Supreme Court interpreted a public initiative as mandating a return to a *M'Naghten*-type NGRI standard. The court's opinion included arguments suggesting that *M'Naghten* is the least-inclusive standard sufficient to serve the purpose of the NGRI defense. This reasoning, in conjunction with the federal statute and the recommendations of the professional organizations, seems to suggest that a *M'Naghten*-type test can be expected to provide a clear standard that is both necessary and sufficient to avoid moral mistakes. That is, it will be neither under-inclusive nor over-inclusive.

In June 1982, the California electorate passed the initiative known as Proposition 8, which has been codified as Section 25 (b) of the California Penal Code. According to Section 25 (b), a defendant is exculpated under the NGRI defense only when "he or she was incapable of knowing or understanding the nature and quality of his or her act *and* of distinguishing right from wrong at the time of the commission of the offense."[31] As written, Section 25 (b) differs from the traditional *M'Naghten* test in that it takes the conjunctive form. The defendant must be incapable of knowing both the nature and quality of his act and the wrongfulness of his act. Despite the fact that the statute is unambiguous on its face, the *Skinner* court interpreted it as a return to the disjunctive *M'Naghten*.[32]

Immediately prior to the passage of Proposition 8, the NGRI defense in California was governed by the MPC test, which the California Supreme Court adopted in *People v.*

---

31   Cal. Penal Code sec. 25 (b) (West Cumm. Supp. 1987) (added by initiative measure, approved by the people, June 8, 1982) (emphasis added).

32   People v. Skinner, 39 Cal. 3d 765, 769, 777, 704 P. 2d 752, 754, 759, 217 Cal. Rptr. 685, 687, 692 (1985).

Drew.[33] Prior to *Drew*, the California rule regarding NGRI was a version of the *M'Naghten* test recognized by the Supreme Court of California in *People v. Coffman*,[34] and applied by the court through *People v. Kelly*.[35]

In *Kelly*, the court stated that "[i]nsanity, under the California *M'Naghten* test, denotes a mental condition which renders a person incapable of knowing or understanding the nature and quality of his act, *or* incapable of distinguishing right from wrong in relation to that act."[36] A defendant would qualify as NGRI under the *Kelly* version of the *M'Naghten* test if he were either unable to know the nature and quality of his act or unable to know the wrongfulness of his act. In contrast, a defendant would qualify under a literal interpretation of Section 25 (b) only if he were both unable to know the nature and quality of his act and unable to know the wrongfulness of his act.

The court's argument for its disjunctive interpretation of Section 25 (b) as a return to the pre-*Drew M'Naghten* test portrays that test as the least-inclusive NGRI standard that will adequately serve the purpose of the defense. The court started with the premise that the essence of a criminal offense in our system of jurisprudence is wrongful intent, and reasoned that the NGRI defense, and the *M'Naghten* test as the measure of minimum cognitive functioning necessary to form wrongful intent, have become fundamental principles of our common law. A conjunctive interpretation would not only abandon the *Drew* test, it would also abrogate the pre-*Drew M'Naghten* test. Given the requirement of wrongful intent for culpability, and the status of the *M'Naghten* test as the measure of minimal cognitive capacity to form such intent, abandoning the *M'Naghten* standard would entail abandoning the requirement of wrongful intent, which in turn would alter the essential nature of a criminal offense. The court con-

---

33 People v. Drew, 22 Cal. 3d 333, 345, 583 P.2d 1318, 1324, 149 Cal. Rptr. 275, 281 (1978); MPC, *supra* note 9, at sec. 4.01.
34 24 Cal. 230 (1864) (adopting the standard as stated in *M'Naghten*).
35 People v. Kelly, 10 Cal. 3d 565, 516 P.2d 875, 111 Cal. Rptr. 171 (1973).
36 *Id.* at 574, 516 P.2d at 881, 111 Cal. Rptr. at 177 (emphasis added).

cluded that absent clear evidence that Proposition 8 was intended to produce such a fundamental change, it should be understood as a return to the disjunctive *M'Naghten* test.[37]

The court's understanding of the relationship between criminal intent and the NGRI defense was central to this reasoning. By criminal intent, the court apparently meant *mens rea* in the special sense in which it corresponds to the culpability requirement for the offense. This requirement would remain, however, even if the NGRI defense were abolished. That is, the court apparently failed to distinguish insanity as a general defense from the role that psychological disturbance can play in a failure-of-proof defense regarding the culpability requirement.

Some states have abolished the insanity defense entirely without abandoning the culpability requirement. In those states, evidence of psychological dysfunction is admissible when it is relevant to failure of proof claims.[38] The court's argument demonstrates the confusion that can arise regarding the NGRI defense when failure-of-proof claims are not distinguished from general defenses, and it suggests that clarification of the underlying structure of offense elements and defenses might avoid some of the difficulties encountered in the pursuit of a satisfactory NGRI formulation.[39]

Having decided that Proposition 8 mandated a return to the disjunctive *M'Naghten* test, the court turned to an interpretation of that standard. The prosecution set out two theories. First, it argued that the nature and quality disjunct and the wrongfulness disjunct actually state the same require-

37 *Id*. at 776–77, 704 P.2d at 759, 217 Cal. Rptr. at 692.
38 Robinson, *supra* note 6, at sec. 173 (a) n.5. For details regarding these three states, see Idaho Code sec. 18–207 (Cumm. Supp. 1986); Mont. Code Ann. sec. 46–14–102 (1985); Utah Code Ann. sec. 76–2–305 (1) (Cumm. Supp. 1986).
39 The court also reasoned that the disjunctive interpretation of sec. 25 (b) would serve the deterrent purpose of punishment as well as would the conjunctive formulation. *Skinner*, 39 Cal. 3d at 777 n.8, 704 P.2d at 759 n.8, 217 Cal. Rptr. at 692 n.8. The court's reasoning regarding this issue was seriously flawed, but these arguments are not central to the purpose of this book. For a more complete discussion of this specific issue, *see* Schopp, *supra* note 2, at 143–46.

ment. Second, the state argued that the wrongfulness disjunct was intended to be satisfied by the knowledge that the act was illegal.[40]

The court quickly dismissed the first claim, reasoning that whereas a defendant who did not know the nature and quality of his act could not know that it was wrong, the defendant who knew the nature and quality of his act would not necessarily know that it was wrong. The court cited the instant case as one in which the defendant knew the nature and quality of his act but believed that he had a right to perform it.[41] Skinner strangled his wife while believing that the words

40 *Skinner*, 39 Cal. 3d at 777–84, 704 P.2d at 759–64, 217 Cal. Rptr. at 692–97.

41 *Id.* at 777–78, 704 P.2d at 759–60, 217 Cal. Rptr. at 692–93. Although the court was willing to accept without debate the contention that one who does not know the nature and quality of his act can not know that it is wrong, this is not completely obvious. Due to the conjunctive form of this requirement, it is possible at least in principle, for an individual to fail to satisfy the nature and quality requirement because he knows the quality (i.e., that it is harmful) but is mistaken about the nature (i.e., the physical characteristics). Suppose A pours powder into B's sugar bowl believing that it is poison that will kill B when B next adds the powder to his tea thinking it is sugar. In fact, A is mistaken; the powder is actually a chemical that explodes when it comes into contact with hot water. When B next adds "sugar" to his tea, he is injured in the explosion. Although A knew that his act was wrong, he did not know the nature and quality of his act because he was mistaken about the nature. Similar cases can be described in which the actor who knew that his act was wrong would fail the "nature and quality" requirement because he knew the nature but not the quality. Such examples raise perplexing legal, moral, and epistemological problems that can not be addressed here.

It is traditional to refer to the M'Naghten test as having two prongs: the nature and quality requirement, and the wrongfulness disjunct. The first of these, however, is itself a conjunctive requirement that is met only when the defendant was able to know both the nature and the quality of his act. In effect, then, the test has three disjunctive requirements. The defendant is exculpated if he is unable to know the nature, the quality, or the wrongfulness of his act. It is this complex nature of the "nature and quality" disjunct that allows the possibility of examples such as the "explosive sugar" one described earlier. Although it may be more accurate to describe the M'Naghten test as a three-prong standard, this book will conform to the traditional practice by referring to it as a two-prong test with a complex "nature and quality" requirement.

41

"till death do us part" in the marriage vows bestowed upon a marital partner a God-given right to kill a spouse who violated, or was inclined to violate, those vows. He understood this "right" as one that carried both legal and moral force.[42] Although Skinner would have been exculpated under either the legal or the moral interpretation of "wrongfulness," the court went on to analyze the wrongfulness requirement, and concluded that in order to be culpable, the defendant must be capable of knowing that the act was morally, and not merely legally wrong.[43]

In summary, the court interpreted Section 25(b) as a return to the previous California version of the *M'Naghten* standard that exculpated a defendant who was unable to know the nature and quality of his act *or* that it was wrongful. In doing so, the court identified the *M'Naghten*-type standard as fundamental to our system of jurisprudence. The court identified *M'Naghten* as the measure of cognitive functioning that is required to form the intent necessary to constitute an offense. The less-inclusive conjunctive interpretation of Section 25(b) was ruled out as inconsistent with our basic principles of jurisprudence. The federal statute and recommendations of professional organizations described earlier advocated *M'Naghten*-type standards, and rejected more inclusive ones as likely to lead to moral mistakes. Taken together, these recent developments seem to recommend *M'Naghten*-type standards as the kind that will provide clear criteria with determinate meaning and that will, therefore, be both necessary and sufficient to minimize moral mistakes; that is, these standards will be neither over-inclusive nor under-inclusive.

2.1.2 Evaluation of recent developments. A review of the past quarter of a century reveals a puzzling pattern of changes. Initially, *M'Naghten* was the dominant NGRI standard. It was severely criticized, however, as overly narrow in focus and,

42 *Id.* at 765–70, 704 P.2d at 752–55, 217 Cal. Rptr. at 685–88.
43 *Id.* at 777–84, 704 P.2d at 759–64, 217 Cal. Rptr. at 692–97.

therefore, under-inclusive. The MPC test was advanced as an improvement on *M'Naghten*, partially because it expressly addressed volition, and thus was more inclusive. The MPC standard, particularly the volitional clause, was then criticized as unclear and likely to lead to "moral mistakes." Recently, *M'Naghten*-type tests have been advocated as a means of avoiding these moral mistakes.

The arguments presented here call into question the *Skinner* court's reasons for interpreting Section 25(b) as a return to *M'Naghten*. It is certainly possible, however, for a court to make the right decision for the wrong reasons. Perhaps the more fundamental question is whether the *M'Naghten* test, which was so highly criticized in the past, can be expected to provide a clear standard and prevent moral mistakes.

At least two problems arise regarding the clarity of the standard. First, the test turns on the defendant's capacity to know or appreciate. As discussed earlier, however, it has never been established what either of these terms means, or whether there is any intelligible difference between the two terms. The second, and perhaps more problematic, difficulty with the *M'Naghten* test is that it turns on the defendant's capacity to know (or appreciate) the wrongfulness of his act.[44]

Three distinct meanings have been attributed to "wrongfulness." "Wrong" may mean: (1) illegal, (2) contrary to the socially accepted moral standard, or (3) contrary to the defendant's subjective moral standard. The first interpretation is accepted in England,[45] and it has been accepted by some courts in the United States.[46] Other authorities consider this

---

44 Most plausible candidates for the NGRI defense will qualify for exculpation under the wrongfulness disjunct, if at all, because the nature and quality disjunct has usually been interpreted narrowly to require only awareness of the physical characteristics of the act and awareness that it was harmful. See sources cited *supra* notes 6–7.

45 R. v. Windle, 2 All E.R. 1, 1–3 (1952); Goldstein, *supra* note 5, at 52; LaFave and Scott, *supra* note 1, at sec. 4.2(b) (4).

46 State v. Foster, 44 Hawaii 403, 426, 354 P.2d 960, 972 (1960) (defendant is exculpated only if he is incompetent to discern the nature and criminality of the act); State v. Boan, 235 Kan. 800, 810, 686 P.2d 160, 168 (1984) (defendant is exculpated only if he was unable to know that his actions were contrary to Kansas law); State v. Andrews, 187

interpretation to be too restrictive, and select one of the two moral variations. The social moral standard, the second interpretation, has been endorsed by the *Skinner* court and others.[47] At least one court has reasoned that there is no effective difference between the legal and social moral interpretations, and thus has explicitly rejected both of these in favor of the third interpretation, the subjective moral standard.[48]

An anticipated advantage of a clear standard with definite meaning is that a jury would be able to apply it consistently and fairly in order to avoid moral mistakes. Given the intent to avoid moral mistakes, it would be consistent with the purpose of the test to select the interpretation of "wrongfulness" that would preclude such mistakes. As indicated previously, the term "moral mistake" is apparently intended to refer to cases in which the decision regarding legal culpability is inconsistent with the defendant's state of moral blameworthiness for the offense with which he is charged. The appropriate interpretation of "wrongfulness," therefore, would be that which avoids decisions regarding the defendant's legal culpability that are inconsistent with his moral blameworthiness for the offense.

On this understanding of the purpose of the NGRI defense, and of the meaning of "moral mistake," the courts are charged with formulating a moral standard. The court should select and apply the interpretation of wrongfulness that inculpates all and only those who are morally blameworthy for the act constituting the offense, and exculpates all and only those who are not morally blameworthy for their offending

Kan. 458, 469, 357 P.2d 739, 747 (1961) (wrong means that which is prohibited by the law of the land).

47 *Skinner*, 39 Cal. 3d at 783–84, 704 P.2d at 764, 217 Cal. Rptr. at 697; People v. Rittger, 54 Cal. 2d 720, 734, 355 P.2d 645, 653, 7 Cal. Rptr. 901, 909 (1960); State v. Berndt, 138 Ariz. 41, 45, 672 P.2d 1311, 1315 (1983); State v. Sanchez, 117 Ariz. 369, 373, 573 P.2d 60, 64 (1977); State v. Corley, 108 Ariz. 240, 243, 495 P.2d 470, 473 (1972). People v. Schmidt, 216 N.Y. at 340, 110 N.E. at 949.

48 United States v. Segna, 555 F.2d 226, 232 (1977) (defendant is not responsible if he believes he is morally justified in his conduct even though he may appreciate that his act is contrary to law and public morality).

actions. The court faces the task of measuring each standard against the moral correctness of the decisions it would produce. This process of standard selection is virtually identical to the procedure followed by many philosophers when they evaluate moral principles.

John Rawls described the process of "reflective equilibrium" by which proposed moral principles are tested against deeply held and carefully considered intuitions regarding real or hypothetical situations.[49] Morally significant cases are evaluated according to the proposed principle. If the principle produces moral evaluations and prescriptions for action that are consistent with these considered moral intuitions, and provides a common foundation for them, the principle is supported. If, however, there is a discrepancy between the considered intuitions and the evaluations or prescriptions provided by the principle, then either the principle must be modified or the intuitions reconsidered in light of the principle and the other intuitions that support that principle.

The process is one of careful reasoning back and forth from principle to shared intuitive evaluations of particular cases. Ideally, the result would be an integrated set of principles that would provide a common foundation for our entire set of morally relevant intuitions, which are themselves duly pruned and integrated. A real or hypothetical situation constitutes a counter-example that defeats a principle if it demonstrates that the principle would require an evaluation or action that is clearly contrary to moral intuitions that remain firmly held after careful consideration.

In the context of selecting a standard for the NGRI defense, the court measures proposed NGRI tests, or interpretations of those tests, against the results that these standards would produce in cases. A satisfactory standard should exculpate all and only those defendants who were not morally blameworthy for their offenses due to their psychopathology. As

49 J. Rawls, A Theory of Justice 19–21, 46–53 (Cambridge, MA: Harvard Univ. Press, 1971).

it pursues this task, the court is applying the method of reflective equilibrium to proposed insanity tests, and searching for a standard that embodies an accurate measure of moral blameworthiness.[50]

Justice Cardozo's reasoning in *People v. Schmidt* can be understood as an example of judicial reasoning that conforms to the process of reflective equilibrium. Cardozo reasoned that a defendant who knew that his act was illegal, but believed that God had ordained it, would not be morally blameworthy. If the "wrongfulness" disjunct of the *M'Naghten* test were interpreted as requiring only that the defendant was capable of knowing that his act was illegal, then such a defendant would be inculpated under the NGRI test. Therefore, "wrongfulness" must mean "morally wrong," not merely "illegal."[51] By this reasoning, Cardozo accepted the case as a counter-example to the moral principle represented by the *M'Naghten* standard with "wrongful" interpreted as "illegal."

A similar pattern of reasoning can be applied to the social and subjective variations of the moral interpretations of the "wrongfulness" standard. Unfortunately, there appear to be counter-examples to both variations. One can propose plausible hypothetical cases in which the defendant appears to be the sort of person who should be considered a reasonable candidate for the NGRI defense, but who would clearly be excluded under these tests, thus resulting in moral mistakes. Consider the following cases.

---

50 The principle of *stare decisis* leads to an important difference between the manner in which this method is applied by philosophers and the manner in which it is applied by courts. If a philosopher encounters a persuasive counter-example to a principle, he may abandon it in favor of some alternative that more adequately accommodates the entire set of cases. In contrast, once a court has announced a principle and decided a case on the basis of it, the mere fact of the decision weighs against discarding the principle. Courts can reverse prior decisions, but the principle of *stare decisis* supports the status quo. In short, it is easier (in principle, if not in practice) for the philosopher to say "I was wrong."

51 People v. Schmidt, 216 N.Y. 324, 339, 110 N.E. 945, 949 (1915).

1. According to the social standard, the defendant would be culpable if he were capable of knowing both the nature and quality of his act and the fact that his act violated the prevailing community standard of morality.

X is psychotic, and as a result of his psychosis, believes that the universe is powered and directed by an impersonal cosmic force represented by the sun and the moon. He understands the television weather reports as messages directed personally to him that worship of the traditional Christian God is misguided. He begins a program to correct this erroneous worship by burning down churches.

X understands the physical nature of his actions, and that they will be harmful to the churches as well as to anyone who happens to be in one when it burns. He also is fully aware that his actions are both illegal and immoral by the prevailing community standard, but he believes that this standard is wrong. In his psychotic view of the world, it seems to him that he ought (morally) to continue. Under the social standard, X would not qualify for exculpation under the NGRI defense.

2. According to the subjective standard, the defendant would be culpable if he were capable of knowing both the nature and quality of his act and the fact that his act was immoral by his subjective standard.

Y is psychotic. He interprets his experiences in traffic and the regulations requiring drivers to yield to pedestrians in crosswalks as indicating that it is legal and moral by the prevailing social standard for drivers to kill pedestrians who cross outside of the crosswalks. By his personal standard, he considers this to be morally abhorrent and he takes it as evidence of the dangerous and immoral society he lives in. Due to his personal moral beliefs, he usually avoids hitting pedestrians wherever they are.

One day, in a moment of anger, he intentionally hits a pedestrian who has crossed in the middle of the block and yelled obscenities at Y. When Y realizes that he has broken the pedestrian's leg, he feels guilty and remorseful because he thinks he has done something morally wrong, but he makes no attempt to escape because he is convinced that his act was legal as well as approved by public moral standards. He is startled and confused when the police arrest him. Under the subjective standard, Y would not qualify for exculpation under the NGRI defense.

3. Some might wish to argue that these cases demonstrate that the wrongfulness standard should require that the defendant is capable of knowing that his act is wrong by both the prevailing social morality and his subjective standard. Note, however, the following example.

Z is suffering a major depressive disorder with psychosis. He believes that Satan has temporarily prevailed in his eternal struggle with God. Consequently, he believes that the next 100 years will be a period of great misery for all good people. He knows that it is illegal to kill and that it is wrong by the prevailing moral standard. In addition, he endorses that standard. Despite his firm belief that it is legally and morally wrong to kill, he finds the thought that his children will experience the same misery of existence that he has already begun to live intolerable. After careful, prolonged deliberation, and with great sadness and remorse regarding the terrible wrong he is doing, he strangles them.

It is tempting to argue that Z did not "really" know that his act was wrong. But Z did know that the act violated the prevailing moral standard, and he did believe that the prevailing standard was the morally correct one. He felt remorse just because he was convinced he was doing a great wrong. If someone were to commit a crime of profit despite knowing that act to be wrong, and feeling guilt regarding it, there would be no apparent reason to think that he did not "really" know that it was wrong. Furthermore, there seems to be no reason to think that one could do what he believes to be wrong for his own benefit, but not for his children's benefit. Z would not qualify as insane under any of the three interpretations of "wrongfulness." He knew that the act was illegal as well as contrary to both the accepted social morality and his own personal moral beliefs.

X, Y, and Z all appear to be legitimate candidates for the NGRI defense. Reasonable people might differ in their final conclusions regarding these three actors, but most people would agree that they are plausible candidates. That is, if one thinks that there is a legitimate role for the NGRI defense, then these actors are among those who would be able to raise a nonfrivolous claim to the defense.

Yet, if we accept the interpretation provided by the authorities cited earlier of the nature, quality, and wrongfulness requirements of the *M'Naghten*-type tests, they all seem to fall clearly outside of the scope of the test. Each knows the physical characteristics of his acts, the harmful quality of those acts, and the fact that those acts are wrong by the respective standards. Although the move toward the cognitive *M'Naghten* test was apparently intended to make the NGRI defense more precise and predictable, and to avoid "moral mistakes," it apparently has not provided a satisfactory standard for these purposes.

Finally, it may well be the case that in practice a court would exculpate the hypothetical actors described here. But to do so, a court would have to manipulate the standard in order to accommodate the cases. A standard that requires distortion in order to serve its function falls short of the intent to develop a test with a clear and definite meaning. In addition, standards that can be distorted to accommodate cases in a manner that is consistent with common intuitions of justice are also likely to be vulnerable to distortion resulting in moral mistakes.[52]

52 This argument should not be taken as an endorsement of the MPC

These examples all involve cases in which a defendant would be found culpable under a strict interpretation of a *M'Naghten*-type test despite the fact that each appears to be the sort of person usually thought to be a plausible candidate for exculpation. This may not be the type of moral mistake that the changes in the standard were intended to avoid. To the extent that the changes were a response to the concerns raised or exacerbated by the *Hinckley* acquittal, they were probably directed primarily toward the problem of acquitting the guilty rather than toward avoiding convictions of the innocent.

There is no apparent reason, however, to think that inculpating those who should be exculpated is any less a moral mistake than exculpating those who should be inculpated. There may be policy reasons for preferring to risk the former sort of error over the latter, but if this change is really based on such policy considerations, then it requires justification in terms of those considerations rather than in the guise of putative moral rectitude.

2.1.3 Conclusions. The history of the NGRI defense reveals a long and frustrating search for a satisfactory standard. The *M'Naghten* test has been the dominant standard for most of the last century and a half. That test was severely criticized, however, and there was a discernible trend away from it and toward the MPC test for approximately twenty years following the introduction of that test.

Recent developments, however, suggest a general trend toward restricting the scope of the NGRI defense and, specifically, a return to standards of the *M'Naghten* type. This

standard because it is not at all clear that these cases could be accommodated by that test either (assuming that it were strictly applied). There is no reason in the accounts of X, Y, or Z to think that any of these actors lacked capacity to conform their behavior to the law. Much of the criticism of the MPC test is directed toward the lack of any clear conception of what would constitute a volitional deficiency. This issue will be addressed again in chapter 6.

move is motivated by a desire for a clear standard with determinate meaning that will avoid moral mistakes. Interpreted collectively, the arguments advanced in support of the 1984 federal statute – Section 25(b) of the California Penal Code as interpreted by the *Skinner* court and the recommendations of the ABA and the APA – seem to suggest that *M'Naghten*-type standards are necessary and sufficient for these purposes.

Unfortunately, there appears to be no good reason to think that either of these goals has been advanced. The analysis in this chapter suggests that we are left with the same fundamental problems that have traditionally plagued the search for a satisfactory standard. If we are to develop an adequate standard, we will probably not do so through recourse to other past tests or public initiatives, but rather through a careful investigation of the structure of our system of criminal liability and a deeper inquiry into the moral foundations of that system as informed by a thorough appreciation of the nature of psychopathology. We will pursue that in Chapters 4, 6, and 7.

2.2 THE STATUS OF THE NGRI DEFENSE

The *Skinner* court failed to distinguish failure-of-proof defenses from general defenses when it reasoned that the *M'Naghten* test was necessary to support the role of criminal intent in our system of criminal justice. The NGRI defense has been interpreted by various writers as a failure-of-proof defense, as a specific excuse that applies one of the usual excusing conditions of ignorance or coercion, and as a status excuse that is uniquely appropriate to those who suffer certain types of psychological disorder. Each of these classifications raises different issues and difficulties regarding the NGRI defense.

2.2.1 NGRI as a failure-of-proof defense. As discussed earlier, criminal liability under the MPC must be based on conduct that includes a voluntary act, and the actor must have acted with the required level of culpability regarding each material element of the offense. Most serious offenses require that the actor acted with a culpability level of purposely, knowingly, or recklessly. When the offense definition fails to specify a culpability requirement, the MPC presumes that the actor must act at least recklessly regarding each material element.[53] The actor acts recklessly with regard to a material element when he consciously disregards a substantial and unjustified risk that the element is present or will result.[54] In order to consciously disregard such a risk, the actor must be aware of it. Thus, the actor must have generally accurate knowledge about the nature of his act and the likely consequences in order to act recklessly.

The actor needs a similar type and degree of knowledge in order to act knowingly or purposely. He acts knowingly when he knows that all material elements of the offense are satisfied with substantial certainty. He acts purposely when he acts for the purpose of performing the acts, or causing the effects that constitute the material elements of the offense.[55]

Technically, the defendant could act purposely regarding a material element while he was in fact mistaken about it, but in such a case he could be guilty only of an attempt. For example, A could shoot at a silhouette in B's window for the purpose of killing B, but succeed only in destroying B's bust of Mozart. In such a case, A acted purposely with regard to the homicide element of causing B's death, but his factual error prevented him from actually causing B's death. A therefore failed to meet a material offense element for any homicide offense, and could be convicted only of attempted homicide.[56] The important point here is that relevant failures

53 MPC, *supra* note 9, at sec. 2.02(3).
54 *Id.* at sec. 2.02.
55 *Id.* at sec. 2.02(2) (b), 2.02(2) (a), respectively.
56 *Id.* at sec. 210.1(1) (regarding homicide) and 5.01(1)(a) (regarding attempts). One could imagine exotic circumstances under which A could purposefully cause B's death despite such errors. Suppose, for example, that in the case discussed here, B heard the shot, entered the room, and died of disappointment when he saw his shattered bust

of knowledge can prevent an actor from acting with the required culpability level in most serious offenses.

The *M'Naghten* test is an ignorance standard that excuses the defendant who does not know the nature, quality, or wrongfulness of his act. If one accepts the argument presented earlier that there is no identifiable difference between "know" and "appreciate" as these terms are used in the NGRI defense, then the MPC standard also contains an ignorance standard.

Some writers have interpreted the NGRI defense as one that exculpates the defendant whose psychopathology produced in him a condition of ignorance that prevented him from acting with *mens rea*. J. Goldstein and J. Katz appear to be interpreting the NGRI defense in this manner when they argue that the defense is really a device intended to allow the state to confine actors who should be free of liability because their psychological disorder prevented them from acting with *mens rea* and thus from fulfilling all offense elements.[57] S. Brakel, J. Parry, and B. Weiner sometimes appear to interpret the NGRI defense in this manner, but it is difficult to be certain because it is not clear whether they use the term *mens rea* in the special or general sense. They initially describe *mens rea* as the requirement of criminal intent that must accompany the forbidden act that constitutes the crime. At this point, *mens rea* is apparently used in the special sense. Shortly thereafter, however, they appear to use the term in the general sense when they describe the doctrine of *mens rea* as

of Mozart. In such a case, courts must address difficult questions regarding the necessary correspondence between the act and the effect. *See,* LaFave and Scott, *supra* note 1, at sec. 3.11. Under most plausible circumstances, however, relevant failure of knowledge will prevent an actor from satisfying all offense elements knowingly.

57 Goldstein and Katz, *Abolish the "Insanity Defense" – Why Not?*, 72 Yale L. J. 853, 864–65 (1963). It is difficult to be certain whether these authors were endorsing this interpretation or advancing the conditional thesis that if the NGRI defense operates in this manner, then it serves primarily to provide a mechanism allowing the state to confine those who are not guilty of a crime. The primary point here is to examine the claim, regardless of whether these authors intended to endorse it.

exempting insane persons and children from punishment because these actors could not comprehend the morality of their actions.[58]

Consider the *M'Naghten* provision that exculpates those who do not know the nature and quality of their act. The courts have interpreted the nature and quality requirements narrowly, such that the nature of an act is defined by its physical characteristics, and a person knows the quality of his offending act if he knows that it is harmful.[59] According to the MPC, "A person is guilty of perjury . . . if in any official proceeding . . . he makes a false statement under oath . . . when the statement is material and he does not believe it to be true."[60] This is approximately equivalent to knowingly making a false statement under oath in official proceedings. Suppose a psychotic defendant knowingly makes a false statement in court while delusionally believing that he is projecting his thoughts in a special manner that is perceivable only by certain spies who are monitoring his brain activity. That is, he does not realize that he is speaking out loud. In such a case, he would qualify for exculpation under the *M'Naghten* test because he did not know the nature of his act.

When an offense is defined in terms of harmful consequences, the actor may fail to know the quality of his act if his psychopathology prevents him from knowing that it is harmful. "A person is guilty of assault if he: (a) attempts to cause or purposely, knowingly, or recklessly causes bodily injury to another."[61] Consider the psychotic defendant who believes that his son is possessed by the devil and that his son will be fine as soon as the devil is driven out. He beats and seriously injures his son with a silver cross, convinced that this will drive the devil out and that only the devil can

58 Brakel, Parry, and Weiner, *supra* note 1, at 708–09.
59 *See supra* chapter 2.1 regarding the narrow interpretation of the nature of an act.
60 MPC, *supra* note 9, at sec. 2.41(1).
61 *Id.* at sec. 211.1(1) (a).

be injured by a silver cross. He would be exculpated under *M'Naghten* because he did not know the harmful quality of his act.

Although both defendants would be excused under *M'Naghten,* they would also have been exculpated in a jurisdiction that had abolished the NGRI defense. The same considerations that would support NGRI findings would also establish failure-of-proof defenses for both defendants because they did not satisfy the culpability requirements for a material element of their offenses. The first defendant did not know that he was speaking, or even that there was a substantial risk of his speaking, whereas the second did not know that he was creating a substantial risk of injury. Cases such as these support the impression that the NGRI defense merely replicates failure-of-proof defenses regarding the culpability requirement.

Similarly, NGRI standards that include a volitional clause at least appear to replicate failure-of-proof defenses regarding the voluntary act provision of the MPC. This impression is tentative for two reasons. First, as indicated in Chapter 1, the exact nature of the voluntary act requirement is not clear; it is hard to be certain, therefore, what would constitute a failure-of-proof defense that addressed it. Second, as described in Chapter 2.1.1, the volitional clause of the MPC test has not been explicated as clearly as one would like either. If, however, the volitional clause is understood as defeating voluntariness in the narrow sense of "voluntariness" employed by the MPC, then it seems to provide a defense in cases that would also have a failure-of-proof defense available.

Whereas this interpretation of the NGRI defense as a subset of failure-of-proof defenses seems plausible regarding certain cases, it encounters serious difficulty with others. On some interpretations, for example, the volitional clause of the MPC's NGRI provision extends beyond the narrow sense of "voluntary" used in the MPC's voluntary act requirement to the broader and more common sense of "voluntariness."

On these accounts, the volitional clause would apply to some defendants who would not be exculpated by the failure-of-proof defense regarding the voluntary act requirement.

In addition, both the *M'Naghten* and MPC standards exculpate the defendant who does not know that his conduct is wrongful. Lack of knowledge of wrongfulness, whether legal or moral, does not establish a failure-of-proof defense unless knowledge of illegality is included among the elements of the offense. Although this is not unheard of, few offense definitions include knowledge of wrongfulness as a material element.[62]

Furthermore, there seem to be defendants who are at least plausible candidates for the NGRI defense but who clearly meet all offense elements. The case of Z at the end of Section 2.1.1 provides an example. By hypothesis, Z purposely strangled his children despite his awareness of the nature, quality, and wrongfulness of his act.

The classification of the NGRI defense as a failure-of-proof defense encounters other difficulties in addition to counterexamples. Procedurally, the state bears the burden of proving all offense elements, but the defendant may have the burden of proving the NGRI defense. Hence, if the NGRI defense is classified as a failure-of-proof defense, then in jurisdictions that place the burden of proving the defense on the defendant, both parties will have the burden of proving the same fact. For example, the state might have the burden to prove that the defendant acted knowingly, whereas he has the burden of proving that he did not. In such a case, if both parties failed to carry their burdens, then both parties should prevail! Additionally, the failure-of-proof interpretation simply renders the NGRI defense superfluous. It would be ironic indeed if so many people had agonized for so long about a vacuous defense.

There is a related interpretation, however, that is sometimes confused with the failure-of-proof hypothesis and

---

62 *Id.* at sec. 212.3. False imprisonment requires knowledge of illegality as an offense element.

that may provide a more attractive account to many who consider the issue. Some argue, in effect, that there is nothing special about mental illness. The idea here is not that the NGRI defense should be understood as a failure-of-proof claim. Rather, proponents of this position hold that mental disorder exculpates only by producing one of the ordinary excusing conditions involving some type of ignorance or compulsion.

2.2.2 NGRI as an application of standard excusing conditions. On this view, the NGRI defense is a general defense. More precisely, it is a specific excuse, but psychological disorder leads to exculpation in the same manner that many other circumstances do, by causing a standard excusing condition. Psychopathology is just one of several disabilities that can result in a state of ignorance or compulsion that constitutes an excusing condition. On this interpretation, psychological dysfunction is analogous to a mistake regarding justification or to duress. This picture is consistent with Robinson's claim that all excuses share a common structure of excusing condition caused by disability. In addition, the usual NGRI standards include ignorance and volitional clauses that correspond to at least three of Robinson's excusing conditions.[63]

Although both the failure-of-proof hypothesis and the view presented here direct attention to ignorance as an important source of exculpation, there is an important difference between the two approaches. On the current "standard excuse" view, the ignorance that exculpates does not have to negate a material element of the offense.

The NGRI defense, on this interpretation, takes a form that is comparable to certain other general defenses. Compare, for example, the ignorance clauses of the standard NGRI tests to the specific excuse that is available to those who act on a mistaken but reasonable belief that their act is justified. This defense would excuse a defendant whose conduct fulfilled

63   Robinson, *supra* note 6, at sec. 161, 173.

all offense elements for assault, but who reasonably believed that his action was necessary to protect himself or others from serious bodily injury.[64] Similarly, ignorance of illegality excuses when it is due to the unavailability of law or an official misstatement of law.[65]

The excusing condition in both of these types of excuses is the defendant's ignorance of the illegality or wrongfulness of his act. Although Robinson's uniform structure of excuses calls for a disability that gives rise to the excusing condition for each excuse, neither of these excuses includes a disability condition. There are additional factors, however, that fulfill the function usually served by the disability requirement. The reasonableness required of the mistake regarding justification limits this excuse to unusual circumstances in which we believe that the defendant actually believed his action was justified because we can see that the belief was reasonable. We tend to think that most reasonable people, including ourselves, would have believed that the action was necessary under the circumstances. Similarly, we believe that an actor really acted in ignorance of the law when that law was unavailable or officially misrepresented.[66] Hence, with these excuses, verifiable circumstances separate that actor in those conditions from the rest of the population in ordinary conditions and support the contention that the excusing condition actually obtained.

The NGRI ignorance clauses exculpate when the actor did not know the nature, quality, or wrongfulness of his actions. Due to the narrow interpretation of the nature and quality clauses, most defendants will escape liability under the wrongfulness provision, if at all. These NGRI cases, in contrast to those involving the excuses described earlier,

64 MPC, *supra* note 9, at sec. 3.04; Robinson, *supra* note 6, at sec. 184.
65 MPC, *supra* note 9, at sec. 2.04(3); Robinson, *supra* note 6, at sec. 182, 183.
66 Notice that this latter defense may be supportable as either an excuse or a nonexculpatory policy defense. It might excuse for the reasons given in the text. Alternately, it could further the policy of encouraging officials to publish the law accurately. It is usually formulated and defended as an excuse.

often occur in circumstances in which most people would know that their act was illegal and wrongful. For this reason, the presence of a disability becomes an important factor in establishing that the excusing condition actually obtained. When A shoots B repetitively while B sleeps, we usually feel quite certain that A knew that his act was wrongful. We may start to entertain doubts, however, when we learn that A psychotically believed that he was acting on direct orders from God. On this view, the NGRI defense excuses in the same manner, and for the same reason that other ignorance defenses do; psychopathology is merely one type of disability that can give rise to the standard excusing conditions.

Those who advocate this position would submit volitional clauses to a similar analysis. The MPC test excuses those who, by virtue of mental disease or defect, lack substantial ability to conform their conduct to the law.[67] This is a direct application of one of Robinson's excusing conditions, and it at least appears to fit well with the claim that all excuses are attributable to either ignorance or compulsion.[68] Robinson identifies this excusing condition as the least compelling of those that he lists, however, because it is often very difficult to distinguish those who were unable to conform their conduct to the law from those who simply did not. For this reason, the disability plays a central role in convincing us that the defendant was actually unable to control his conduct. One can draw certain parallels between duress, in which the defendant must show that he was subject to such coercion that no reasonable person would have resisted, and this clause of the NGRI defense, in which the defendant must show that he was so disturbed that he could not have conformed.[69]

This "standard excuse" interpretation of the NGRI defense, however, encounters difficulty with both ignorance

---

67 MPC, *supra* note 9, at sec. 4.01.
68 Robinson, *supra* note 6, at sec. 161(a).
69 *Id.* at sec. 161(a), 173(e).

and volitional clauses. Although Robinson and others are correct in pointing out the problem involved in distinguishing those who can not conform from those who simply do not conform, the central issue is much deeper than this. We simply have no idea what we mean by an inability to conform. We clearly do not mean that the actor lacked the physical ability to control his movements. If, for example, A struck B as a result of an unexpected and unforeseeable seizure that deprived A of conscious control of his limbs, A would clearly fulfill the condition of being unable to conform his conduct to the law. In such a case, however, A would be exculpated under a failure-of-proof defense regarding the voluntary act requirement.

When we shift our attention to cases in which the defendant was severely psychopathological, it seems natural to say that he was so crazy that he was unable to control himself. It remains unclear, however, what we mean by that. Surely, if the defendant is severely disturbed, something is wrong; but the mere fact that something is wrong does not provide reason to think that one's capacity to conform is impaired, nor does it clarify the nature of such an impairment. Puzzles such as these motivated the recent trend away from volitional tests and back toward *M'Naghten*-type standards.[70]

The interpretation of the ignorance clauses as applications of the more general excusing conditions also encounters difficulty. The comparison of the NGRI ignorance clauses to the excuses associated with reasonable mistake as to justification or nonculpable ignorance of the law suggests that the NGRI defense merely supplies one more condition under which the defendant can confidently be exonerated of responsibility for his ignorance regarding the illegality of his conduct. Many jurisdictions have adopted either the social or subjective moral interpreta-

---

70 *See supra* chapter 2.1.1. This issue will be addressed more completely in chapter 6.3.

tions of "wrongful" in the NGRI defense, however, and we have no comparable general excuses for "nonculpable ignorance of immorality."

Some readers might think that the law ought to provide such a general excusing condition regarding ignorance of immorality. I take no position on that issue here. The key point here is that the law does not currently recognize such an excusing condition, but various jurisdictions apply social or subjective moral interpretations of the wrongfulness clause of the NGRI defense. As long as this discrepancy remains, one cannot plausibly argue that the NGRI defense is merely an application of ordinary excusing conditions to mentally disordered defendants.

Finally, there appear to be certain plausible examples of legitimate NGRI defendants who do not fall under any of the standard ignorance or volitional clauses. Even if one interprets the ignorance and volitional clauses of the *M'Naghten* and MPC tests as applications of more general ignorance or compulsion excuses, Z acted in a calculated and effective manner, following careful reflection, and with full knowledge of the nature, quality, and wrongfulness of his act.[71] Although some NGRI defendants seem to fit the more general ignorance and compulsion categories, others are more difficult to accommodate under this model. Joel Feinberg tentatively endorsed this model, but he then identified certain cases that seem to raise some questions regarding the adequacy of the "standard excuse" interpretation. These cases usually involve actors who seem intuitively to be psychologically disturbed in ways that are relevant to culpability but not satisfactorily described in terms of ignorance or compulsion.[72] Such cases have led some writers to suggest a third classification for the NGRI defense. They suggest that this defense is a status excuse.

71 *See supra* chapter 2.1.2.
72 J. Feinberg, Doing and Deserving 272 (Princeton: Princeton Univ. Press, 1970).

2.2.3 NGRI as a status excuse. Writers who categorize the NGRI defense as a status excuse often direct attention to the similarity this defense bears to the defense labeled "infancy" or "immaturity." The dominant approach to this defense either exempts all defendants under a certain age from criminal liability, or vests jurisdiction over those below some specified age in a special juvenile court.[73] Such statutes require neither an excusing condition regarding the conduct in question nor a disability, unless one considers the age itself as a disability. Those who would apply this approach to the NGRI defense contend that we excuse seriously psychologically disturbed actors from criminal liability because they are so disturbed. That is, their status as severely disordered persons renders them inappropriate subjects for evaluation and punishment by the criminal justice system. They are simply the wrong kind of being for that system to deal with.

Herbert Fingarette advances a conception of insanity and an approach to the NGRI defense that seems to portray the defense as a status excuse, but certain aspects of his theory are more compatible with a specific excuse interpretation. Fingarette contends that the NGRI defense goes to the status of the person as responsible.[74] He contends that the NGRI defendant is not a fit subject for criminal condemnation or punishment. Rather, such a defendant is outside the law in the sense that the entire prosecutory process is inappropriate for that person. The NGRI defense is not an excuse, but rather a claim that this person is not the sort of being to whom the criminal justice system can appropriately be applied.[75] On this interpretation, the NGRI defense is analogous to a jurisdictional claim that the criminal courts have no jurisdiction over certain disordered persons.

Douglas Husak has criticized this approach, however, on

73 *See supra* chapter 1.2.
74 Fingarette, *supra* note 1, at 157, 214.
75 Fingarette and Hasse, *supra* note 7, at 73, 208–09.

the grounds that Fingarette's recommended procedure is inconsistent with his own claim that the NGRI defendant is outside of the proper scope of the prosecutory process. Husak argues that Fingarette's procedure, which calls for a trial on the substantive charges and a decision on the insanity issue only if the defendant is found guilty on at least one criminal count, is inconsistent with the claim that the defendant is outside the prosecutory system. Husak contends that both this substantive trial on the facts and the court order for confinement of NGRI acquittees require that the defendant is not outside the law in the sense that Fingarette claims.[76]

Perhaps Fingarette could respond to these criticisms by altering his procedure or by arguing that these procedures are consistent with his status claim because even if one accepts the contention that NGRI defendants are outside the prosecutorial process, the court would have to hold hearings to establish that this status applied to this defendant. He might argue further that the court could confine a defendant for whom this status had been established as an exercise of the state's police powers in order to protect the public. He might alter his recommended procedure in order to allow the question of NGRI status to be raised earlier in the process, as one would expect of a true status claim.

Putting procedural issues aside, however, Fingarette's analysis of the concept of insanity and of the NGRI defense does not consistently support the status excuse interpretation over the specific excuse model. The key difference between specific excuses and status excuses lies in the requirement of an excusing condition that applies to the specific behavior that constitutes the offense. Robinson's structure of specific excuses requires such an excusing condition regarding the conduct in question, whereas status excuses exempt the de-

---

76 D. Husak, The Philosophy of Criminal Law 196–97 (Totowa, NJ: Rowman & Littlefield, 1987).

fendant from punishment on the basis of membership in some specified category.[77]

Whereas Fingarette sometimes describes the NGRI defendant as holding a status that places him outside the law or beyond the prosecutory process, he also defines insanity and the NGRI defendant in terms of deficits of certain capacities with regards to the specific offense charged. In these passages, the NGRI defense fits the model of a specific excuse. NGRI defendants are described, for example, as lacking "the mental capacity for rational control of that conduct."[78] Fingarette proposes the following definition of criminal insanity: "The individual's mental make up at the time of the offending act was such that, with respect to the criminality of his conduct, he substantially lacked capacity to act rationally."[79] He also requires that the defendant be unable to act rationally with respect to the moral-legal status of his act or the criminality of his act.[80]

These passages suggest a conception of the insanity defense that is quite compatible with Robinson's structure of specific excuses. The defendant suffers some psychological disorder that constitutes the disability. This disability causes an impairment of his capacity to act rationally; that is, it gives rise to an excusing condition. Finally, this excusing condition must apply to the criminality of the conduct with which the defendant is charged.

Fingarette describes the key deficit as impairment of the "capacity to act rationally." In at least some cases, this may be explicated in a manner that is compatible with Robinson's four excusing conditions. That is, the defendant may have been unable to react rationally because he was ignorant of the nature, quality, or wrongfulness of his act, or because he was unable to conform his conduct to the law. Fingarette argues, however, that at least some appropriate NGRI de-

---

77 See supra chapter 1.2.
78 Fingarette and Hasse, supra note 7, at 73.
79 Fingarette, supra note 1, at 211.
80 Id. at 238, 241.

fendants do not meet these descriptions. These candidates are neither ignorant in the specified ways nor unable to control their conduct, but they are not able to respond rationally.[81] It is not clear exactly what we mean by the claim that they are unable to act rationally, but it hardly seems fair to criticize Fingarette on that ground, because we are also unable to elaborate satisfactorily on what we mean when we say that the defendant lacked the capacity to conform his conduct to the law.

If the impairment of the capacity to act rationally regarding the particular act in question cannot be given full effect in terms of Robinson's four excusing conditions, Fingarette may have shown that this set of four excusing conditions is incomplete. A complete account of recognized excusing conditions may require the addition of one or more conditions that constitute the inability to act rationally regarding a particular act. If, however, this inability to act rationally is such that it can ultimately be articulated as some type of psychological impairment regarding the act in question, then Fingarette's conception seems to take the form of a specific excuse rather than a status excuse.

Fingarette seems to describe a status defense at some points and a specific excuse at others. There is no reason to expect his account to conform to the system of defenses described in Chapter 1, or to that put forward by Robinson or Moore. The point, however, is that it is difficult to establish precisely what type of defense Fingarette and others have in mind, and this lack of clarity regarding the status of the NGRI defense in a system of defenses contributes to the difficulty encountered in developing a satisfactory formulation.

Moore advances a conception of the NGRI defense that falls clearly into the status excuse category. He argues that standard tests share a fundamental error. "They assume that legal insanity is an excuse for the particular acts done,

---

81 Fingarette and Hasse, *supra* note 7, at 23–65.

not a general status attached to a class of human beings who are not responsible agents."[82] Moore argues that the insane, like infants, are not moral agents or proper subjects of moral evaluation. "[T]he very status of being crazy precludes responsibility."[83]

In summary, Moore and possibly Fingarette reject both the failure-of-proof and specific excuse models of the NGRI defense. Their alternative account of the NGRI defense as a status excuse has certain advantages. For one, it seems to avoid the need to develop a precise account of the types of excusing conditions and disabilities that are sufficient to excuse. The frustrations encountered by the extended effort to formulate such a standard may suggest that the status excuse category is more likely to be satisfactory. In addition, this approach appeals to the intuition that certain types of psychopathology exculpate in a gross, obvious manner. When the actor is extremely psychotic, cognitively disorganized, and socially primitive, an examination to determine whether he lacked specific knowledge or capacities seems to miss the point. Approaching these defendants as responsible moral agents seems fundamentally unfair, futile, and likely to weaken the moral force of the criminal law for the rest of us who are moral agents.

Unfortunately, the status approach also encounters difficulties. First, those who advocate this approach need some clear description of the type of people who should fall within the scope of this exculpatory status and some justification for choosing the boundaries that are chosen. The apparent advantage gained by avoiding the task of formulating specific excusing conditions may seem illusory as one attempts to define and defend the category of persons to be included in the exempted status. This problem is exacerbated by the need to complete this program without appeal either to social policies or to implicit excusing conditions. If the exempted category were defined and justified in terms of some social

---

82 Moore, *supra* note 2, at 222.
83 Moore, *Causation and the Excuses*, 73 Calif. L. Rev. 1091, 1139 (1985).

policy that would be promoted, such as avoiding recidivism or costly, futile punishment, then the status excuse would be indistinguishable from the nonexculpatory defense. Both types of defenses would constitute strategies for pursuing social goals without regard to the blameworthiness of the defendants.[84]

Similarly, if the exempted category were defended by arguing that people in this category are certain, or virtually certain, to lack the capacities required for criminal liability regarding any behavior, then the status excuse would not differ in principle from the specific excuse. It would, in effect, constitute a conclusive presumption that a specific excuse applies to all conduct by the members of this category. Such a presumptive excuse might be defended on the grounds that the presence of the excusing condition is highly probable in this group and the exceptions are very difficult to identify.

There may be good reason to think that certain categories of people, such as children or the severely disturbed, should be exempted from criminal liability because they suffer impairments that differ significantly from the four standard excusing conditions listed by Robinson. This would only establish, however, that Robinson's list is incomplete, not that status excuses are fundamentally different types of defenses from specific excuses.

Second, the defender of the status approach must address the dilemma raised by the clearly psychotic defendant whose pathology is apparently unrelated to his crime. Suppose that A is delusionally convinced, despite strong evidence to the contrary, that his wife is unfaithful. One day he robs a bank for reasons completely unrelated to his delusions. In fact, he was a thief long before his reality testing deteriorated. Either A is included in the NGRI status group or he is not. If he is, why should he be exempted from responsibility by virtue of impairment that is apparently unrelated to the crime? If, however, A is excluded from the NGRI group, what criteria

84   *See supra* chapter 1.2.

for membership in this group appropriately defines an NGRI status defense but excludes a clearly psychotic defendant? The criteria cannot require that the defendant's pathology constitute an excusing condition regarding the conduct in question because such a requirement would recast the defense as a specific excuse.

2.3 SUMMARY

The NGRI defense has been categorized as a failure-of-proof defense, a specific excuse, and a status excuse. All three interpretations have some appeal, but all three encounter difficulty. The search for a satisfactory standard is closely related to this categorization issue. Although the *Skinner* court did not explicitly categorize the NGRI defense as a failure-of-proof defense, it concluded that abandoning the *M'Naghten* standard would entail abolishing the culpability requirement for criminal liability. This view led the court to interpret Section 25 (b) as a return to *M'Naghten*. In contrast, if one interprets the NGRI defense as a failure-of-proof claim but assumes that the state would retain its burden to prove all offense elements in the absence of the defense, then it appears to be redundant.

Those who categorize the NGRI defense as a specific excuse are likely to formulate a standard that specifies the necessary disabilities and excusing conditions, and if they think that Robinson's list of appropriate excusing conditions is exhaustive, they will develop a test that employs those conditions. Finally, writers who categorize the defense as a status excuse will describe the class of defendants who should be exempted from punishment. For example, Moore would ask the jury, "Is the accused so irrational as to be nonresponsible?"[85] Morse advocates a status interpretation according to which a defendant would be NGRI if he was "so extremely crazy and the craziness so substantially af-

---

85 Moore, *supra* note 2, at 245.

68

fected the criminal behavior that the defendant does not deserve to be punished."[86]

This complex debate regarding the correct categorization of the NGRI defense and its appropriate formulation is inseparable from the system of offense elements that defines the offenses from which defendants seek exculpation. The continuing disputes regarding the NGRI defense are related to the ongoing lack of clarity regarding the underlying structure of offense elements. For example, the MPC includes a vaguely articulated voluntary act requirement for criminal liability, and it advances an NGRI standard with a volitional clause that exculpates those who are unable to conform their conduct to the law.[87] If one interprets the volitional clause as exculpating all those who, by virtue of mental disease or defect, do not perform their illegal conduct voluntarily, then this clause seems to establish a failure-of-proof defense. Psychotic behavior is not listed among the examples of involuntary action, however, and it is not obvious whether or not such conduct is the product of effort and determination in the same manner as ordinary human action is.

The recent trend away from volitional clauses in the NGRI defense has not been accompanied by attempts to abolish the voluntary act requirement, suggesting that some legislators and commentators view the former as different from, and more objectionable than, the latter. Those who advocate abolition of volitional clauses argue that it is impossible to distinguish actors who were unable to conform to the law

---

86 Morse, *Excusing the Crazy*, 58 S. Cal. L. Rev. 777, 820 (1985). Although Morse generally presents his recommendation as a status excuse, the requirement that "the craziness so substantially affected the criminal behavior" suggests that this formulation assumes some attributes of a specific excuse. It seems to require that the craziness in some unspecified way gave rise to the behavior constituting the objective elements of the offense. On this interpretation, Morse has identified a disability (craziness) and a required relation between the disability and the offending behavior. This seems to suggest that Morse's status excuse is actually a specific excuse with an unspecified excusing condition.

87 MPC, *supra* note 9, at sec. 2.01, 4.01(1).

from those who simply did not conform. Similarly, it is very difficult to categorize some actions as voluntary or involuntary according to the MPC provision. The point is not that the voluntary act requirement and volitional clauses are redundant, but rather that we lack a clear conception of either one or of the relationship between the two, and that this lack of clarity contributes to the perennial questions regarding defenses that appeal to these provisions. This effect is not limited to the NGRI defense; it also pervades the discussion about automatism.

Chapter 3

Problematic defenses: Automatism

Automatism is a defense against criminal liability for those defendants who perform illegal conduct in a state of unconsciousness or semi-consciousness.[1] The defense may apply to "behavior performed in a state of mental unconsciousness or dissociation without full awareness."[2] Although the paradigmatic cases of automatism are those involving convulsions, reflexes, or other movements that are apparently performed without any conscious direction, the defense also applies to those who perform complex actions in coordinated, directed fashion, but with substantially reduced awareness.[3] Courts have recognized the defense in cases in which the defendant's impaired consciousness was associated with epilepsy, somnambulism, concussion, or physical or emotional trauma.[4]

Although relatively rare, the defense has been accepted sufficiently often to establish it as a recognized criminal defense in the United States and Britain. Courts vary widely, however, in their theoretical accounts of the defense. As with the NGRI defense, the difficulties encountered by courts as they attempt to formulate and apply the automatism defense

1   W. LaFave and A.W. Scott, Jr., Substantive Criminal Law sec. 4.9 (St. Paul, MN: West Pub. Co., 1986).
2   Black's Law Dictionary 122 (rev. 5th ed., St. Paul, MN: West Pub Co., 1979).
3   Fulcher v. State, 633 P.2d 142, 144 (1981 Wyo.); LaFave and Scott, *supra* note 1, at sec. 4.9 (a); Annot., 27 A.L.R.4th sec. 2 (1984).
4   LaFave and Scott, *supra* note 1, at sec. 4.9(b); Annot., 27 A.L.R.4th sec. 2 (1984).

reflect the courts' inability to satisfactorily define the place of this defense in the larger system of offense elements and defenses.

3.1 THE AMERICAN APPROACH

American courts have not settled on a consistent interpretation of the automatism defense. Some have treated automatism as a variation of the general excuse of insanity, interpreting epilepsy as a defect of reason that prevented the defendant from knowing the nature and quality of his act.[5] The court adopted this approach in *People v. Higgins* although the defendant did not manifest the usual symptoms of mental illness such as hallucinations or delusions, but rather clouded consciousness, dizziness, pounding sensations in the head, shaking, and disturbed memory.[6] Somnambulism has also been addressed by some courts as a form of insanity.[7]

Other courts, however, have accepted the automatism defense while expressly denying that it is a form of the insanity defense. Some of these courts have stated that automatism is a separate defense from the insanity defense without identifying the theoretical basis for automatism.[8] Other courts have rejected the insanity defense interpretation, and accepted automatism as a defense purporting to show lack of intent, mental element, or *mens rea*.[9] These cases are somewhat perplexing in that these terms all usually refer to the culpability requirement of the offense. Interpreted in this manner, automatism appears to be a failure-of-proof defense

5 Cook v. State, 271 So. 2d 232 (Fla. Dist. Ct. App. 1973); Cooley v. Commonwealth, 479 S.W.2d 89 (Ky. 1970); People v. Higgins, 5 N.Y.2d 607, 186 N.Y.S.2d 623, 159 N.E.2d 179 (1959).
6 *Higgins*, 5 N.Y.2d at 612, 186 N.Y.S.2d at 626, 159 N.E.2d at 183.
7 Tibbs v. Commonwealth, 138 Ky. 558, 128 S.W. 871 (1910); Bradley v. State, 102 Tex. Crim. 41, 277 S.W. 147 (1925).
8 People v. Martin, 87 Cal. App. 2d 110, 197 P.2d 379 (1948); People v. Freeman, 61 Cal. App. 2d 110, 142 P.2d 435 (1943); Carter v. State, 376 P.2d 351 (Okla. Crim. 1962).
9 See respectively, State v. Welsh, 8 Wash. App. 719, 508 P.2d 1041, 1043–44 (1973); State v. Caddell, 287 N.C. 266, 215 S.E.2d 348 (1975); Government of Virgin Islands v. Smith, 278 F.2d 169, (1960).

with the burden of persuasion on the state. Yet, in *State v. Caddell*, the court endorsed this interpretation of automatism while placing the burden on the defendant.[10]

Still other courts have addressed automatism as a failure-of-proof defense that goes to the voluntary act requirement. According to *Jones v. State*, automatism applies to involuntary acts totally beyond the control and knowledge of the defendant.[11] One court described the defense as one that asserts lack of intent (apparently interpreting it as a failure-of-proof defense regarding the culpability requirement), but quoted with approval the language of another court interpreting automatism as a failure-of-proof defense addressing the voluntary act requirement, "an 'act' committed while one is unconscious is in reality no act at all. It is merely a physical event or occurrence. . . . "[12]

In *People v. Newton*, the court stated that unconsciousness is a complete defense that negates the defendant's capacity to commit any crime at all.[13] This suggests that automatism is a failure-of-proof defense regarding the voluntary act requirement, because if it were a defense negating the culpability element, the defendant would still be able to commit crimes of strict liability, and if it were a specific excuse, it would only apply to those acts for which the disability caused an excusing condition. Alternately, it is possible that the court was contemplating a status excuse, although the defendant was neither a minor nor a member of any other category of persons that would ordinarily provide a likely class for categorical exclusion from criminal liability. In addition, this interpretation encounters the difficulties reviewed in Chapter 1.2 regarding the appropriate foundation and boundaries of status excuses.

In *Fulcher v. State*, the court expressly stated that automatism is separate from the insanity defense, and adopted a

10 *Caddell*, 287 N.C. at 290, 215 S.E. 2d at 363.
11 Jones v. State, 648 P.2d 1251, 1258 (Okla. Crim. 1982).
12 *Welsh*, 8 Wash. App. at 323, 508 P.2d at 1044.
13 People v. Newton, 8 Cal. App. 3d 359, 377, 87 Cal. Rptr. 394, 406 (1970).

standard intended to leave open the question whether it goes to the voluntary act or the mental fault requirement. Although this characterization seems to commit the court to the claim that automatism is a failure-of-proof defense, the court also referred to it as an affirmative defense, placing the burden of persuasion on the defendant.[14] The commentators, like the courts, are divided. The MPC's examples of actions that fail to meet the voluntary act requirement include several conditions, such as convulsions and somnambulism, that usually give rise to the automatism defense.[15] This suggests that those who wrote the code would interpret automatism as a failure-of-proof defense regarding the voluntary act requirement. Some commentators endorse the MPC position, describing automatism as a failure-of-proof defense going to the voluntary act requirement with the burden of persuasion on the state, whereas at least one writer rejects both the insanity defense and failure-of-proof interpretations, suggesting a separate general defense of impaired consciousness.[16]

In summary, interpretations of the automatism defense in the United States have varied widely across courts, and some individual court opinions have been internally inconsistent. The courts have failed to establish any settled doctrine regarding automatism, and the decisions relevant to this defense constantly reflect the underlying uncertainty regarding the structure of offense elements and defenses. Various courts define different relationships between the automatism defense and the system of offense elements, and in some cases the court invokes procedures that are inconsistent with the relationship enunciated.

The British courts, in contrast to their American counter-

14   Fulcher v. State, 633 P.2d 142, 147 (Wyo. 1981).
15   American Law Institute, Model Penal Code and Commentaries, sec. 2.01(2) (official draft and revised comments, 1985). The code includes reflex, convulsion, unconsciousness, sleep, and hypnotic state as examples of conditions that might give rise to involuntary acts.
16   *See, respectively,* LaFave and Scott, *supra* note 1, at sec. 4.9(b); P.H. Robinson, Criminal Law Defenses, sec. 172 (St. Paul, MN: West Pub. Co., 1984).

parts, have developed a relatively settled approach to the automatism defense. Unfortunately, this settled approach also reveals considerable confusion regarding the structure of offense elements and defenses. The British interpretation turns on a highly questionable distinction between sane and insane automatism, and it defines the relationship between the insanity and automatism defenses in a manner that is difficult to sustain.

3.2 THE BRITISH APPROACH

The British NGRI defense employs the *M'Naghten* test which, as described previously, exculpates the defendant for an offense committed while he was (1) suffering from a disorder of reason, (2) caused by a disease of the mind such that (3) he did not know the nature and quality of his act or that it was wrongful.[17] Defendants who raise the automatism defense but meet all three conditions of the *M'Naghten* test are classified under the rubric of insane automatism and adjudicated under the NGRI standard, whereas those who do not meet all three requirements are treated as having raised the defense of sane automatism, which challenges the voluntary act requirement.[18] This distinction is of immense practical significance to the defendant because a successful claim of sane automatism establishes a failure-of-proof defense, resulting in an unqualified acquittal, whereas a defendant who is exculpated under the NGRI defense is subject to indefinite commitment to a mental health institution.[19]

17 *See supra* chapter 2.1.
18 British courts and commentators would describe this requirement as the act requirement rather than the voluntary act requirement because they define an act as a willed bodily movement. Thus, the term "voluntary act" would be redundant as the British law accepts the term "act." Generally, the term "act", as accepted by the British criminal law corresponds to the "voluntary act" of the MPC. *See*, G. Williams, Textbook of Criminal Law chapter 2, sec. 2 (London: Stevens & Sons, 1978); G. Williams, Criminal Law: The General Part sec. 8 (2d ed., London: Stevens & Sons, 1961).
19 *See, generally*, Beck, *Voluntary Conduct: Automatism, Insanity and Drunkenness*, 9 Crim. L. Quart. 315 (1966–67); Holland, *Automatism and Crim-*

As the British courts have interpreted the automatism defense, a defendant who asserts it contends that he did not know the nature and quality of his conduct. In *R. v. Charlson*, the defendant contended that he had acted in an epileptic seizure. The court reasoned that one who acts during a seizure is not responsible for his act if it was automatic and unconscious. In such a case, the court reasoned that the defendant would not know what he was doing or be in conscious control of his conduct.[20] In *R. v. Kemp*, all parties agreed that the defendant who suffered from arteriosclerosis did not know what he was doing, and thus did not know the nature and quality of his behavior.[21] The court accepted testimony in *R. v. Sullivan* to the effect that the defendant had acted in the post-ictal stage of an epileptic seizure that rendered him unaware of his movements. According to the court, he had acted unconsciously and involuntarily, and thus he did not know what he was doing.[22] In short, all courts agreed that the defendants in question satisfied the *M'Naghten* ignorance clause regarding the nature and quality of their conduct.

The *M'Naghten* test requires a defect of reason (DOR) that gives rise to the ignorance that exculpates. The defendant must be deprived of the power of reason to such an extent that at least one of the ignorance clauses applies. The test does not cover those who fail to notice the nature, quality, or wrongfulness of their acts through momentary confusion or absent-mindedness. That is, the relevant ignorance must reflect an impairment of the capacity to reason, not a mere failure to exercise that capacity.[23]

This British interpretation of *M'Naghten* seems to fit nicely into Robinson's structure of excuses. The ignorance clauses

inal Responsibility, 25 Crim. L. Quart. 93 (1982–83); Jennings, *The Growth and Development of Automatism as a Defense in Criminal Law*, 2 Osgoode Hall L. J. 370 (1962).

20 R. v. Charlson, 1 All E.R. 859, 861, 862, 864 (1955).
21 R. v. Kemp, 3 All E.R. 249, 249–51 (1956).
22 R. v. Sullivan, 2 All E.R. 673, 675–76 (1983).
23 R. v. Clarke, 1 All E.R. 219, 221 (1972).

articulate the acceptable excusing conditions, and the DOR is the disability that causes these conditions. This interpretation, however, leaves no role for the disease of mind (DOM) clause in the *M'Naghten* test. As articulated, *M'Naghten* requires that the defendant suffer a DOR from a DOM. Robinson accommodates all three factors by interpreting the DOM as the disability that causes the appropriate types of ignorance that constitute the excusing conditions. The DOR requirement, in Robinson's view, apparently modifies the DOM clause by limiting the defense to persons whose DOM is sufficiently serious to include a DOR.[24]

Robinson's interpretation seems consistent with the requirement articulated by the *Clarke* court that the defendant's disorder be a major one that deprives him of the power of reason.[25] It is somewhat problematic, however, in that the British apparently contemplate a causal relation between the DOM and the DOR. According to the *Sullivan* court, the defendant must be "labouring under a 'defect of reason' *resulting from* 'disease of mind'," and "the meaning of the expression 'disease of mind' *as the cause of* 'a defect of reason' remains unchanged."[26] Similarly, the court in *R. v. Kemp* found that the defendant suffered from a DOR caused by a DOM.[27]

The word "disease" can be used in either a narrow or a broad sense. In the narrow sense a disease is specifically a disorder of the body, "[a] condition of the body, or of some part or organ of the body, in which its functions are disturbed or deranged; a morbid physical condition." In contrast, a disease in the broad sense is "[a] deranged, depraved, or morbid condition (of mind or disposition, of the affairs of a community, etc.); an evil affectation or tenancy."[28] To be deranged is to be disordered or disarranged, and something

---

24 Robinson, *supra* note 16, at sec. 173(a), (b).
25 R. v. Clarke, 1 All E.R. 219, 221 (1972).
26 R. v. Sullivan, 2 All E.R. 673, 677 respectively (1983) (emphasis added).
27 R. v. Kemp, 3 All E.R. 249, 250 (1956).
28 Oxford English Dictionary, vol. I, p. 748 (compact ed., Oxford: Oxford Univ. Press, 1971).

is depraved when it is corrupted, perverted, or rendered bad or worse.[29] Thus, a disease in the narrow sense is a physical disorder of the body that disturbs its functioning, whereas a disease in the broad sense is a disorder of any process or system that corrupts it or renders it worse.

When the word "disease" is limited to its narrow sense in which it means a physical disorder of the body, the causal interpretation of the relationship between the DOM and the DOR seems plausible. On this account, *M'Naghten* would require a physical disorder of the body that affects the faculties that constitute the mind in such a manner as to cause a DOR. The British courts, however, explicitly deny this narrow interpretation of "disease." According to the *Sullivan* court, "it did not matter whether the cause of the impairment was organic, as in epilepsy, or functional."[30] Similarly, the *Kemp* court ruled that "it was immaterial whether the disease had a mental or physical origin."[31]

The British courts have opted for the broad sense of "disease" in which the term stands for a disorder or malfunction of a process or system. The British courts have interpreted the term "mind" as used in *M'Naghten* as referring to the mental faculties of memory, reasoning, and understanding. A DOM, therefore, is a disorder or malfunction of these mental faculties. On this interpretation, however, a DOR is not caused by a DOM, rather a DOR is a DOM. Disorders of reason, memory, understanding, or some combination of these three constitute DOMs. It is possible that a particular DOR will be caused by a DOM insofar as one DOM may cause another, but there will never be a DOR without a DOM because a DOR just is a DOM.

Once one realizes that any DOR is a DOM, then it seems reasonable to interpret the DOR as the disability in Robinson's structure of excuses. The ignorance clauses continue to identify the excusing conditions. On this account, the

29 *Id.*, at 694 and 692 respectively.
30 R. v. Sullivan, 2 All E.R. 673, 677 (1983).
31 R. v. Kemp, 3 All E.R. 249, 250 (1956).

DOM requirement indicates that the *disorder* of mind must take the form of an impairment of the capacity to reason and not merely a failure to reason. That is, the DOM clause in *M'Naghten* clarifies the DOR requirement by making it clear that a person suffers a DOR only if he is actually unable to perform the specified mental functions adequately. The DOM clause does not add an additional requirement or limit the NGRI defense to a certain subset of DORs; rather, it clarifies what DOR means. Thus, when one interprets the key terms in *M'Naghten* as the British courts have, a defendant meets the requirements of the NGRI defense if he satisfies one of the ignorance clauses as a result of a DOR. Furthermore, any defendant who raises an automatism defense but meets the requirements of the *M'Naghten* test is addressed under the NGRI defense.

Although the insane automatism defense in effect collapses into the NGRI defense, the British courts also recognize a variation of the defense called sane automatism. They have drawn the distinction between sane and insane automatism by appealing to the DOM requirement of the *M'Naghten* test. Defendants who are deemed to be fit candidates for exculpation because they acted in ignorance of the nature or quality of their action, due to a DOR, are addressed under the *M'Naghten* standard if they suffered a DOM and under the sane automatism defense if they did not.[32] According to the *Sullivan* court, a defendant is not guilty due to sane automatism when he acted under temporary impairment of his mental faculties due to some external physical factor. A blow to the head causing a concussion or a therapeutic administration of anesthetic would qualify as such a factor.[33]

At first glance, it appears that sane automatism differs from insane automatism in that the latter is caused by a DOM, whereas the former is the product of a temporary impairment from external physical factors. The courts have explicitly de-

32 R. v. Kemp, 3 All E.R. 249, 251 (1956).
33 R. v. Sullivan, 2 All E.R. 673, 677 (1983); R. v. Quick, 3 All E.R. 347, 352 (1973).

nied, however, that the temporary nature of the disorder is significant. A defendant who acted in ignorance of the nature or quality of his action due to a DOR from a DOM is insane under the British standard whether the disorder is permanent, transient, or intermittent.[34] That is, any DOM that gives rise to a permanent, transient, or intermittent DOR that causes the defendant to satisfy one of the *M'Naghten* ignorance clauses satisfies the British *M'Naghten* requirement. The distinction, then, apparently rests on the source of the disorder. If it is the product of some identifiable external event, then the sane automatism defense applies, but if the source of the DOR is internal to the actor, then the defendant falls within the scope of the NGRI defense.

Unfortunately, the internal/external distinction quickly loses its appeal. The idea that one can contrast a DOM with an external cause of impairment seems plausible when "disease" is used in its narrow sense in which it means a disorder of the body. In that case, the distinction could be explicated in a manner similar to the distinction between a disease and an injury. The courts closed this option, however, when they rejected the narrow sense of "disease." External events, such as concussive blows to the head or administrations of anesthetic, do not cause the actor to satisfy the ignorance clauses in the absence of a DOR; rather these events give rise to a temporary DOR, resulting in the required type of ignorance. In short, once one accepts the broad sense of "disease," then any DOR constitutes a DOM and any external event that produces a DOR does not provide an alternative to a DOM; rather, it explains the source of this particular DOM.

The internal/external distinction produces practical as well as conceptual difficulties. If one applies the distinction consistently, then certain physical disorders, such as hypoglycemia, qualify as diseases of the mind that ground the insanity defense. No one, however, suggests that hypogly-

---

34   R. v. Sullivan, 2 All E.R. 673, 677 (1983); R. v. Kemp, 3 All E.R. 249, 250 (1956).

cemia is a DOM or that diabetics are insane according to the usual meanings of "DOM" and "insanity." In order to deal with this anomaly, the courts have either recognized hypoglycemia as a potential source of sane automatism or ignored the obvious causal role of hypoglycemia in an actor's conduct while identifying alternate events to label as "the cause."[35] In effect, internal disorders are diseases of the mind that ground the insanity defense, except when they are not. Although the British courts, in contrast to their American counterparts, have established a relatively settled approach to the automatism defense, the putative foundations for this approach raise serious questions. Upon close examination, neither the DOM requirement nor the internal/external distinction seems capable of bearing the weight required.

The courts' opinions in these cases seem to indicate that the distinction between sane and insane automatism does not rest on any principle of law, but rather on the court's judgment regarding appropriate disposition. According to the *Bratty* court, "Any mental disorder which has manifested itself in violence and is likely to recur is a disease of the mind. At any rate it is the sort of disease for which a person should be retained in hospital rather than be given an unqualified acquittal."[36] The *Sullivan* court reasoned that the British legislation regarding the insanity defense was intended to protect the public from recurrences of dangerous behavior. External circumstances that produce dangerous conduct are not usually of a type that are likely to recur, but internal conditions that generate such behavior are more likely to continue or recur.[37] As described earlier, however, the internal/external criterion becomes untenable in some cases, and the courts appear to decide individual cases on the basis of their judgment regarding the appropriate disposition for this particular defendant.

35 *See, respectively,* R. v. Bailey, 2 All E.R. 503 (1983); R. v. Quick, 3 All E.R. 347 (1973).
36 Bratty v. A.-G. for N. Ireland, 3 All E.R. 523, 534 (1963).
37 R. v. Sullivan, 2 All E.R. 673, 677–78 (1983). *See also,* R. v. Kemp, 3 All E.R. 249, 251 (1956).

Apparently, the British courts attempt to separate those defendants who are safe to release from those who are not. The former group are acceptable candidates for the sane automatism defense, whereas the latter group is relegated to the NGRI defense, which provides for indefinite commitment in England. Hence, any particular defendant's status as appropriate to either the NGRI or automatism defenses is not a matter of that defendant's culpability, or of the presence or absence of a DOM; rather, the defense that will be available to each defendant depends on the court's opinion regarding the appropriate disposition.

Courts routinely and legitimately interpret statutes according to the apparent legislative purpose. One can distinguish, however, two levels of generality at which this procedure can be applied. At the more general level, the courts can interpret the meaning and intent of statutes on the basis of the apparent purpose of the statute and then consistently apply that interpretation to all defendants. The *Skinner* court followed this practice when it interpreted the intent of the conjunctive Section 25(b) as a return to the disjunctive *M'Naghten* test.[38]

This procedure does not insure that the court will accurately interpret the legislative intent. Indeed, in some cases there may not be any coherent legislative intent for the courts to discover, either because the legislature did not consider the question to be interpreted or because there was no consensus in the legislature. This more general approach does, however, provide an approach that remains relatively consistent across defendants.

At the less general level, the courts could ask in each particular case, "What treatment of this defendant would best promote the purpose of the statute?" This approach would allow for case-by-case determination of the most effective disposition of each defendant without the constraints posed by requiring a consistent rule.

The British courts appear to be interpreting the NGRI and

38   *See supra*, chapter 2.1.1.

automatism rules at the more general level when they articulate criteria such as the presence of the DOM or the internal/
external distinction for the application of the NGRI or automatism defenses. When these criteria fail and the courts
resort to an evaluation of the best disposition of this particular
defendant, however, they move to the less general level of
interpretation. At this level, courts are deciding cases on the
basis of the preferable outcome in this specific case. This
approach violates what some jurists consider to be the fundamental principle of judicial decision-making.

Herbert Wechsler contends that the main constituent of
the judicial process is the requirement that judges decide
cases, and justify those decisions, on the basis of principles
of sufficient generality and neutrality to transcend the results
of the immediate case. This requirement of entirely principled
decision-making differentiates judicial decisions from legislative decisions. Judges must justify their decisions by appeal
to principles that are neutral as to outcome preference in this
particular case and in general that they can be applied to
all other cases of this class. This requirement of principled
decision-making protects the rule of law by preventing
judges from merely pursuing their personal preferences.[39]
When British judges decide between the sane and insane
variations of automatism on the basis of their evaluation of
the proper disposition of this particular defendant, they en-
danger this fundamental principle of judicial decision-
making.

In summary, the British have developed a relatively settled
approach to automatism, but it apparently has no coherent
foundation. The presence or lack of a DOM has been identified as the key distinction between the automatism and the
NGRI defense, but it appears to be an entirely illusory criterion. The internal/external distinction fails to account for
hard cases such as hypoglycemia. Neither the excusing conditions nor the types of pathology that establish the disability

---

39 H. Wechsler, Principles, Politics and Fundamental Law 17–27 (Cam-
    bridge, MA: Harvard Univ. Press, 1961).

adequately differentiate the two defenses. When the limits of these proposed criteria are exposed, the courts apparently resort to decisions that are driven by disposition preference regarding that particular case rather than by any general principle of law.

3.3 CONCLUSIONS

Chapter 1 examined the MPC's system of offense elements and identified the voluntary act and culpability requirements as aspects of criminal offense definitions that are directly concerned with the psychological processes of the defendant. The exact role that these processes play in each of those requirements and the relationship between them remained unclear. In addition, three types of defenses that directly involve the psychological processes, or impairment of those processes, were identified. These defenses included the failure-of-proof defenses regarding the voluntary act and culpability requirements and the specific excuses. Status excuses may be a fourth type of defense in this category.

Chapters 2 and 3 examined the recent history and current status of two problematic defenses. Chapter 2 demonstrated that the NGRI defense has been the subject of a constant unsuccessful search for a satisfactory standard, and that its status in a system of defenses remains unclear. These two issues are closely related insofar as the various tests proposed, applied, and rejected reflect different presuppositions regarding the appropriate role of the NGRI defense in a comprehensive system of offense elements and defenses.

Chapter 3 reviewed the similarly unsatisfactory state of the automatism defense. In the United States, the automatism defense has been classified as a failure-of-proof defense going to either the voluntary act requirement or to the culpability level. It has also been identified as part of the NGRI defense, and at least one commentator has called for a separate general defense of impaired consciousness. The British, in contrast, have developed a relatively settled approach to automatism, but that approach seems to have no coherent foundation.

Several factors contribute to this general picture of confusion. The psychopathology that gives rise to these defenses is not fully understood, and at least some of the court decisions are partially the product of concern regarding the ongoing dangerousness of the defendants. In addition, the moral basis for criminal responsibility remains a contentious issue. One significant source of these difficulties lies in the lack of clarity regarding the underlying structure of offense elements and related defenses that was identified in Chapter 1.

Chapter 4 will advance a conceptual structure for the analysis of offense elements. This structure will not by itself resolve all of the puzzles described earlier. Rather, it provides a mechanism for explicating more clearly the nature of the offense elements and the relationships among them. Later chapters will reinterpret the insanity and automatism defenses in light of this structure in order to demonstrate that the structure presented in Chapter 4 can illuminate some of the recalcitrant issues that have rendered these defenses so problematic. Finally, Chapter 7 will argue that this structure is morally defensible.

Chapter 4

Actions, reasoning, and offenses

This chapter will propose an analysis of the MPC offense elements that is intended to clarify the nature and purpose of the objective offense elements and of the voluntary act and culpability requirements. This analysis employs philosophical action theory as a conceptual framework with which to explicate both the nature of these offense elements and the relationships among them. Section 4.1 will summarize the relevant parts of Alvin Goldman's causal theory of human action, and Section 4.2 will analyze the MPC offense elements in light of this theory of action. Section 4.3 will respond to certain criticisms that have previously been leveled against causal theories of action, and will demonstrate that the MPC offense elements can be understood as intended to insure that criminal guilt is attached only to acts that are suitably attributable to the actor in his capacity as a practical reasoner. Finally, Section 4.4 will summarize the analysis of the entire chapter.

4.1 ACTION THEORY

Alvin Goldman has advanced a theory of human action that individuates actions as a particular person's exemplifying an act-type at a particular time.[1] Act-types are defined in terms

---

1   A. Goldman, A Theory of Human Action (Princeton: Princeton Univ. Press, 1970). The sketch presented here includes only the central features of the theory that are necessary for the analysis of criminal

of certain properties that can be exemplified by an actor at a specified time. Examples of act-types include moving one's finger, writing a letter, making a speech, or firing a gun. In contrast, green is a property of grass or dollar bills, but it is not an act-type because it is not a property that a person can exemplify. Painting oneself green would be an act-type because an actor could exemplify that property at a particular time.[2]

Although all act-types are properties that can be exemplified by a specific person at a particular time, it is not the case that all such properties are act-types. A person can exemplify the properties of being tall, blond, or a capricorn at a particular time, but being tall, blond, or a capricorn does not constitute an action, and these properties are not act-types. Only a subset of the properties that can be exemplified by an actor at a particular time are act-types. In order to identify this subset, one must first develop the concepts of an act-token, a basic act, and level-generation.

An act-token is the exemplifying of an act-type by an actor at a particular time. John's moving his finger at a specified time (t_n) or John's firing his gun at t_1 are examples of act-tokens. Two act-tokens are identical only if they consist of the same actor's exemplifying the same act-type at the same time. On this theory, John's moving his finger at t_1, John's firing his gun at t_1, and John's killing James at t_1 are each different act-tokens.[3] This aspect of the theory may seem counter-intuitive initially, and some theorists prefer to characterize John's moving his finger, firing his gun, and killing James as three different descriptions of the same act. Goldman has given theoretical support for his approach, however, and it will prove useful in the analysis of criminal offenses.[4]

Level-generation is a relation between an ordered pair of

offenses. Refinements, technical details, and supporting arguments are included in the book, but excluded here for the sake of brevity.

2 *Id.* at 10.
3 *Id.* at 10–12. Throughout this book, the terms "act" and "action" will refer to act-tokens.
4 *Id.* at 1–10.

act-tokens by the same agent at the same time that captures the intuitive notion of "S did A_2 by doing A_1." A_1 generates A_2 when there is some set of conditions (C) such that S's doing A_1 in condition C at t_1 entails S's doing A_2 at t_1, although neither C nor A_1 by itself entails A_2.[5] For example, John's moving his finger under the condition that his loaded gun is in his hand generates John's firing his gun; which, under the condition that James is standing in front of John, generates John's killing James; which, under the conditions that John did so intentionally and without justification or excuse, in a jurisdiction with a law against murder generates John's murdering James. It would be common to describe such a situation by saying that John killed James by shooting him.

It is important to distinguish generation from causation. When A_1 generates A_2, the two acts occur simultaneously and the first act constitutes the second under the conditions. When A_1 causes A_2, the two acts occur sequentially and the first gives rise to the second, but it does not constitute the second. In the example given, suppose that John killed James by shooting him and then fled across the U.S.-Mexican border in order to avoid capture. In such a case, John's killing James would have generated John's murdering James because the act of purposefully killing someone without justification or excuse in a jurisdiction with the usual type of penal code constitutes murder. In contrast, John's killing James causes but does not generate John's act of leaving the country because the two acts occur in sequence, and the conditions were not such that killing James in those circumstances would constitute leaving the country.[6]

Generational relations can be diagrammed on an act-tree such as the one illustrated in Figure 1, which reveals the generational relations among the acts in the John-killing-James example. When one act generates another, the gen-

5 *Id.* at 20–22, 38–40. Goldman describes four types of level generation at 22–30.
6 *Id.* at 23–25.

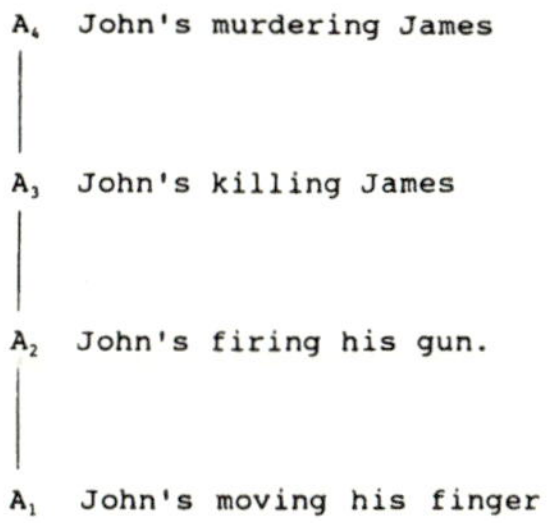

A₄   John's murdering James

A₃   John's killing James

A₂   John's firing his gun.

A₁   John's moving his finger

Figure 1. Act-tree

erated act is placed above the generating act, and the two are connected by a solid line. More complex act-trees illustrate the relations among more complex sets of actions, but this simple tree will suffice for the present. Figure 1 diagrams the generational relationships among four acts, all of which occur simultaneously, and each of which generates (but does not cause) the act directly above it on the tree.

A_1 of Figure 1, unlike the other three acts shown, is not generated from any lower act. It is a basic act. Basic act-types are the sort of act-property that can be exemplified at will. If an act-property is a basic act-type for S at t_1, then in standard conditions as to that property, if S wanted to exemplify it, S would do so without recourse to causal or level generational knowledge. Examples of basic act-properties include raising one's arm, turning one's head, or planning a trip. Basic act-types are individualized to specified actors at specified times. Raising one's arm is a basic act-type for most actors at most times, but it is not for a paraplegic at any time, or for other actors while the arm is temporarily anesthetized for surgery. The central characteristic of a basic act-type is that it is the kind of act-property that an actor can exemplify merely by deciding to, without any further knowledge.[7]

S performs a basic act-token when S exemplifies a basic act-type at a particular time at will without level-generating it from any more basic act. Some events may be basic act-

7   *Id.* at 64–69.

tokens, or they may not be, depending on whether they are done at will. A cough is a basic act-token when done intentionally as a signal to a confederate, but it is not if it occurs reflexively in response to dust.[8] Basic act-tokens are done at will in that they are produced directly by the wants and beliefs of the actor in the ordinary or characteristic way that wants and beliefs cause actions. They are inherently intentional in the sense that it is part of the concept of a basic act that it is caused by the wants of the actor in the manner that intentional acts are caused.[9]

Admittedly, this idea that basic acts follow directly from the decision of the actor in the manner that intentional acts ordinarily follow from the actor's wants is not as clearly explicated as one would like. Consider, however, the following example. Mary and Jane are discussing a proposed zoning regulation that is to be the topic of a town meeting that night. Mary announces that she intends to oppose the regulation. Jane asks how Mary intends to do that, and Mary answers, "I will oppose it at the meeting." "But how," asks Jane, "will you do that?" "I will vote against it." "But how will you vote against it?" "I will raise my hand when the moderator asks for those who oppose the regulation." "But how will you raise your hand?" At this point, Mary can only answer "I just will" because in ordinary circumstances one does not raise one's hand by doing anything else; one just decides to raise one's hand. Raising one's hand is a basic act because it is the type of act that one performs simply by deciding to. Under ordinary conditions, one's hand raises immediately upon the decision to do so. There are no intermediate steps,

8   *Id.* at 70–72.
9   Throughout this chapter I shall use the term "want" as either a verb or a noun, when it may seem more natural to use the term "desire." "Desire," however, suggests an inclination that is relatively intense or emotion laden, whereas the term "want" suggests a broader type of inclination as "being inclined toward" or "finding an act to be fitting or appropriate." It is part of the nature of wants that they have a tendency to cause acts, although not all wants actually cause an act. *See, generally, id.* at 49–125.

and no causal or generational knowledge is employed. Although there may be a physiological explanation for this process by which a decision leads to a raised hand, most actors do not know it and certainly do not employ it in order to raise their hands. This issue will be addressed further in Section 4.3.

The notions of a basic act, act-token, and level-generation enable one to identify those cases of an actor's exemplifying a property at a particular time that constitute actions. As indicated earlier, some properties can be exemplified by an actor at a particular time without constituting an action. For example, Sam may exemplify the property of being tall, or of being a capricorn at a particular time, but these are not acts. Intuitively, these cases are not acts because they are not something the actor does; they are not the product of his beliefs and wants in the same way that an action is. Roughly, an exemplifying of a property by an actor is an act-token only if it is a basic act-token or if it is level-generated from a basic act-token.[10]

This conception of action reserves an important role for the wants, beliefs, and intentions of the actor. All act-tokens are either basic act-tokens, which are inherently intentional, or they are generated from basic act-tokens under certain circumstances. Hence, all act-tokens are produced, either directly or indirectly through level-generation, by the wants and beliefs of the actor in the characteristic way that actors' wants and beliefs cause acts.

S can do basic act A_1 intentionally either directly from a want to do A_1, or from a want to do A_2 and a belief that A_1 will generate A_2. When S does basic act A_1 because he wants to do A_2 and believes that A_1 will generate A_2, S does A_1 in order to do A_2. For example, John moved his finger in order to fire his gun, in order to kill James. Completed acts can be diagrammed on act-trees such as Figure 1, whereas hypo-

10 *Id.* at 44–48. Goldman provides a more precise and comprehensive account, but this formulation is sufficient for the purpose here.

thetical future acts can be diagrammed on projected act-trees that represent the acts S believes he could perform by doing basic act-token A_1.

When S combines a projected act-tree from A_1 to A_n with a want to do A_n, S forms an action-plan. In the earlier example, John formed an action-plan for the killing of James when he combined his want to kill James with his projected act-tree representing his beliefs that he could kill James by firing his gun, which he could do by moving his finger. Note that the concept of an action-plan does not require that John reflected on the various steps in his plan, or even that he articulated each separately. In this case, John may have shot James immediately upon hearing James call him a coward. An action-plan only requires that John wants to kill James and believes that he can accomplish that act by performing the lower acts on the projected act-tree.

All action-plans begin with a basic act, which, as described here, is inherently intentional. All acts that are performed as part of the action-plan, in order to perform A_n, and in the manner conceived of in the action-plan, are also intentional. Other acts that are generated by the acts in the action-plan may be foreseen by the actor when he formulates the plan. Those acts that are generated by the acts in the action-plan, and are foreseen by the actor, but are neither A_n nor done in order to perform A_n, are anticipated but not intentional. If John knew that his killing James under the conditions that James and his wife were highly antagonistic toward each other would generate John's pleasing James's wife, but John did not kill James in order to please James's wife, then John's pleasing James's wife was an anticipated, but not intentional act.[11]

In summary, when S does basic act-token A_1 in order to do A_n, S intentionally does A_1, A_n, and any other acts that

11 *Id.* at 49–62. Note that this usage departs from the meaning of "intentional" as the term is used in intentional torts, where knowledge that a given result is virtually certain to follow an act is sufficient to render it intentional. In Goldman's terms, such an act is anticipated, not intentional.

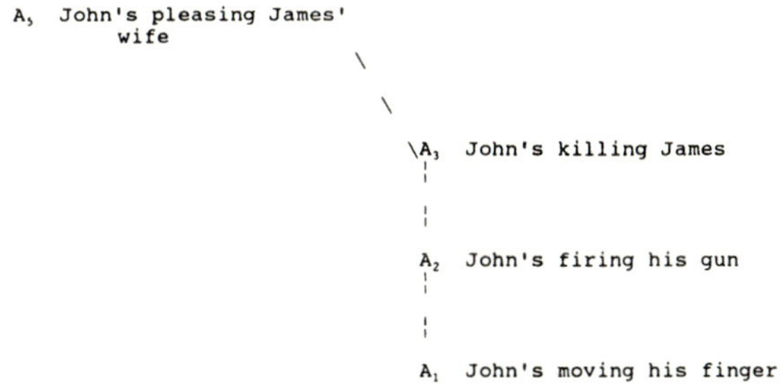

```
A₃  John's pleasing James'
        wife
                                \

                                 \
                                  \A₃  John's killing James
                                    ¦
                                    ¦
                                    ¦
                                  A₂  John's firing his gun
                                    ¦
                                    ¦
                                    ¦
                                  A₁  John's moving his finger
```

Figure 2. Projected act-tree

are part of the action-plan, and done as conceived of in the action-plan in order to perform A_n. Other acts, whether anticipated or unanticipated, that are generated by the action-plan are not intentional. Those that are anticipated, however, are part of the projected act-tree. All intentional acts are caused by the actor's wants and beliefs in the manner that wants and beliefs characteristically cause actions.

Action-plans can be diagrammed as projected act-trees. Generated acts are placed directly above the generating act if they are intended as part of the plan, whereas they are placed diagonally to the side if they are anticipated but not intended. All acts are connected by broken lines to indicate that they are projected. Although act-trees include all relevant acts, projected act-trees include only the intended and anticipated acts.[12] Figure 2 is a projected act-tree representing John's action-plan to kill James.

It may be helpful to compare briefly the act-tree (Figure 1) with the projected act-tree (Figure 2). Both begin with a basic act because all act-tokens, whether actual or projected, must either be basic act-tokens or be generated from basic act-tokens. All act-tokens on both diagrams are below the acts they generate. Actual acts on the act-tree are connected with solid lines, whereas projected acts on the projected act-tree are connected by broken lines. Finally, the act-tree includes

12   *Id.* at 56–63.

all acts that were actually generated from the basic act, whereas the projected act-tree includes only the intended and anticipated acts. The intended acts are placed on the projected act-tree directly above the acts from which they are expected to be generated, whereas the anticipated acts are placed diagonally above and to the side of the act from which they are generated.

John's murdering James occurs as A_4 on the act-tree because the act-tree includes all acts that were actually generated by the basic act. A_4 does not appear on the projected act-tree because John neither intended nor anticipated that his killing James would constitute murder. Had John been relatively sophisticated legally and realized that killing James under these conditions would constitute murder, then A_4 would appear on the projected act-tree directly above A_3 if John acted for the purpose of murdering James, or diagonally above A_3 if John only anticipated that his killing James would constitute murder.

4.2 AN ACTION THEORY ANALYSIS OF OFFENSES

A criminal code provides a list of offenses, the objective elements of which identify the proscribed conduct as well as the circumstances and results of that conduct.[13] For example, perjury is defined in terms of conduct and circumstances as "in any official proceeding he makes a false statement under oath ... when the statement is material," whereas criminal homicide is defined in terms of results as conduct that "causes the death of another human being."[14] Objective elements of offenses are properties of acts. Offenses, as described by their objective elements, are proscribed act-types that can be exemplified by a particular actor at a particular time. For example, Anne satisfies the objective elements for the crime of perjury when she exemplifies the act-type of

13 American Law Institute, Model Penal Code and Commentaries, sec. 1.13(9) (official draft and revised comments, 1985). See part II of the MPC for a list of offenses.
14 *Id.* at sec. 241.1(1), 210.1, respectively.

making a false material statement under oath in an official proceeding. Similarly, John satisfies the objective elements of the crime of criminal homicide when he exemplifies the act-type of causing the death of another human being (James).

In order to establish that John's act constitutes an offense, the state must prove both that John exemplified the proscribed act-type (objective elements) and that he did so with the specified level of culpability. The culpability level may be described as a required relation between the act-token that exemplifies the proscribed act-type and an action-plan. Each of the culpability levels of purposely, knowingly, recklessly and negligently describes a different relation between the proscribed act and the action plan.

In the John-killing-James example, assume the following conditions. John fired his gun for the purpose of killing James, knowing that this constituted murder. John knew that Rick was standing near James, and that a shot might hit Rick, but John fired anyway, wounding Rick. Ned was also standing near James, but John never thought about the possibility that a shot would hit Ned, which it did. John anticipated that James' wife would be glad that James was dead, although John did not shoot for that reason. When John pulled the trigger, he startled a fly that had come to rest on his finger without his noticing it. Figures 3 and 4 illustrate respectively the projected act-tree that represents John's action-plan, and the act-tree that represents his actual acts.

As a projected act-tree, Figure 3 contains only intended and anticipated acts. Acts 1–3 are intentional actions and part of the action-plan. Acts 4–6 are anticipated but not intended, and are diagrammed diagonally to the side to indicate that they are not intentional. The action-plan consists of the intended acts on the projected act-tree and John's decision to kill James. That is, the anticipated acts on the projected act-tree are not part of the action-plan, which includes only the intentional acts on the projected act-tree and the decision to perform the acts represented by that projected act-tree.

As an act-tree, Figure 4 includes all relevant acts, including

95

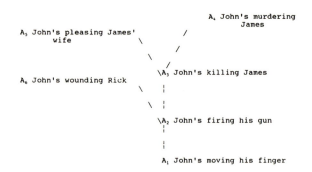

Figure 3. John's projected act-tree

the basic act and all acts that were level generated from it. As this tree indicates, one act-token may generate several other acts. John's firing his gun generates his killing James as well as his wounding Rick and Ned. Both vertical and diagonal lines indicate that the lower act generates the higher one. Vertical and diagonal lines do not carry the intentional versus anticipated significance that they do in the projected act-tree.

The relation that each culpability element requires between the act-token that exemplifies the proscribed act-type and the action-plan is illustrated by Figures 3 and 4. If an offense requires that the defendant acted purposely or knowingly regarding the objective elements, then the act that exemplifies those act-properties must be part of the projected act-tree as intended or anticipated, respectively. Purposeful acts are not only part of the projected act-tree, they are also part of the action-plan. Those acts on the projected act-tree that are basic acts, the target act, or done as part of the action-plan in order to perform the target act are purposeful acts. In this case, acts 1–3, if done in the manner conceived in the action-plan, are intentional in Goldman's terms or purposeful in MPC terms.[15]

---

15 In this book I will use the terms "purposefully" and "intentionally" interchangeably.

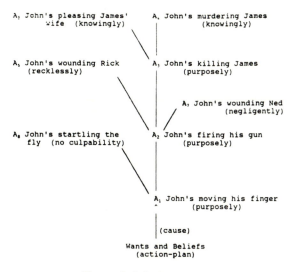

Figure 4. John's act-tree

Acts that appear both on the act-tree and at the end of diagonal lines on the projected act-tree are anticipated acts that were performed either knowingly or recklessly. Here, acts 4 and 5 were performed knowingly, whereas act 6 was done recklessly. The MPC lists knowingly and recklessly as qualitatively different culpability levels. The definitions in the code reveal, however, that they actually reflect different degrees of confidence regarding the probability of anticipated events.[16]

When the objective elements of an offense are defined in terms of the characteristics of the actor's conduct, the actor acts knowingly if he is aware that his conduct has those characteristics, and he acts recklessly if he consciously disregards a substantial and unjustifiable risk that it might have those characteristics. For example, Anne knowingly made false statements before an official proceeding if she were aware that her statements were false, but she made false

---

16   MPC, *supra* note 13, at 2.02(2) (b), (c).

statements recklessly if she consciously disregarded a substantial and unjustifiable risk that they were false.

When the objective elements of an offense are defined in terms of results, the actor acts knowingly if he is aware that these results are practically certain to follow from his acts, and he acts recklessly if he consciously disregards a substantial and unjustifiable risk that those results will follow from his conduct. For example, John caused James' death knowingly if he was practically certain that his firing his gun would cause James' death, but John caused harm to Rick recklessly because he consciously disregarded the substantial and unjustifable risk that a shot would hit Rick.

Thus, both acts done knowingly and those done recklessly are anticipated acts on a projected act-tree. When the actor anticipated that the act constituting the offense was almost certain to occur, we say that he committed the offense knowingly, but when he only anticipated a serious and unjustifiable risk that it would occur, we call it a reckless offense.

This interpretation is consistent with the MPC provision that allows a defendant to establish a failure of proof defense if he acted out of ignorance or mistake that negates the required culpability element for the offense.[17] In such a case, the required relation between the act-token that exemplifies the offense and the action-plan would not obtain. If the actor failed to anticipate the possibility that his basic act would generate the act constituting the offense, then that act would not appear on the projected act-tree, and the actor would not be guilty of committing the offense knowingly or recklessly. If, however, the actor anticipated the act as one which might be generated by his basic act, but not as one that was practically certain to occur, then it would appear on the projected act-tree as an anticipated act, and the actor would be guilty of committing the offense recklessly but not knowingly.

If the actor did not anticipate that an act would occur as part of the act-tree, or that there was a substantial and un-

---

17 *Id.* at sec. 2.04; P.H. Robinson, Criminal Law Defenses sec. 62 (St. Paul, MN: West Pub. Co., 1984).

justifiable risk that it would occur, then he acted negligently if his failure to anticipate it was the result of a gross deviation from a reasonable standard of care. The reasonable standard of care is that which the reasonable law-abiding citizen would exercise in the actor's situation in light of the nature and purpose of his conduct and the circumstances he is aware of.[18]

When the actor violates such a standard of care, the act that exemplifies the proscribed act-type is not a part of the projected act-tree, but it does stand in a specified counterfactual relation to that projected act-tree. It is an act that would have been on the projected act-tree if John had exercised reasonable care. That is, had the actor exercised the care that a reasonable law-abiding citizen would have exercised in light of the nature of his conduct and the circumstances, the actor would have realized that his act created a substantial and unjustifiable risk that the act-token exemplifying the act-type that constitutes the objective elements of the offense would occur. Act 7 in Figure 4 is such an act because a reasonable law-abiding citizen would realize that shooting a gun in the general direction of Ned creates a substantial risk that a bullet will hit Ned and, thus, that under these circumstances, firing the gun is likely to generate the act of shooting Ned.

Finally, if the act occurs as part of the act-tree, but bears no relation to the projected act-tree, there is no culpability and the actor cannot be guilty unless the offense is one of strict liability. Act 8 in Figure 4 is such an act.

In summary, each of the four standard culpability levels defines a different relation between the act-token that exemplifies the act-type that constitutes the objective elements of the offense and the projected act-tree selected by the actor in forming the action-plan. The action-plan is inherently intentional in that it consists of basic acts, which are inherently intentional, and acts that are intended to be generated from those basic acts. The projected act-tree that

18 MPC, *supra* note 13, at 2.02(2) (d).

the actor decides to pursue as his action-plan represents the intentions, wants, and beliefs of the actor, and therefore it represents him as a decision-maker or a choosing being. The act-tree diagrams the acts that the actor actually performed.

When the culpability element specifies a required relation between the actor's act that exemplifies the proscribed act-type and the projected act-tree that he selects to act on, it specifies a required relation between the act exemplifying the objective offense elements and the actor's wants, beliefs, and intentions. Thus, the culpability element specifies the required relation between the act and the psychological processes that represent the actor as a decision-maker. To require that an offense be committed purposely is to require that the actor performed the basic act for the purpose of committing the proscribed act. To require that the offense be committed knowingly or recklessly is to require that the actor performed the basic act while anticipating that the proscribed act was practically certain to occur or that there was a substantial and unjustifiable chance that it would occur. Finally, crimes of negligence require that with reasonable care the actor would have known that his basic act would likely generate the proscribed act. In short, the culpability requirement in an offense definition reflects society's judgment regarding how directly the proscribed action must be related to the processes that represent the actor as a decision-maker before he will be held accountable for that action as that offense.

Hyman Gross has argued that the continuum of culpability reflects the degree of dangerousness of the act in the sense that the higher degrees of culpability involve greater actor control over the harm caused by the act. He contends, for example, that an offense committed purposely is more blameworthy than one committed knowingly because in the former type of case the actor exerts more control over the harm producing situation and leaves less to chance. Hence, the harm caused is more directly attributable to the actor.[19]

It is not clear, however, in what sense an actor exerts more control when he acts purposely than when he acts knowingly, nor does it seem likely that purposeful offenses are necessarily, or even generally, more dangerous than those committed knowingly. Recall that an actor acts knowingly when he anticipates that the offense is practically certain to be generated by his act. Yet an actor may act purposely while realizing that the probability of his succeeding is much lower than substantial certainty. The hypothetical bank robber in Chapter 1 who killed the bank guard by setting off an explosion in order to gain access to the vault acted under circumstances that rendered the guard's death substantially certain, yet the robber caused the guard's death knowingly, not purposely.

Compare that defendant to one who plants a time-bomb in one of his victim's two cars and then hopes that his victim drives that car to work this morning. Assume that the victim drives each car to work approximately half of the time and that the assassin has no grounds on which to predict which the victim will drive that day. Should he succeed, this killer would have caused the death of his victim purposely, but he would have exerted less control and left more to chance than the bank robber who killed knowingly.

The difference between the purposeful killing and the knowing killing does not lie in the degree to which we can accurately attribute the harm to the actor or to chance. Rather, the difference lies in the manner in which the killing reflects the wants, beliefs, and intentions of the actors. The purposeful killing more accurately reveals the wants and intent of the killer than does the killing performed knowingly. Although these two killings involve different relationships between the act of killing and the actor's

19 H. Gross, *A Theory of Criminal Justice* 82–88 (New York: Oxford Univ. Press, 1979).

wants and intentions, it does not necessarily follow that these differences lead to different degrees of blameworthiness or accountability.

The relative blameworthiness of actors who act purposely or knowingly can be determined only in the context of an underlying theory of responsibility and a complete description of the acts, motives, and circumstances in each case. The MPC, for example, treats both purposeful and knowing homicide as murder.[20] Aggravating or mitigating circumstances may support the judgment that any particular purposeful homicide is more or less blameworthy than any particular one committed knowingly.

There may also be an evidentiary issue that supports the policy of distinguishing between purposeful and knowing offenses. Both purpose and knowledge are mental states that must be inferred from other evidence unless the defendant admits holding such a state of mind. Purpose, however, will ordinarily be reflected in overt action designed to achieve that end, whereas the actor who acts knowingly may perform no overt action that reveals his knowledge. The examples of the bank robber and the car bomber discussed here illustrate this pattern.

All other considerations being equal, we might generally tend to treat purposeful wrongdoing more seriously than the same conduct performed knowingly, not because it is necessarily more blameworthy, but because we have more confidence in our judgment that the act was performed purposely than we have in our corresponding judgment that an act was performed knowingly. When we conclude that an actor acted purposely, we will usually be able to identify specific words or deeds that support this conclusion. In contrast, when the defendant has acted knowingly but not purposely, we may find it more difficult to be certain that the actor was actually aware of the circumstances or likely consequences that constituted the objective elements of the offense.

20 MPC, *supra* note 13, at sec. 210.2(1) (a).

The defendant whose behavior instantiates the objective elements of an offense with the required level of culpability fulfills necessary but not sufficient conditions for criminal guilt. The MPC also requires that the conduct on which the defendant's liability is based include a voluntary act. According to the MPC, voluntary acts are the product of the effort or determination of the actor.[21] "Determination" means "the mental action of coming to a decision – the fixing or settling of a purpose," whereas "effort" means "a strenuous putting forth of power, physical or mental."[22] In modern usage, however, "effort" is used more broadly to include exertions of power that are not strenuous.[23] Conduct that is based on the actor's determination and effort, therefore, is conduct that involves a putting forth of power on the basis of some decision or purpose.[24]

It is important to remember that this conception of a voluntary act as expending effort on the basis of some decision or purpose differs significantly from the usual, broader use of "voluntary." According to Feinberg's analysis of the broad conception of voluntariness as described in Chapter 1, an ascription of voluntariness is defeated by a sufficient degree of coercion, impairment, or ignorance.[25] Under Feinberg's conception, for example, the bank president who rationally agrees to drive the robber to the bank, open the safe, and

21 *Id.* at sec. 2.01.
22 Oxford English Dictionary (compact ed., Oxford: Oxford Univ. Press, 1971).
23 Oxford English Dictionary (supp. 1977).
24 MPC, *supra* note 13, at 2.01. This section could be read to require only that the act be the product of either decision or the putting forth of effort. If the exertion of power were sufficient, however, the examples of involuntary acts in the section would be voluntary. Convulsions and reflexes put forth power; it is the decision that is lacking. When the exertion of effort is the product of decision, it seems reasonable to attribute that exertion to the person as agent. In contrast, convulsions include an expenditure of energy, but we usually distinguish these movements from normal or voluntary actions just because there is no decision that ties the exertion to the person as a decision-maker. I will read this section, therefore, as requiring that the power be put forth as a result of determination or decision.
25 *See supra* chapter 1.1.

103

hand over the money because the robber is holding a gun to his head is not acting voluntarily.

This bank president's behavior would, however, meet the MPC conception of a voluntary act. The president would have expended effort on the basis of a decision to pursue a particular purpose. Although the president decided to act in this manner for unusual and coercive reasons, his decision produced his acts in the manner that an actor's effort and determination produce ordinary human activity. Power expended on the basis of an actor's decision or purpose in this manner is the product of an action-plan and reflects the actor's wants and beliefs that give rise to that action-plan. According to Goldman, all acts that are either basic acts, or acts performed as part of an action-plan in order to perform some target act, are intentional.[26]

Unintentional acts, whether anticipated or not, are also part of an act-tree and generated from a basic act. Although these other acts are not fully intentional in the sense that Goldman uses that term, they are weakly intentional in the sense that they are all part of some act-tree that is rooted in a basic act that is intentional. That is, all acts are weakly intentional in the sense that they are generated by an inherently intentional basic act. On Goldman's theory, then, all behavior that qualifies as action is at least weakly intentional; either it is an inherently intentional basic act, or it is generated from such an act. All acts are weakly intentional because they are produced, either directly or indirectly, by the action-plans of the actor.

In short, voluntary acts in MPC terms must be intentional acts in Goldman's terms, but they are not necessarily voluntary in the broader sense understood by Feinberg and common usage. Understood in this light, the MPC requirement that conduct constituting an offense include a voluntary act requires that the act-token constituting the offense be at least weakly intentional; that is, it must occur as part of an act-tree that is rooted in a basic act. The basic act is inherently

26 *See supra* chapter 4.1.

intentional in that the actor's decision to perform the basic act produces it directly in the manner that an actor's action-plans characteristically produce actions. The basic act that forms the root of the act-tree in the actor's action-plan provides the voluntary act required by the MPC, provided that the action-plan produces the basic act in the characteristic manner that wants and beliefs produce ordinary human action.

The voluntary act requirement is intended to select conduct that is within the control of the actor in the sense that ordinary human conduct is, but reflex and convulsion are not.[27] In H.L.A. Hart's terms, involuntary conduct is not governed by the will of the actor. The conduct is not "really" human action at all because the vital link between mind and body is missing.[28]

Similarly, in Goldman's theory, an "act" that is not at least weakly intentional is not an act at all. When an action-plan gives rise to an act-tree, grounded in a basic act in the way that wants and beliefs characteristically give rise to human action, then the actor's will, or psychological processes, produces action in the manner that people produce ordinary human action. The voluntary act provision requires only that the action-plan representing the actor's wants and beliefs give rise to the basic act that roots the act-tree in the characteristic manner. It does not mandate that the actor select the action-plan that is most likely to fulfill his wants, or that the actor reason from his wants and beliefs to the action-plan through unimpaired reasoning processes. The actor who selects an action-plan through fallacious reasoning or the psychotic actor who forms an action-plan on the basis of delusional process may act voluntarily as long as the action-plan that represents the actor's wants and beliefs gives rise to the act-tree in the ordinary way.

In order to accurately interpret the voluntary act requirement, one must carefully separate two similar but distinct

27 MPC, *supra* note 13, at sec. 2.01 and comments p. 215.
28 H.L.A. Hart, Punishment and Responsibility 105–07 (1968).

105

claims. The MPC's voluntary act clause requires that the conduct that constitutes the offense *include* a voluntary act, *not* that the act constituting the offense *be* a voluntary act. Complex actions constitute act-trees including a basic act and other acts generated from that basic act. The requirement that the conduct constituting the offense *include* a voluntary act addresses the basic act that roots the act-tree rather than the generated act that exemplifies the act-type that constitutes the offense. If one misconstrues this requirement, reading it as mandating that the act constituting the offense *be* a voluntary act, then this reading, in conjunction with the realization that a voluntary act in MPC terms is intentional in Goldman's terms, seems to suggest that all offenses must be committed purposely. Such an interpretation seems to rule out offenses performed knowingly, recklessly, or negligently. It also blurs the distinction between the voluntary act and culpability requirements, because on this reading both provisions address the relationship between the act constituting the offense and the wants, beliefs, and intentions of the actor. It is then tempting to conclude that any act that fails to satisfy the voluntariness or culpability requirements must violate both.

When one recalls, however, that the voluntary act provision requires that the conduct constituting the offense *include* a voluntary act, it becomes clear that the voluntary act requirement addresses the relationship between the action-plan that represents the actor's wants, beliefs, and decisions and the basic act that roots the act-tree that includes the act constituting the offense. In contrast, the culpability requirement addresses the relationship between the actor's action-plan and the act that instantiates the objective elements of the offense. Stated intuitively, the voluntary act provision requires that the actor *did something* through the ordinary processes by which people produce acts, whereas the culpability element addresses the required relationship between what the actor did and what he intended to do; that is, the relationship between the act constituting the objective elements of the offense and the projected act-tree that the actor selected to act upon. In principle, various types of pathology might prevent the actor from fulfilling either of these two requirements, or both of them. I shall argue in Chapters 5, 6, and 7 that both provisions are necessary but not sufficient, in order to accommodate the various forms of psychopathology that are relevant to moral responsibility.

On this interpretation, the requirements of objective offense elements, voluntary act, and culpability address three different aspects of human action as illustrated in Figures 3 and 4. In order to fulfill the objective offense elements, the actor's act-tree (Figure 4) must include an act-token that exemplifies the proscribed act-type in terms of conduct, circumstances, and results. In order to meet the voluntary act requirement, the act constituting the offense must be part of an act-tree, and the basic act rooting that act-tree must be produced in the characteristic manner by an action-plan representing the wants and beliefs of the actor. The focus here is neither the wants and beliefs nor the act-tree, but rather the process by which the action-plan representing the former produces the latter. Finally, the culpability level specifies the necessary relation between the projected act-tree (Figure 3) and the act-token that exemplifies the objective offense elements and appears as part of the act-tree (Figure 4) that is produced by the action-plan.

Reflection on this interpretation reveals the insight contained in the LaFave and Scott argument that the culpability element must actuate the offending conduct.[29] I have argued in Chapter 1 that this claim does not work precisely as stated, particularly when the specified culpability level is knowledge, recklessness, or negligence. It contains the insight, however, that the actor's wants and beliefs must actuate his conduct in a particular manner. The culpability element is not identical with these psychological processes that actuate the conduct, however; rather it specifies the required relation

---

29 W. LaFave and A.W. Scott, Jr., Substantive Criminal Law sec. 3.11, 3.11(a) (St. Paul: West Pub. Co., 1986).

between the action-plan and the conduct constituting the offense.

Hart claimed that any condition that defeated the voluntary act requirement would also negate the culpability level; or in effect, that the culpability level entails voluntariness.[30] This claim is accurate for the clear cases of involuntary movement. When the body moves as a result of reflex or convulsion, there is no action-plan, and therefore the movement can not have been related to the actor's wants and beliefs in the specified way, and the action-plan cannot have given rise to the movement. The difficult cases, however, are those such as somnambulism and epilepsy, which include coordinated and apparently directed behavior, suggesting that there is some sort of action-plan. These cases produce the problematic claims of automatism, which will be addressed in Chapter 5.

4.3 ACTION AND PRACTICAL REASON

Sections 4.1 and 4.2 have sketched the central points of Goldman's theory of action and advanced an explication of the MPC's structure of offense elements in terms of that theory of action. I argued in Section 4.2 that the nature of the objective offense elements and of the voluntary act and culpability requirements, as well as of the relationships among these three components of offenses, can be understood more clearly when interpreted in terms of action theory. Goldman's theory of action is a causal one in that it presents a conception of action in which the causal role of the actor's wants and beliefs is central. Although act-tokens on an act-tree generate rather than cause other acts on that tree, the actor's wants and beliefs cause the act-tree. Causal theories of action have been criticized, however, as subject to the problem of deviant causal chains. This section will address this problem and discuss the relationship among the causal

30 Hart, *supra* note 28, at 107.

theory, the MPC offense structure, and the role of practical reason in personal agency.

4.3.1 Actor as practical reasoner. Michael Moore criticizes causal theories of action, including Goldman's, as vulnerable to the problem of deviant causal chains.[31] There are certain cases in which a person's movements are caused by his wants and beliefs through a distorted process that leads us intuitively to think that the movement was not an action despite the fact that it was caused by his wants and beliefs. Moore and others contend that these cases constitute counter-examples to any causal theory of action that identifies action with behavior caused by the wants and beliefs of the actor.

Consider, for example, a variation of the now familiar John-killing-James case. Suppose that the young and healthy James insults John, who is sick and elderly. John becomes very angry at James, wants to kill him, and decides to get his gun and do so. His anger and decision, however, cause him to become so excited that he suffers a heart attack and falls to the floor gasping for breath. James becomes frightened because he thinks he may be blamed for John's heart attack, so James runs from the room, trips on the stairs, and falls to the bottom of the stairs where he dies from a broken neck. Here, John's wants, beliefs, and decision caused his movement of falling to the floor gasping for breath, and that movement was a causal factor in James' death. It seems clear, however, that neither John's falling to the floor nor his causing James' death was an action.

Goldman acknowledges the problem of deviant causal chains for causal theories and responds by placing a constraint on the manner in which the actor's wants and beliefs must cause his acts. He contends that the actor's wants and beliefs must cause his actions in the "characteristic manner in which desires and beliefs flow into intentional acts."[32]

---

31 M. Moore, Law and Psychiatry 72 (Cambridge: Cambridge Univ. Press, 1984).

32 Goldman, *supra* note 1, at 62; *see, generally* 56–63.

Unfortunately, Goldman provides no account of this characteristic manner. He merely appeals to our intuitive understanding of the manner in which our wants and beliefs lead to actions and argues that providing a detailed explanation of this process falls within the scope of the empirical sciences rather than philosophy.[33]

Moore rejects the "characteristic manner" response as ad hoc and vacuous because the only account of the causal relationship involved in action that Goldman provides is that it is the kind of causal process that produces action. This seems to reduce to the claim that acts are caused by the kind of process that causes acts. Moore concludes that any causal theory of action falls prey to deviant causal chains unless it can provide a substantive account of the type of causal process involved in want and belief causation of acts.[34]

Moore's objections to causal theories of action occur in the context of his larger project, which addresses issues of legal agency and responsibility. Moore contends that the legal conception of a person is the same as the moral one, and that for both legal and moral purposes, a person is a practical reasoner. By a practical reasoner, Moore means one who acts for reasons and whose actions can be explained by reason-giving explanations.[35] On Moore's view, a satisfactory theory of human action must both causally explain acts and rationalize them. An explanation rationalizes an act when it portrays that act as the rational thing to do given the actor's beliefs and desires.[36]

Moore objects to the manner in which causal theories such as Goldman's explain acts in terms of belief-desire sets. He contends that these explanations rely on a conception of state causation, whereas an adequate explanation of actions attributable to persons as practical reasoners requires explanation in terms of personal agency. He argues that explanations in the form of state causation, including those

33   *Id.* at 56–63.
34   Moore, *supra* note 31, at 72–73.
35   *Id.* at 48–49, 100.
36   *Id.* at 9–14.

that refer to the actor's mental states, fail to rationalize acts. Such explanations, therefore, do not provide reason-giving accounts that satisfy legal and moral purposes. Moore contends that in order to fulfill legal and moral purposes, one needs an explanation of acts in terms of personal agency; that is, "the notion of a person bringing about some state of affairs."[37]

He also contends that causal theories provide inadequate accounts of intentionality because causation by belief-desire sets is neither necessary nor sufficient for intentional action. He argues that the problem of deviant causal chains establishes that causation by belief-desire sets is not sufficient for intentional action, and the fact that people can act intentionally for no further reason demonstrates that such causation is not necessary.[38]

Moore does not advance a fully formulated theory of action or intentionality. He does contend, however, that the notions of a basic act, intentionality, and reason-giving explanations are linked in important ways. Explanations of intentional acts must be reason-giving ones that connect the acts to the actor as a practical reasoner. He proposes the following epistemic indicator of a basic act: "An actor's bodily movement is a basic action only if he knows that he can perform that movement as an action and knows that he is doing so on that particular occasion."[39] By characterizing a basic act in terms of what the actor knows, rather than causation by belief-desire sets, Moore apparently intends to emphasize the role of the reasons the actor has for acting.

I shall argue that several of Moore's criticisms of causal theories miss their mark because he misinterprets certain aspects of Goldman's theory and because his own epistemic indicator of basic action falls prey to one of the problems he identifies for Goldman. Moore is correct, however, when he argues that the "characteristic manner" constraint on belief-

37 *Id.* at 72, *see, generally,* 14–18.
38 *Id.* at 78.
39 *Id.* at 73, *see, generally,* 79–80.

desire causation is inadequate and when he contends that reason-giving explanations are central to law and morality. Ideally, one would like an account that combines Moore's insights with Goldman's. An explication of the "characteristic manner" in which beliefs and desires cause intentional action that also provides a reason-giving account of action would do this nicely. First, I will examine Moore's criticisms of Goldman and attempt to identify the common ground as well as the important differences between the two positions. Then I will return to the task of providing an account of the manner in which a person's beliefs and desires may cause his acts by virtue of their status as reasons.

Moore contends that causation by belief-desire sets is neither necessary nor sufficient for intentional action. That such causation is not sufficient would not be a problem for the causal theory if the "characteristic manner" constraint could be elaborated in some satisfactory manner. Moore's claim that such causation is not necessary is based on his contention that people can act intentionally for no further purpose. He is correct in his assertion that people can act intentionally for no further reason. People usually act intentionally for some further purpose, but they sometimes perform intentional acts just because they want to. For example, people often raise their hands because they want to signal for attention and believe that this is an effective way to do so, but anyone who has had a limb immobilized in a cast has raised or bent that limb shortly after the cast was removed just because he wanted to.

Although Moore is correct in claiming that people do perform intentional acts for no further reason, this does not present a problem for Goldman's causal theory. On Goldman's account, intentional acts are either basic acts that are inherently intentional or they are generated from basic acts according to an action-plan. Basic acts or other acts in an action-plan that are done in order to do the target act are done for some further reason, but the target act is also intentional, and it is not necessarily done for any further reason. Furthermore, a basic act, such as bending the limb just removed from the cast, can be performed just because the actor wanted to. Such an act would meet the requirement of being caused by a belief-desire set because it would follow directly from the actor's belief that he could perform it simply by deciding to and his decision to do so.

Moore is also correct in identifying the problem of deviant causal chains and in arguing that the "characteristic manner" constraint is not fully satisfactory. With no adequate account of this characteristic manner, the constraint seems only to require that beliefs and desires cause action in the manner that they cause action. Unfortunately, Moore's epistemic indicator appears to suffer the same malady. According to the epistemic indicator, the actor must know that he can perform the movement as an action and that he is currently doing so. But what constitutes knowing that he can perform it as an action; that is, what does the actor have to know in order to know that he can perform the movement as an action? Just as the "characteristic manner" constraint gives us no information about how the belief-desire set must cause the action, the epistemic indicator gives us no account of what the actor must know in order to know that he can perform the act as an action.

Moore rejects causal theories such as Goldman's because these theories employ a notion of state causation, whereas Moore contends that we need an explanation in terms of personal agency in order to rationalize acts and satisfy legal and moral purposes. Moore admits that traditionally the notion of personal agency causation has not been explicated in any very informative way.[40] He attempts to give it some content through his epistemic indicator, but, as indicated earlier, it is not clear that this indicator is particularly helpful.

Although Moore seems to believe that state causation and personal agency are incompatible, Goldman contends that any plausible notion of personal agency would take the form of a state causation account. He argues that if persons author their own acts, they must do so by virtue of some state they

40   *Id.* at 72–73.

occupy. It seems plausible to contend that persons initiate their own acts by virtue of their beliefs, wants, and decisions. If people do not author their own actions through their psychological states and processes, then personal agency seems to be entirely mysterious in that we have no other account of how it might work.

There appears to be no obvious reason to think that personal agency is incompatible with state or event causation. Claims about agent causation usually take the following form: "John caused the death of James." Moore is correct in noting that legal proscriptions usually take such a form. Consider similar attributions of event and state causation respectively: "John's firing his gun at James caused the death of James," "John's desire to kill James and his belief that he could do so by shooting James caused the death of James." All three statements form a consistent set in that one can endorse all three simultaneously without contradiction. In addition, the second and third statements elaborate on the first in that they tell us how John caused James's death, and they provide a partial explanation of why he did so. A more complete statement of John's beliefs and desires that led him to kill James would also provide a more complete rationalization of the act. It seems, therefore, that state causation theories are compatible with personal agency, and that they can actually provide the reason-giving type of explanation that Moore requires.[41]

Furthermore, Moore's conception of practical reasoning is very similar to Goldman's. Moore builds his model of practical reasoning on his understanding of a person performing an intentional act for a reason. He elaborates the concept of a person performing an intentional act for a reason in the

---

41 Some writers apparently reject state causation elaborations of personal agency because they understand such accounts as incompatible with free will and personal responsibility. If one holds that mental states such as beliefs and desires are subject to deterministic explanation, and that personal agency and responsibility are incompatible with such explanation, then one has a motive for resisting mental state accounts of personal agency. These issues will be addressed more fully in chapter 7.

following manner. A person (P) performs an intentional act (A) for a reason when: (1) P desires that some state of affairs (S) obtains, (2) P believes that his doing A will produce S, and (3) P's doing A is caused by P's desire for S and his belief that his doing A would produce S. Moore contends that this interpretation rationalizes P's doing A because it portrays A as the rational thing to do in light of P's desires and beliefs. It also provides a causal explanation for P's doing A because step 3 calls for a causal connection between A and what P believes and desires.

According to Moore, the process of practical reasoning is a pattern of inference by which the actor reasons from his reasons for acting to an intentional act that he identifies as an effective means to the end represented by his reasons for acting. Consider the following example:

PR1 1. I am cold and I want to be warm.
2. I can become warm by donning the sweater.
3. (Conclude) I don the sweater.

Premise 1 identifies the state of affairs that the actor wants to achieve, and premise 2 selects an intentional act that provides an effective means to the end established in 1. The conclusion (3) takes the form of a directive to perform the intentional act selected in 2. Moore contends that the practical syllogism rationalizes the decision to act represented by the conclusion because it provides a reason-giving explanation for that intentional act.[42]

Although Moore rejects causal theories such as Goldman's because they explain actions by appeal to state causation by belief-desire sets rather than through an account of personal agency, his own account of what it means for a state of affairs to be a reason for intentional action includes causation by belief-desire sets in step 3.[43] It is this step, and the causal

42 Moore, *supra* note 31, at 13–14.
43 *Id.* at 79. Moore's conception of intentional action differs from Goldman's. Moore claims that an actor intentionally causes the death of another only if the death was a consequence of the actor's basic act,

115

process it represents, that serves the explanatory function that Moore claims is necessary. Moore does not include Goldman's "characteristic manner" constraint on the causal process, but he must accept it in order to avoid exactly the same kind of problems with deviant causal chains that all causal theories encounter. Despite Moore's emphasis on the process of practical reasoning and reason-giving explanations for action, his account of what it means for a consideration to be a reason for an intentional action, and thus, his account of practical reasoning, seems to encounter exactly the same concern regarding unexplained causation by belief-desire sets that Goldman confronts.

Goldman also advances an account of practical inference that is quite compatible with Moore's process of practical reasoning. He develops his model of practical inference by comparing it to cognitive inference in which one reasons to the truth of propositions. Consider the following example:

1. All wool clothes are warm.
2. This sweater is made of wool.
3. (conclude) This sweater is warm.

Here, the reasoner believes that 3 is true because he believes that 1 and 2 are true. The term "because" has both logical and causal force. It has logical force because 1 and 2 provide good reasons to believe 3. Premises 1 and 2 do not cause premise 3, but the reasoner's believing that 1 and 2 are true

and the actor knew that it would be. This account seems to exclude purposeful killings that were committed under conditions in which the actor was not practically certain of success. I assume, however, that Moore would want to include such cases as that of the assassin with the time-bomb discussed in Section 4.2 in the category of intentional acts. Moore advances epistemic criteria for both basic acts and intentional acts. The point, however, is that as long as intentional acts are done for some reason, such epistemic criteria supplement rather than replace the causal provision included in Moore's account of what it means for a consideration to be a reason for an intentional act. Even in cases in which the actor performs an action just because he wants to, his wanting to is the reason for his action and the causal connection between the actor's want and his action applies.

116

(and his belief that 3 follows from 1 and 2) causes him to believe that 3 is true.[44]

The pattern of practical reasoning is analogous in both form and force to cognitive inference. Consider the following slight variation of PR1.

PR2   1. I am cold and I want to be warm.
       2. I can become warm by donning this sweater.
       3. I want to don the sweater.

Here, the reasoner wants to don the sweater because he wants to be warm and believes that he can become warm by donning the sweater. "Because" has logical force in that the want in 1 and the belief in 2 give him good reason to want to don the sweater (3); he has reasoned to a sufficient condition for fulfilling his want identified in 1. "Because" also carries causal force in that it is his wanting to be warm (1) and his believing that donning the sweater constitutes a sufficient condition for satisfying that desire (2) that cause him to want to don the sweater (3).[45]

The processes of practical reasoning or inference described by Moore and Goldman are quite similar. Both reason from premises about wants and about beliefs regarding effective means for satisfying those wants. Their conclusions differ somewhat in that Moore's conclusion is a directive to action, whereas Goldman's is a want to perform the act constituting the means to the end identified in the premises. Little seems to rest on this distinction, however, because Moore's directive to action would lead to action only if there were no stronger conflicting directives resulting from competing practical syllogisms. Similarly, Goldman's want to perform the means to the original end would presumably motivate a decision to act on that want as long as the reasoner was not aware of any stronger competing wants.

Perhaps, most importantly, both writers attribute logical

---

44   Goldman, *supra* note 1, at 100–01.
45   *Id.* at 102–03.

and causal force to the process of practical reasoning. On both accounts, the process carries logical force in that the wants represented in the first premise, in conjunction with the beliefs about effective means to fulfilling those wants included in the second premise, provide the reasoner with good reason to want to perform the action indicated by the conclusion. In Moore's terms, practical reasoning rationalizes the actor's acting on the conclusion of the syllogism by giving him good reason to do so. Similarly, both accounts portray the process of practical reasoning as carrying causal force in that the agent's wanting to achieve the end stated in premise 1 and his believing that the action identified in premise 2 will provide an effective means to that end cause him to want to act on the want or directive represented by 3 as a means to satisfying the want stated in 1.

Although Moore rejects causal theories generally and Goldman's theory specifically, this entire review of Moore's criticisms of Goldman suggests that the two positions are much more compatible than first impressions might suggest. Moore's rejection of Goldman's theory seems to be partially attributable to some misinterpretation of that theory as well as to the deviant causal chain problem and the inadequacy of the "characteristic manner" constraint. Moore advances his epistemic criteria for basic and intentional acts as an alternative to the unexplained causal hypothesis, but it is not clear that this epistemic approach is any more informative than the "characteristic manner" provision, and Moore's theory seems to retain the same unexplained causal requirement in the account of reasons for intentional actions.

Both writers advance accounts of practical reasoning that involve reasoning from wants and beliefs about effective means of satisfying those wants to actions that are expected to constitute means to the identified ends. Both rely on a notion of basic acts that are inherently intentional and on a process by which other intentional acts are generated by the basic act. Both are concerned with the logical and causal force of practical reasoning and reasons for action.

The differences between these two theories reflect the different purposes that the writers are pursuing. Moore is primarily concerned with a theory of rational agency for legal and moral purposes. He concentrates, therefore, on intentional action and the role of wants and beliefs as reasons that rationalize actions. In contrast, Goldman is primarily interested in developing a broad theory of human action that can accommodate intentional action and be applied to legal and moral issues but that is not limited to these concerns. Thus, Goldman concentrates on the more general causal processes that underlie all action. Both theories, however, contain the undeveloped causal provision that explains actions as the causal product of the actor's wants and beliefs, and both are concerned with the actor's beliefs as reasons for intentional action. Goldman addresses this issue in terms of the logical force of practical inference, whereas Moore writes of rationalizing actions.

It seems, then, that Moore has accurately identified the inadequacy of Goldman's theory with the unexplained "characteristic manner" provision. The theory fails to address important legal and moral questions because without an account of this "characteristic manner," we have no means of identifying those persons whose behavior cannot legitimately be attributed to them as the actions of moral agents. Moore's epistemic criteria do not provide a satisfactory alternative, however, both because we have no account of what the actor has to know in order to fulfill these criteria and because the mysterious causal connection between the actor's belief-desire sets and his intentional action remains.

Moore seeks a theory of personal agency because he is primarily concerned with legal and moral issues that are usually framed in terms of the actor's reasons for acting. He apparently rejects causation by belief-desire sets because he sees this type of state causation as incompatible with an account of personal agency in which a person acts for reasons. Ideally, however, one would want an explanation of the causal process by which the actor's wants and beliefs cause him to act on the conclusions of his practical reasoning, and one would want that explanation to reflect the role that

119

these beliefs and desires play as reasons for action. Such an account of the "characteristic manner" in which the actor's wants and beliefs cause his acts would avoid deviant causal chains and explain the causal force of these wants and beliefs by virtue of their being reasons for acting. This account would fulfill Moore's purpose of representing legal and moral agents as practical reasoners who engage in intentional acts that are rationalized by their reasons for acting, and it would do so in the form of a causal theory such as that put forward by Goldman and Sections 4.1 and 4.2.

4.3.2 Causal explanation and reasons for action. Fred Dretske has advanced a theory of behavior in which reasons for acting provide a causal explanation of behavior by virtue of their nature as reasons.[46] In this subsection, I will argue that Dretske provides the kind of explication of the "characteristic manner" in which belief-desire sets cause action that is needed for the purpose of this book. Goldman's causal theory, supplemented by Dretske's explanation of the manner in which reasons cause acts, provides the framework that allows one to clarify the nature and function of the MPC's structure of offense definitions. This framework suggests that the MPC approach can reasonably be understood as defining offenses in such a manner as to require that a person can be held criminally liable for an act only if it is appropriately attributable to him as a practical reasoner. On this account, the voluntary act and culpability requirements identify two ways in which an act can fail to issue in the requisite manner from the actor as a practical reasoner.

Dretske defines behavior as a process in which an internal cause (C) in a system (S) produces movement (M) in that system. One must distinguish the behavior from the product of that behavior. Linda is a ten-year-old child in a fifth-grade class. The teacher asks for a volunteer to answer a question. Linda knows the answer and wants to respond, so she raises her hand. Linda's rising arm is the movement in this case.

---

46   F. Dretske, Explaining Behavior (Cambridge, MA: MIT Press, 1988).

This movement could have occurred for purely external reasons such as the boy behind Linda grabbing her hand and holding it up. In that case, there would have been movement, but no behavior by Linda because there would have been no internal cause for the movement. When Linda's arm rises as a result of some cause internal to Linda, however, the process of that cause producing the movement is behavior.[47]

Behavior includes but is not limited to action. If, for example, Linda's arm had moved as a result of muscle spasms or convulsion, a cause internal to Linda would have produced movement. In such a case, Linda would have behaved, but she would not have acted. Actions are behaviors in which M constitutes S's exemplifying an act-type, C takes the form of the wants and beliefs of the actor, and C produces M in the characteristic manner that wants and beliefs cause actions.

Just as behavior differs from the movement that is the product of that behavior, causal explanations for behavior differ from causal explanations of movement. Neurobiology explains Linda's arm movement. One might explain how Linda's arm went up, for example, by referring to certain muscle contractions and efferent neurological impulses. Such an explanation explains M, but it does not respond to the question, "Why did Linda raise her arm?."[48]

When asked to explain not just the arm movement but Linda's raising her arm, one might provide answers to two separate questions. First, one might explain why Linda raised her arm *then* rather than at some other time. In responding to that question, one would cite a triggering cause such as the fact that the teacher asked for a volunteer. Second, one might explain why Linda *raised her arm* rather than doing

---

47   *Id.* at 3. Although I will continue to refer to the product of behavior as "movement" or M, Dretske recognizes that M can take the form of movement, change, or nonmovement. *See id.* at 29.

48   A purely biological explanation may suffice for behaviors that are not actions. For example, a neurobiological account may fully explain both M and C's producing M when M is caused by a seizure. We are primarily concerned here, however, with those behaviors that are also actions.

something else such as yelling "me," raising her leg, or running to the navy recruiter's station. In this case, one cites a structuring cause such as Linda's desire to answer the question and her knowledge that this teacher calls on students who raise their hands. That is, an explanation cites a triggering cause when it explains an event by identifying some other event that caused the explanandum to occur at the time it occurred, whereas it cites a structuring cause for the event when it explains why *that event* occurred rather than some alternative.[49]

When we want to explain behavior, and not merely movement, we cite triggering or structuring causes. Structuring causes that explain behavior that are actions take the form of reasons for action. Linda raised her hand rather than doing something else because she wanted to answer the question and she believed that raising her hand was an effective means of doing that in these circumstances. Linda's beliefs about the most effective means of achieving her end constitute a structuring cause of her behavior by virtue of their content; that is, her beliefs caused her to act as she did because of what they represented.[50]

Dretske defines a representational system (RS) as a system "whose function is to indicate how things stand with respect to some other object, condition, or magnitude."[51] An RS may indicate whether object O is in condition A or B by occupying state a when O is in condition A and state b when O is in B. For example, a room thermometer is a simple RS that indicates the temperature in the room. The state of the thermometer, measured by the level of mercury on the scale, represents the condition of the room in terms of temperature. The RS carries information about its O in that the RS's being in state a represents the information that O is in condition A.[52]

Beliefs are representational structures in an RS. They rep-

49 Dretske, *supra* note 46, at chapter 2.
50 *Id.* at 51–52.
51 *Id.* at 52.
52 *Id.*

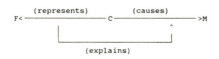

Figure 5. Beliefs as causes of movement

resent the circumstances that the person encounters and his condition in those circumstances. The actor's beliefs partially determine what he does. The content of the beliefs represent facts about the person's environment and about his own condition in relation to that situation. In Linda's case, for example, the content of her beliefs represented facts about her environment (the teacher asked for a volunteer) and about her own condition (that she knew the answer to the question). If Linda's beliefs constitute part of the internal cause C that produces M, then C has both representational and causal functions; C represents conditions (F) and it causes M.

In order to explain the characteristic manner in which the actor's beliefs cause his actions, we need an explanation of the process by which C causes M that makes use of the fact that C represents F. According to such a theory, C would cause M by representing F. We could then say that the actor's beliefs cause his action in the characteristic manner that beliefs cause acts just in case C caused M by virtue of C's representing F according to the process identified by the theory. Figure 5 illustrates this process.[53]

Dretske contends that during the process of associative learning, internal states C become associated with F and acquire control over M when that M in F promotes success in F. That is, C represents F and M succeeds in F, so C becomes the mental event that elicits M in F. C elicits M in F just because C represents F and M has previously been rewarded in F. By virtue of its representational content, C becomes the link that connects M to F. On this account, C is a structuring

53 *Id.* at 79–88. Figure 5 is taken from Dretske's Figure 4.2 at 88.

cause of M in F because C represents F. Once C, which represents F, becomes associated through learning with the success of M in F, C becomes a reason to do M in F. C's representational content therefore becomes both a structuring cause that explains M and a reason for performing M.[54]

C elicits M because M has succeeded in situations represented by C previously, not because M will succeed in this case. Once C becomes established through learning as the internal state that represents F and associates M with success in F, it may cause M in some cases when O is not actually in F. O might encounter F', which differs from F in relatively subtle ways that render M unlikely to succeed. In such circumstances, O may register F' with C and thus perform M, which will not succeed. Either O will learn to discriminate between F and F' – representing F with C, which elicits M, and F' with C', which elicits M' – or O will continue representing both F and F' with C, in which case the associative link between M and success will weaken. In the latter case, C's role as a structuring cause and rationalization for M will fade.

On this theory, Linda learns through experience that M (raising her hand) succeeds in F (the teacher asking for volunteers) and that M' (yelling "me") does not succeed in F. C, which includes the belief set that represents F, then serves as a structuring cause of M, and it provides Linda with a reason for performing M instead of M'. In short, C both causes and rationalizes M by virtue of its representational content.

Although C includes O's relevant beliefs, it is not constituted entirely of beliefs. Linda's beliefs would not cause her to raise her hand if she did not want to answer. Suppose Linda is shy or does not know the answer. C would still represent F, but it would not elicit M. C, the internal cause of M, can be divided into beliefs (B) and desires (D). Linda's beliefs (B) represent F (the conditions that the teacher has asked for a volunteer, and that raising one's hand constitutes

54   *Id.* at 95–107.

volunteering). "D" stands for Linda's receptivity to the reward (R) of being called on. When Linda is in state D and experiences B, then the conjunction of B and D cause Linda to respond with M in order to secure R. If, however, Linda is shy or unprepared, B continues to represent F, but B does not elicit M because she is not in state D.[55]

This account provides a causal explanation for Linda's performing M in F, and it rationalizes that action. In addition, it provides an analysis of Linda's acting for reasons that makes use of the notion of state causation. According to this theory, C both provides a structuring cause for M and rationalizes M just because C consists of O's being in belief-state B and receptivity-state D. Therefore, O's acting for reasons is explained in terms of state causation involving the relationship between C (including both B and D) and M, which has previously succeeded in satisfying D in conditions represented by C.

In summary, belief-desire sets (C) cause actions (M) as reasons for those actions when the actor is in state D, B represents F, and M has previously succeeded in F by achieving R, which satisfies D. C causes the actor to perform M (rather than any M') because the beliefs that the actor is in F and that M has succeeded previously in F by satisfying D provide reasons that constitute structuring causes for the actor's doing M and that rationalize the decision to do M in order to achieve R. On this account, B both causes and rationalizes the decision to do M by virtue of B's representational content, which forms the link between M in F and R as a means of satisfying D.

Recall the John-killing-James example. John is in state D regarding the prospective R (James's death) in that he is angry at James and wants to kill him. John believes (B) that he is in conditions F such that M (firing his gun at James) will produce R. Aggressive actions similar to M have successfully achieved rewards such as R, fulfilling wants such as D, in the past. The belief-desire set C has therefore ac-

55 *Id.* at 109–15.

quired control of M in that B represents F and the D for R has previously been fulfilled by acts such as M in F. The representational content of C serves as the learned link between M in F and satisfaction of D by achieving R. C serves as a structural cause for M, eliciting M rather than some M' in F, and the representational content of C provides John's reason for performing M in F in order to elicit R. Thus, C both causes and rationalizes M in F.

It is important to recognize that we do not have to suppose either that John has been rewarded specifically for killing someone in the past or that aggressive behavior has previously paid off in the long run, all things considered. For C to elicit M, it is enough that behavior like M has succeeded in satisfying states similar to D. Episodes in which acts similar to M in conditions similar to F have resulted in some satisfaction of states like D may establish C as the internal state linking F to M by representing F and eliciting M.

The actor with the capacity to form abstract concepts and draw fine distinctions will generally be capable of responding more precisely to important similarities and differences among stimulus conditions. A cognitively more sophisticated actor, therefore, will be more successful than the relatively less sophisticated one in satisfying D by achieving R in light of variations in the stimulus conditions F, F', F", and so on.[56]

Compare this analysis to that of the variation of the same example given previously to exemplify a deviant causal chain. In that version, John's beliefs, desires, and decision to kill James caused John to suffer a heart attack, which then contributed to James's death as James ran from the scene.[57] In that case, John's beliefs represented F – including the fact

---

56 A comprehensive account of the external contingencies and cognitive processes that would determine whether the actor will actually perform M in any particular case would extend well beyond the scope of this book, although chapter 7 will discuss this issue to some degree. *See id.* at 134–36 and 141–46 for Dretske's account of response generalization.

57 *See supra,* chapter 4.3.1.

that he had been insulted, that he could kill James, and so on. His belief-desire set (C) caused his heart attack, and thus his falling to the floor gasping for breath (M). C caused M by virtue of its being a source of stress, however, rather than through its representational content. M could have been caused in the same manner by John's belief that he had just lost all his money in the stock market. That is, C caused M, but it did so as a triggering cause rather than as a structuring cause; it caused M to occur now, but it did not provide John with reasons to perform M. C caused M without providing John with reasons that rationalized John's doing M in order to achieve R and satisfy D.

We can imagine a third variation in which John intentionally killed himself because he wanted to cause James trouble and believed that his own death would achieve this result. In that case, however, C would have provided a structuring cause for John's performing M (inducing his own death) and C would have provided reasons that rationalized John's doing M in order to achieve R and satisfy D.

The key points in this analysis are the following. An actor's wants and beliefs cause his actions in the characteristic manner that wants and beliefs produce intentional action when C causes M by virtue of its representing F and forming the internal link between M in F and previous instances of satisfying D (or similar states) by achieving R (or similar rewards). In such cases, C constitutes a structuring cause for M that provides reasons that rationalize the actor's doing M in F in order to satisfy D by achieving R.

This account of reasons as causes that rationalize the agent's behavior reconciles Goldman's causal theory of action with Moore's recognition that legal and moral systems usually address the person as a practical reasoner. In addition, it responds to Moore's criticism of causal theories by providing an explication of the "characteristic manner" in which the actor's wants and beliefs cause actions. This explanation renders mental state causation of action consistent with agent causation and addresses the problem of deviant causal chains. When deviant causal chains occur, the actor's wants and beliefs may serve as a triggering cause rather than as a structuring cause, and either C's causal force is independent of its representational content or the representational content does not rationalize M; that is, C does not cause M by providing the actor with reasons for doing M in F in order to satisfy D by achieving R.

This analysis does not render the actor infallible because C rationalizes M whenever it portrays M as rational in light of the actor's wants and beliefs. This requirement would be met, for example, if Linda raised her hand because she wanted to elicit the teacher's attention and believed that this act would achieve this purpose. Suppose that today's substitute teacher does not respond to raised hands. Linda's act would be ineffective, but her wants and beliefs would constitute a structuring cause for it and rationalize it nonetheless.

Finally, this account does not rest on the contention that Goldman and Dretske have advanced unassailable theories. It only contends that these writers provide reason to think that their theories or some similar alternatives can supply an adequate account of human action as caused by reasons that rationalize those actions. Revised versions of these theories or more satisfactory alternatives could support the interpretation of the MPC offense structure advanced in this chapter.

4.4 SUMMARY AND CONCLUSIONS

This chapter has advanced an interpretation of the MPC's structure of offense elements that is intended to clarify the nature and purpose of the primary requirements of this structure and the relationships among these provisions. This interpretation is grounded in a causal theory of action that represents acts on act-trees consisting of basic acts and other acts level-generated from basic acts. Projected act-trees illustrate hypothetical future acts consisting of basic acts, target acts, and other acts that are expected to be level generated from basic acts. These other generated acts may be either intentional or anticipated.

The actor forms an action-plan when he decides to perform a basic act in order to do a target act. The action-plan consists of the intent to perform the target act and all intentional acts on the projected act-tree that the actor selects. When the actor acts on an action-plan, the beliefs and desires represented by that action-plan cause the basic act and the rest of the act-tree in the manner that beliefs and desires characteristically cause acts. Beliefs and desires characteristically cause acts by virtue of their representational content. These mental states provide a structuring cause for acts when their representational content supplies the actor with reasons that rationalize those acts as a means to satisfying a want by achieving some identified result. When an actor acts on an action-plan under ordinary conditions, his beliefs and desires cause his acts in this characteristic manner. The actor's basic-act and all other acts that are level-generated from that basic act form an act-tree.

When the actor selects an action-plan from among the array of available projected act-trees, he engages in a process of practical inference. In doing so, he acts as a practical reasoner, and the resulting act-tree can appropriately be attributed to him as a practical reasoner. MPC offense elements can be understood as specifying the required connection between the act-token that exemplifies the act-type constituting the offense and the actor as a practical reasoner. This interpretation suggests that the criminal law applies only to those with the capacities to function as practical reasoners, and that acts constituting offenses can give rise to criminal guilt only if they are appropriately attributable to the actor as a practical reasoner.

The objective elements in the offense definitions identify the proscribed act-types. The culpability requirement defines the required relation between the projected act-tree that the actor selects to act upon and the act-token that constitutes the offense. Under ordinary conditions, the projected act-tree that the actor selects for his action-plan represents the actor as a practical reasoner, so the culpability element identifies the required relation between the act-token constituting the offense and the actor as a practical reasoner. It specifies the manner in which the act exemplifying the objective offense elements must represent the actor as a practical reasoner in order to establish criminal guilt for that act as that offense.

A failure-of-proof defense demonstrating that the defendant lacked the required type of culpability establishes that the act-token constituting the objective elements of the offense is not sufficiently related to the projected act-tree that represents the defendant as a practical reasoner to allow attribution of that offense to that defendant as a practical reasoner. The standard defense of ignorance or mistake exculpates the defendant for the same reason.[58] Ignorance or mistake regarding fact or law that negates the required culpability element precludes the required connection between the defendant's conduct constituting the objective offense elements and his status as a practical reasoner.

If one understands the structure of MPC offense requirements as limiting criminal liability to cases in which the offense as defined in the code is appropriately attributed to the defendant as a practical reasoner, then failure-of-proof defenses involving ignorance or mistake will undermine that attribution. In contrast, claims such as that of reasonable mistake regarding justification, which exculpate the defendant by virtue of ignorance or mistake without challenging the attribution of the offense to him as a practical reasoner, must be general defenses rather than failure-of-proof defenses. A reasonable mistake regarding justification, for example, would give rise to a specific excuse in Robinson's system of defenses by virtue of his third excusing condition involving nonculpable ignorance of wrongfulness.[59]

Finally, the voluntary act provision requires that the be-

---

58 MPC, *supra* note 13, at sec. 2.04(1).
59 Robinson, *supra* note 17, at sec. 25(b) (regarding the four excusing conditions) and sec. 184(a) (regarding mistake as to justification).

havior constituting the offense be part of an act-tree produced through an action-plan in the characteristic manner by the defendant's wants and beliefs. This constitutes the requirement that the offense occur as part of an act-tree that is rooted in a basic act that is produced in the characteristic manner by the actor's beliefs and desires in their capacity as reasons that explain and rationalize the actor's decision to perform the basic act as part of an action-plan. When this requirement is met, the actor's beliefs and desires led him to act on some action-plan in his capacity as a practical reasoner. Thus, the actor produced an act-tree in his capacity as a practical reasoner, and any act-token on that tree is accurately attributed to him as a practical reasoner because it is at least weakly intentional. A failure-of-proof defense addressing this requirement denies that the conduct constituting the objective elements of the offense is part of an act-tree arising from a basic act that was produced by the defendant's wants and beliefs in the characteristic manner.

Chapter 1 reviewed the MPC system of offense elements and a proposed structure of defenses. It concluded that neither the individual offense elements, the relationships among them, nor the relationships among the offense elements and defenses was clear. Chapters 2 and 3 contended that current approaches to the defenses of insanity and automatism are inadequate, and that these deficiencies are at least partially attributable to the lack of clarity described in Chapter 1. Chapter 4 has advanced a conceptual framework intended to improve our understanding of the MPC system of offense requirements. Chapters 5 and 6 will apply this framework to the automatism and insanity defenses in order to demonstrate that it can clarify some perplexing issues regarding these defenses.

Chapter 5

Automatism

This chapter applies the action theory framework presented in Chapter 4 to the automatism defense. It contends that automatism is most appropriately understood as a failure-of-proof defense regarding the voluntary act requirement. This chapter is intended to serve two purposes: First, it advances a theoretically consistent approach to the types of cases that usually give rise to claims of automatism, and second, it demonstrates that the conceptual framework advanced in Chapter 4 can serve as a useful tool for clarifying difficult issues regarding criminal defenses.

5.1 INTRODUCTION AND CONTEXT

Chapter 3 reviewed current approaches to the automatism defense in the United States and Britain, concluding that neither the American courts nor their British counterparts have addressed this defense in a satisfactory manner. The American courts have yet to establish any settled interpretation. Some courts have interpreted the defense as a failure-of-proof defense going to either the culpability or voluntary act requirements, whereas others have treated automatism as a variation of the insanity defense or as some other unspecified general defense. Individual decisions have sometimes been internally inconsistent, describing automatism as a failure-of-proof defense but placing the burden of persuasion on the defendant.

Unlike their American counterparts, the British courts have

developed a relatively settled approach. Unfortunately, this approach involves an unsustainable distinction between sane and insane automatism. British and Canadian courts treat some cases as instances of sane automatism, whereas they address others under the rubric of insane automatism, despite the fact that the defendants apparently acted with similar functional impairment, and the courts have found no firm theoretical ground for this distinction.[1] This is particularly problematic because the cases are categorized on the basis of the internal or external origins of the underlying disability that causes the excusing condition, yet it is the functional impairment rather than the underlying disabling condition that justifies excuses.[2] The decision to treat some but not all cases of automatism under the insanity defense is apparently a practical response to the perception that certain defendants should be confined as dangerous, and to a legal standard that allows commitment only if the defendant is acquitted under the insanity defense. No satisfactory theoretical foundation for this practice has been advanced.

The British courts attempted to distinguish sane from insane automatism by separating the defendants who suffered a disease of the mind from those who did not. The British courts apparently treat the presence or lack of a disease of the mind as the key issue because they apply the *M'Naghten* standard to the insanity defense. They reason that a defendant who acts in a state of significantly impaired consciousness does not know what he is doing and therefore does not know the nature and quality of his act. Given that the defendant does not know the nature and quality of his act, he falls within the scope of *M'Naghten* if, but only if, this ignorance is the result of a disorder of reason caused by a disease of the mind. Thus, automatism falls within the scope of insanity if the defendant suffers a disease of the mind but requires a separate defense if he does not.[3]

1 *See supra*, chapter 3.2.
2 P. H. Robinson, Criminal Law Defenses sec. 25(b) (St. Paul, MN: West Pub. Co., 1984).
3 *See supra*, chapter 3.2 for a more complete analysis.

Defendants who did not know what they were doing do not need either the insanity or automatism defenses. A defendant who did not know what he was doing almost certainly did not perform the objective elements of the offense purposely, knowingly, recklessly, or negligently. One might be able to imagine unusual hypothetical cases in which an actor performed an offense with the requisite culpability level despite not knowing what he was doing. For example, one could imagine a defendant who purposely causes the death of another by placing poison in the victim's tea, although he believed that he was causing the death of that person by placing sugar in the tea and thereby inducing a diabetic coma. Arguably, such a defendant killed his victim purposely without knowing what he was doing.

In most plausible conditions, however, the defendant who did not know what he was doing did not do *that act* purposely or knowingly. Similarly, such an actor is highly unlikely to have consciously disregarded an unjustified risk that he was performing the proscribed offense. Thus, he did not perform it recklessly. Finally, if one assumes that the automatism defendant lacked the capacity to know what he was doing, then he did not act negligently.[4] It seems, then, that automatism defendants have access to a wealth of defenses by virtue of the fact that they performed the conduct constituting the objective elements of the offense without knowing what they were doing.

Unfortunately, when one reviews the cases, there seems to be no good reason to believe that the defendants did not know what they were doing. One can imagine situations in which the defendant would raise the automatism defense regarding behavior that occurred in such a manner that he did not know what he was doing. A defendant who was charged with assault because he suffered a seizure during which he fell to the ground and consequently tripped another

---

4 *See supra*, chapter 1.1 for a more complete treatment of the MPC culpability levels. Crimes of strict liability may constitute the unusual exception to this claim.

person would not have known what he was doing. In such a case, however, he would have a failure-of-proof defense because his conduct did not include a voluntary act as the MPC defines it. The problematic cases of automatism are those in which the defendant acted in such a manner as to indicate that he not only knew what he was doing; he acted in that way for the purpose of performing the act constituting the objective elements of the offense.

The defendant's mental states at the time of the offense are usually inferred on the basis of evidence regarding his behavior and speech. In order to determine whether the defendant acted purposely, the court must review the entire set of words, actions, and circumstances surrounding the offense.[5] Automatism cases sometimes involve acts done in a skilled, coordinated manner, apparently for the purpose of achieving some specific end. For example, some defendants have drawn guns, pointed them at their victims and shot them repeatedly, or struck their victims repeatedly and then pushed them from the car in which both had been sitting and driven away.[6] Such cases involve behavior that was apparently done in a directed, effective manner to achieve a purpose. Other defendants have not only performed the act constituting the offense in an apparently purposeful manner; they have engaged in preliminary behavior apparently intended to arrange circumstances in such a manner as to facilitate the offense. For example, one defendant called the victim over to the window, ostensibly to see an animal swimming in the water below, then struck the victim with a mallet and threw him from the window.[7]

These events simply do not provide evidence from which to infer that the defendants did not know what they were doing. Rather, these facts seem to indicate that the actors

5 W. LaFave and A.W. Scott, Jr., Substantive Criminal Law sec. 3.5(f) (St. Paul, MN: West Pub. Co., 1986).
6 *See, respectively,* Fain v. The Commonwealth, 78 Ky. 183 (1879); People v. Newton, 8 Cal. App. 3d 359, 87 Cal. Rptr. 394 (1970); People v. Higgins, 5 N.Y.2d 607, 186 N.Y.S.2d 623, 159 N.E.2d 179 (1959).
7 R. v. Charlson, 1 All E.R. 859 (1955).

knew what they were doing and acted as they did precisely for the purpose of performing the act constituting the objective elements of the offense. In terms of the model presented in Chapter 4, these actors apparently selected a projected act-tree as their action-plan precisely because it was expected to produce an act-tree including the behavior constituting the offense. Unless this appearance is seriously misleading, these defendants knew what they were doing, and they performed their offenses purposely. Thus, neither a failure-of-proof defense regarding the culpability element nor the "nature and quality" disjunct of the *M'Naghten* test would apply.

Although the automatism defense was raised in these cases, one could defend the contention that automatism applies to defendants who did not know what they were doing, and argue that the defense should not apply to cases such as these. Alternately, one might advance an account of automatism that accommodates these cases but does not involve the claim that the defendants did not know what they were doing. Section 5.2 will pursue the latter approach.

5.2 ACTION THEORY ANALYSIS

At first glance, these defendants appear to meet the voluntary act requirement. If they selected an action-plan in order to perform the offense that they actually completed, then apparently the actor's wants and beliefs caused the act-tree that included the conduct constituting the offense. On the action theory analysis of the MPC advanced in Chapter 4, however, the voluntary act provision requires not only that the actor's wants and beliefs cause the basic action and the acts that are generated from it, but also that they do so in the characteristic way that wants and beliefs cause acts.

The central question, then, is whether conduct that is apparently purposeful is caused by the agent's wants and beliefs in the manner that is characteristic of ordinary human activity. In light of the analysis presented in Chapter 4, this requirement is satisfied if, but only if, the actor's wants and beliefs caused his action by virtue of their representational content as reasons for actions in the manner that reasons cause the actions of practical reasoners. This provision does not require that the actor reasoned correctly or that he did what the ideally rational practical reasoner would have done. It does require, however, that the actor's wants and beliefs caused the action through the normal causal process.

The defense of automatism is appropriate when the offense involves behavior performed "in a state of mental unconsciousness or dissociation without full awareness, i.e., somnambulism, fugue."[8] Normal consciousness includes the person's awareness of himself, his environment, and the relation between the two.[9] The difficult cases in which the defense of automatism is raised are those in which some event, such as physical trauma or an epileptic seizure, has induced some degree of clouding of consciousness. When consciousness is clouded, the person experiences a state of reduced wakefulness and awareness. His ability to perceive and apprehend his environment and his situation in it is impaired, leaving him with an incomplete and inaccurate grasp of his environment and his place in it.[10] In effect, the person is deprived of access to information regarding himself, his environment, and the relationship between the two. This condition of partial isolation from access to orienting information is directly relevant to the process by which an actor's wants and beliefs characteristically produce his actions.

As described in Chapter 4, when a person acts according to an action-plan, he performs a basic act in order to generate some higher act on his projected act-tree. At any particular time, the normal agent has a variety of action-plans open to him, and a rough hierarchy of wants that motivate him to pursue certain action-plans. He selects an action-plan to pur-

---

8 Black's Law Dictionary 127 (rev. 5th ed., St. Paul, MN: West Pub. Co., 1979).
9 Blair, *The Medicolegal Aspects of Automatism*, 17 Med. Sci. Law. 167 (1977).
10 *Id*; L.C. Kolb, Modern Clinical Psychiatry 115–16 (8th ed., Philadelphia: Saunders, 1973).

sue by deliberating about one or more action-plans, comparing his wants and aversions regarding each plan and its likely consequences. Although it is the nature of wants that they tend to cause acts, only some wants actually produce action because the deliberating agent can compare projected act-trees and select from among them.[11]

When an agent selects and pursues an action-plan, he engages in a process of practical inference from his want to perform an act and his beliefs regarding which acts will generate that act.[12] Recall the following example of a very simple practical reasoning sequence discussed in chapter four.

PR2 1. I am cold and want to be warm.
     2. I can become warm by donning the sweater.
     3. (conclude) I want to don the sweater.

The simple practical inference in PR2 provides the reasoner with a brief action-plan; he decides to put on the sweater in order to make himself warmer. Under ordinary conditions, including the ready availability of a sweater, the reasoner will put the sweater on with no further reflection. PR2 is an example of a brief, simple, practical inference that most people have completed and acted upon without any careful reflection. Consider, however, PR3, which takes a form very similar to PR2.

PR3 1. I am broke and want to have more money.
     2. I can get more money by robbing the bank.
     3. (conclude) I want to rob the bank.

Most people have experienced the sensation of being cold and wanting to be warmer. Many people have also been broke and wanted more money. Most people also believe that they can make themselves warmer by donning a

---

11 A. Goldman, A Theory of Human Action 99–121 (Princeton: Princeton Univ. Press, 1970).

12 Id. at 99–109. See supra, chapter 4.3 for a more comprehensive discussion of practical reasoning.

sweater, and that they can get money by robbing a bank. Yet most people act on the conclusion of PR2 without further consideration, whereas relatively few act on the conclusion of PR3.

Although PR2 would often lead immediately to the act of donning the sweater, PR3 would usually elicit further deliberation, which occurs when the actor is unsure whether he wants to perform the act indicated by the conclusion of the practical inference.[13] The inferences represented in PR2 and PR3 may each be elicited by the reasoner's immediate awareness of his wants to be warmer and richer respectively. In each case, however, the reasoner also has a variety of other standing wants and beliefs that form the context for his decision. For example, the actor may have standing background wants to be promoted at work, to take a vacation, to buy a new car, to lose ten pounds, to please his spouse, to be liked and respected by others, to be a good person, and so on.

Practical inferences such as PR2 may lead to immediate action, whereas those such as PR3 lead to further deliberation because the former raise no apparent conflicts with competing wants whereas the latter do. Assume that the reasoners who perform the inferences in PR2 and PR3 have identical sets of background wants and beliefs. Under normal conditions, the reasoner who performs the inference in PR2 may act without considering any further wants because the inference has no apparent relevance to them, and thus elicits no awareness of them.

The reasoner who draws the inference in PR3, however, is likely to become immediately aware of potential conflicts with his other wants because the content of the premises and conclusion will elicit associations with related wants and beliefs. For example, the idea of robbing the bank may elicit thoughts about the possibility of being shot by pursuing police, being sent to jail, losing the respect and affection of others, or simply not being the sort of person the actor wants to be.

13   *Id.* at 103.

The reasoner may have strong standing wants not to be shot, jailed, or shamed in both cases, but the wants and beliefs involved in PR3 will elicit awareness of these standing wants, whereas those involved in PR2 will not. The process of practical inference is a causal one in that the agent's wants and beliefs cause him to form the wants that comprise the conclusions of the practical inferences, as well as to become aware of, and deliberate about, the relationships among various courses of action and his larger set of background wants and beliefs.

This discussion of the process of deliberation in light of the actor's comprehensive set of wants and beliefs demonstrates that practical reasoning becomes much more complex than the simple example of PR2 would suggest. In simple cases the reasoner merely reasons from a want to an act that provides a means to satisfying that want. The agent engages in a process of deliberation when he encounters doubt regarding the best thing to do. He comes to a decision when he resolves that doubt by selecting a projected act-tree to adopt as an action-plan.

The doubt that leads to deliberation may simply reflect the agent's lack of certainty regarding the most effective means for accomplishing a particular end. For example, Linda may want to impress the teacher, but she may be unsure whether she can best accomplish that by running errands or by remaining in class so she can volunteer to answer questions. Alternately, however, deliberation may involve competing ends and various means to those ends. Suppose for example, that Linda wants to impress the teacher, but she also wants to avoid being considered a teacher's pet by her classmates. In such a situation she must consider not only whether a particular action will constitute a sufficient condition for satisfying one want but also the effect of that act on her other wants.

Complex deliberation can involve too many considerations to be reviewed simultaneously. The actor must address part of the problem while holding other aspects in memory. For example, the actor might consider possible means to satisfy one want, select the most efficient act for that purpose, and then consider the likely effects of that act on each of the competing wants. Suppose, for example, that the actor decides that act A_1 would provide the best means of satisfying want W_1. He also realizes, however, that A_1 would prevent satisfaction of W_2. Finally, he concludes that A_2 would come close to satisfying W_1 and it would also achieve partial satisfaction of W_2, whereas no other available act can be expected to satisfy W_1 or W_2 without frustrating the other. Hence, the actor pursues an action-plan that includes A_2 as a target act but does not involve A_1.

Extended evaluation of several possible acts and their likely effects on a complex network of wants requires the ability to store some information in memory while evaluating other alternatives. Then the reasoner must recall the stored information and consider it while holding other data in storage. The reasoner gradually recalls and evaluates information about various alternatives in light of assorted wants in order to select the act that best serves the complex set of wants.[14]

The reasoner cannot, of course, evaluate every possible act in light of all possible wants without becoming paralyzed in perpetual deliberation. The efficient agent needs some mechanism for storing information and then recalling that which is relevant to the decision in question. The agent who is contemplating act A_1 as a means to satisfy want W_1 must consider A_1 in light of all and only the other wants likely to be affected by A_1. If the actor fails to consider wants likely to be affected by A_1, he risks self-defeating acts, but if he indiscriminately reviews all possible acts in light of all his wants, he risks endless deliberation. The reasoner needs a selective information retrieval system that will call to mind the wants likely to be significantly affected by the acts he is considering. The reasoner who is considering bank robbery as a means of acquiring more money must retrieve and review his standing wants to avoid being shot or jailed, but considering his long-standing desire to memorize the batting

14   *Id.* at 103–04.

averages of the 1923 New York Yankees will only prolong and confuse the process of deliberation.

The process of associative learning provides a plausible model of a retrieval system that will serve the practical reasoner. Recall that according to Dretske's theory, mental state C elicits movement M in conditions F because M has previously succeeded in F by achieving reward R, satisfying receptivity state D. Hence, when F recurs, C includes the association of M with successful satisfaction of D in F, and this association provides the actor with a reason that serves as a structuring cause of M in F.[15]

Suppose, however, that M has previously frustrated an alternative want D' in F by preventing the actor from achieving the reward R' that satisfies D'. C consists of receptivity state D for R and beliefs B regarding conditions F and the relationship between M in F and R. D for R causes the actor to pursue R, but B provides the reason for pursuing R *by performing M;* that is, B is a structuring cause of M in F. If the actor encounters F and the associated beliefs B, C will elicit M if the actor is in state D, but C will provide the actor with a reason to avoid M if the actor is in D'. If D and D' are compatible states, the actor may be in both simultaneously. In such a case, F and the associated B will provide the actor with reasons to perform M and to avoid performing M. Conflicting reasons should trigger a process of deliberation in which the actor searches his memory for some alternative M' that will satisfy both D and D' in F, or at least one that will provide the best net satisfaction of D, D', and other relevant wants.

The associative process described here provides an overly simplified account of the kind of retrieval mechanism the practical reasoner needs in order to deliberate effectively. The actor in state D encounters conditions F, which are represented by state B. B and D comprise C, which elicits M (or the avoidance of M) due to the past success (or failure) of M in F as a means for satisfying D. An unimpaired adult de-

15 *See supra,* chapter 4.3.

velops a very complex set of wants and beliefs and a broad repertoire of behavior.

Goldman's causal theory reserves the causal role of wants and beliefs for occurrent wants and beliefs. Occurrent wants and beliefs are mental events that are active in consciousness. For example, under ordinary conditions, one who is cold will be consciously aware of that fact, of his desire to be warm, and of his belief that donning the sweater would satisfy that desire. In contrast, standing wants and beliefs are propensities or dispositions to have certain occurrent wants or beliefs under certain conditions.[16] Most people, for example, have a standing want to avoid paying fines, but that want does not become occurrent until flashing lights appear in the rear view mirror.

Complex practical deliberation requires the capacity to store some information while attending to other considerations and then to retrieve the stored information for continued review. The actor must be able to select relevant standing wants and beliefs in order to recall them to occurrent status. The associative process describes a mechanism through which the actor can perform this operation. Internal state C elicits M, which has been associated with success in F in the past. M, however, is also associated with the frustration of D' in F. Hence, as the reasoner deliberates about the appropriate action to take in F, his receptivity state D and belief B elicit a potential action-plan including M, but his awareness of this projected act-tree will also elicit awareness of his standing want D' and the belief B' that M has been associated with frustration of D' in F.

The ordinarily competent practical reasoner will occasionally fail to consider relevant wants or waste time on irrelevant issues. Generally, however, the unimpaired adult considers most of his relevant wants and beliefs just because his mental states that represent various conditions and potential actions retrieve associated standing wants and beliefs to occurrent status.

16 Goldman, *supra* note 11, at 86–91.

In summary, complex practical reasoning involves an extended causal process of deliberation in which the actor reviews a variety of possible behaviors in an effort to select those that are likely to satisfy his most pressing wants at the least cost to his other wants. As the actor considers various potential acts, the internal states that represent those acts and the other conditions and desires of which he is aware recall to occurrent status additional standing wants and beliefs with which they have become associated. Given sufficient time and interest, the actor will eventually become aware of and review a broad array of potential acts in light of his complex network of relevant wants and beliefs. Throughout this process, mental states play a causal role in eliciting awareness of additional wants and beliefs and in providing reasons that serve as structuring causes for the actor's decision to perform a particular action and as a rationalization for it.

On this analysis, the normal agent is a practical reasoner with a complex system of interacting wants and projected act-trees. He compares them and chooses the action-plan that is most consistent with his overriding wants and aversions. This decision to pursue a particular action-plan produces the basic act, which in turn generates the higher level acts on the act-tree, which if the actor's beliefs were accurate, will be consistent with his projected act-tree. This process of deliberation illustrates the actor's role as a rational being directing his life through practical reasoning in what Hart calls a choosing system – that is, a system of law in which the rational agent can maximize his own ability to determine his own future through choice.[17]

The criminal law is intended to influence the decisions of such agents by proscribing certain behavior and prescribing penalties in order to alter the agent's evaluation of some projected act-trees by virtue of their anticipated consequences. That is, by attaching a criminal penalty to a partic-

---

17 H.L.A. Hart, Punishment and Responsibility 44–46 (Oxford: Oxford Univ. Press, 1968).

ular act, the legislature attempts to discourage agents from performing that act by adding a consequence that will render the act inconsistent with a strong want for most actors.

A central ingredient in this account of a competent practical reasoner is access to a relatively complete array of information regarding himself, his environment, and the relationship between the two – that is, normal consciousness. A person who acts in a state of impaired consciousness is acting in a state of distorted awareness and attention such that his acts may be caused by an action-plan, but the plan is selected with access to only a small and nonrepresentative portion of his wants and beliefs. The actor's wants and beliefs do not cause his acts, therefore, in the manner characteristic of ordinary human activity. Such an actor acts on an action-plan, and thus the relation specified by the culpability level between the act-token constituting the objective elements of the offense and the action-plan can obtain. Yet, the act is not voluntary because the process by which the actor's wants and beliefs cause the act is impaired by his state of clouded consciousness, which limits and distorts his access to his own wants and beliefs.[18]

18 It is important here to recall the relationship among movement, behavior, and action. On the Goldman–Dretske view, advanced in chapter 4, any motion of the body is a movement, whereas behavior is internally caused movement and an act is behavior that is caused in the characteristic manner by the actor's wants and beliefs. An act as defined by the MPC might be movement, behavior, or action in Goldman–Dretske terms. A voluntary act in MPC terms is an act in Goldman–Dretske terms.

When I say, therefore, that the act of a person who suffers clouded consciousness is not voluntary, I mean that the act (MPC) is not voluntary (MPC) and therefore it is not an act in Goldman–Dretske terms. Stated strictly in Goldman–Dretske terms, the behavior performed by a person who is suffering from clouded consciousness is not an act because it is not produced by the person's wants and beliefs through the ordinary causal process of deliberation. This behavior can stand in the relation to an action-plan that is required by the culpability element, however, because the person does engage in behavior with some purpose. Perhaps one should describe these action-plans as "behavior-plans," but whichever term one employs, the required relation between behavior and plan remains.

This interpretation does not imply that normal actors actually reflect on all available action-plans before acting. The critical factor is not the array of wants and beliefs that the actor actually considers, but rather his access to them. Clouded consciousness impairs the reasoner's access to his own standing wants and beliefs about the nature of the world, himself, and the relationship between the two. This impairment distorts the causal process by which the actor's wants and beliefs cause his acts by providing reasons for action.

It is important here to distinguish the causal process by which the actor's action-plan produces the act-tree from the causal process of deliberation through which the actor's comprehensive set of wants and beliefs produces the action-plan and, thus, the act-tree. The former involves the wants and beliefs that the actor decides to act upon and the causal process by which his basic act follows from the decision to perform it. This process occurs in any instance in which an actor acts pursuant to an action-plan. The decision to perform the basic act produces that act and all other acts generated by it. There is no obvious reason to think that this process operates differently for the person who suffers clouded consciousness than it does for the person who experiences ordinary consciousness.

The latter process of deliberation, however, is markedly affected by clouding of consciousness. The process of deliberation, through which the actor selects an action-plan designed to maximize satisfaction of the broad array of wants, involves an associative process in which his consideration of possible action-plans elicits occurrent awareness of related wants and beliefs. Thus, the associative process of deliberation provides the retrieval system through which the actor recalls standing wants and beliefs to occurrent status so they can play a role in selecting an action-plan designed to represent the relatively comprehensive set of wants and beliefs.

Clouded consciousness impairs this process because the person with limited access to his own standing wants and beliefs forms action-plans and acts upon them without the opportunity to have those decisions affected by the likely consequences of those actions on his relatively comprehensive set of wants. Thus, the extended causal process of deliberation through which the actor's comprehensive set of wants and beliefs produces the action is limited and distorted by clouded consciousness. That process is limited in that the actor's action-plan is selected in light of only some of the relevant wants and beliefs, and it is distorted in that this subset of wants and beliefs is not representative of the comprehensive set.

Consider, for example, a hypothetical factory worker, Fran, who suffers clouding of consciousness due to low blood sugar or an epileptic seizure. As a result, she stops working, and the assembly line grinds to a halt. Suppose the foreman yells at Fran, who is aware only that she is angry, that she wants the foreman to stop yelling at her, and that she can stop the yelling by hitting the foreman with her wrench. She hits the foreman with the wrench in order to stop the yelling.

In this case, the usual connection between Fran's action-plan and her act obtains, but the act does not bear the usual causal relation to Fran's comprehensive set of wants and beliefs. The action-plan is selected and acted upon without benefit of the associative process that usually causes the actor to become aware of related standing wants and beliefs such as her desires to keep her job, to avoid jail, or to conform to her own moral standards. In short, the broad causal process through which the actor's relatively comprehensive set of wants and beliefs produces her action-plan and, thus, her act is distorted for the actor who suffers clouded consciousness. This distortion prevents the attribution of the act to the wants, beliefs, and processes that represent the actor as a practical reasoner.

The normal practical reasoner sometimes makes choices that are ill-advised or self-defeating. This might occur, for example, because the actor is mistaken about the likely consequences of an action-plan, or because a short-term desire exerts a stronger motivating force than a long-term want that actually has greater total impact on the actor's complete network of wants. In such cases, however, the actor selects an action-plan through a causal process of deliberation that allows access to the comprehensive set of wants and beliefs.

In contrast, the actor who selects an action-plan in a state of impaired consciousness acts without the benefit of the causal force that would ordinarily be exerted by certain wants and beliefs that constitute reasons for acting in a certain manner. The actor who suffers substantially impaired consciousness is deprived of much more than knowledge of some specific relevant fact; such an actor acts without benefit of the comprehensive network of standing wants and beliefs that provide a consistent context for various specific decisions.

Suppose, for example, that the reasoner who draws the inference in PR3 suffers from some disorder of consciousness such that he is temporarily deprived of access to his own overriding wants to avoid being shot, jailed, or shamed.[19] In such a case, the process of practical reasoning culminating in the want to rob the bank would not elicit awareness of these wants, and consequently they would not be available to counter the motivating force of the want to have more money. The agent's wants, beliefs, and decisions would produce actions, but they would not do so in the manner of ordinary human activity because the full array of background wants and beliefs would not be available to the reasoner during the process of deliberation. Certain relevant wants that form an important part of the actor's comprehensive network of standing wants would not exert the causal force that they ordinarily would because they would be beyond the reach of the associative retrieval process.

On this interpretation, the failure-of-proof defense regarding the voluntary act requirement differs markedly from the defense based on mistake or ignorance. The standard mistake or ignorance defense addresses the culpability requirement

---

19 This example is not intended to be a realistic one. More plausible applications will be considered later in the discussion of epilepsy and hypnosis.

by showing that mistake or ignorance prevented the actor from forming the appropriate state of mind.[20] This mistake or ignorance must involve a material fact regarding the offense. For example, the defendant who leaves a restaurant wearing another patron's coat because he honestly and reasonably believes that it is his coat would have a failure-of-proof defense regarding the culpability element to a charge of theft, which only applies to the offender who takes or controls the property of another with the purpose of depriving that other person of his property.[21]

The interpretation of the voluntary act requirement advanced here does not address knowledge or ignorance regarding material facts of the offense. Rather, it involves the actor's access to his own standing wants and beliefs that would usually play an important role in the process of deliberation for the actor in his capacity as a practical reasoner. Deprivation of access to these wants and beliefs distorts the causal process by which the actor's mental states cause his selection of an action-plan, and therefore his behavior is not produced by his effort and determination in the manner of ordinary action.

On this account, neither the culpability level nor voluntariness entails the other. The voluntariness requirement is met when the basic act that roots the act-tree is caused by the actor's wants and beliefs in the manner that wants and beliefs characteristically cause ordinary human activity. The culpability level is satisfied when the specified relation between the act exemplifying the objective elements of the offense and the action-plan obtains. Clear cases of involuntary behavior, such as reflex or convulsion, will not meet either requirement because there is no action-plan. The problematic cases of the automatism defense involve disorders such as epilepsy that cloud consciousness and give rise to behavior that apparently manifests the specified culpability level.

20 American Law Institute, Model Penal Code and Commentaries sec. 2.04 (official draft and revised comments, 1985).
21 *Id.* at sec. 223.2(1).

5.3 APPLICATIONS

Epilepsy is a physiological disorder characterized by disturbance of consciousness, as well as by several other physical and psychological symptoms. The primary diagnostic criterion of epilepsy, however, is loss or disturbance of consciousness. Epileptics suffer three different types of seizures: grand mal, petit mal, and psychomotor or temporal lobe seizures.[22]

Temporal lobe epilepsy is perhaps the type that is most likely to become an issue in criminal trials because these episodes may be manifested by a variety of behavioral symptoms including aggression and violence, yet they lack the clearly convulsive characteristics that mark the grand mal seizures. Patients who suffer temporal lobe epilepsy may experience substantial clouding of consciousness, confusion, and bewilderment. Some victims also experience brief affective changes including states of vague alarm, fear, or rage. A few epileptics will engage in outbursts of violence that may be strikingly brutal. The clinical impression has been described as that of delirium with liberation of aggressive, and occasionally self-destructive impulses.[23]

The complex interaction of physical and psychological factors that combine to form an epileptic disorder are not entirely understood. The earlier description suggests an interpretation that if it is roughly accurate, would support the analysis of automatism advanced in this chapter. If the victim of an epileptic seizure experiences states of terror and rage while in a condition of clouded consciousness, he may be motivated by intense affect while he is effectively isolated from the comprehensive set of wants and beliefs that usually

---

22 Kolb, *supra* note 10, at 242–45.
23 *Id.* at 245–50; Sherwin and Geschwind, *Neural Substrates of Behavior,* in The Harvard Guide to Modern Psychiatry 59, 66–68 (A. M. Nicholi, Jr., ed., Cambridge, MA: Harvard Univ. Press, 1978). Delirium is a pathological reaction in which the individual manifests a variety of symptoms, including variable states of consciousness with impaired orientation and memory.

serve to inhibit unacceptable impulses. He may, for example, experience a sudden state of fear and rage, directed at the person physically closest to him, while in a state of clouded consciousness that effectively prevents access to his usual complex of inhibitory wants and beliefs regarding his own moral standards, the kind of person he is or wants to be, the identity of this other person, and the likely consequences of his actions. Fran (the factory worker described earlier) provides an example of this pattern.

As described previously, the fully functioning agent selects from a broad array of available action-plans through a process of practical reasoning that allows him to pursue certain dominant wants in light of the available alternatives and the likely consequences of each. If the account presented earlier is approximately correct, the acts that occur during an episode of temporal lobe epilepsy are the product of an action-plan, but the actor's wants and beliefs do not produce that action-plan, and hence the behavior, in the manner characteristic of ordinary human activity. Rather, certain wants and beliefs produce the actor's actions while he is isolated from access to the broad array of wants and beliefs that would ordinarily provide a context for his affective states and allow him to inhibit the unacceptable impulses. Clouded consciousness prevents these inhibitory wants from playing their usual role in the associative process of deliberation.

Many rational adults have felt the urge to punch someone who seemed to be treating them in a particularly insulting, unfair, or injurious manner. Most people refrain from acting on that urge most of the time. The desires not to be arrested, go to jail, look like a thug, be ostracized, feel guilty, suffer some other untoward consequences, or fail to be the kind of person one wants to be can be instrumental in promoting self-control in these situations. If a person acts on an aggressive impulse because he does not care about any of these inhibitory considerations, then his aggressive act represents him as a practical reasoner. If he generally cares about these matters, but in this case his desire to hit was stronger than the inhibitory considerations, then his act reflects his wants

151

and beliefs regarding that situation. If, however, he generally cares about these considerations but his clouded consciousness prevents him from recalling these standing wants to occurrent status, then his aggressive act does not accurately reflect his comprehensive network of relevant wants and beliefs because it is caused by a nonrepresentative subset of them through a distorted causal process.

The important point is not merely that this act was not the most rational thing to do in light of the actor's comprehensive set of wants and beliefs; normal people often perform acts that are less than optimally rational in this sense. Rather, the central point is that in cases of substantially disturbed consciousness, the causal process by which the actor's relevant wants and beliefs cause acts is distorted. The reasons the actor actually has are not available to play their appropriate causal role as reasons for action. Hence, the act is not appropriately attributed to the actor in his capacity as a practical reasoner.

Some episodes of temporal lobe epilepsy can include delusions, hallucinations, and schizophreniform psychosis.[24] In these cases, the epileptic is suffering dysfunction that is consistent with the kind of psychopathology that is usually referred to as mental illness, mental disease, or disease of the mind. The insanity defense seems more appropriate than the automatism defense for defendants manifesting these types of impairment because they suffer impairment in their ability to process their wants and beliefs rather than lack of access to these mental states.[25]

Alternately, these delusions and hallucinations may deprive the epileptic of knowledge regarding a material element of the offense, and thus give rise to a failure-of-proof defense regarding the culpability element. The fact that epileptics can suffer different types of functional impairment, and that these different types of impairment seem to render the victim

---

24 Kolb, *supra* note 10, at 249–50; Sherwin and Geschwind, *id.* at 68.
25 This topic will be addressed more thoroughly in chapter 6.

appropriate for different defenses, supports Robinson's claim that defenses are more appropriately categorized by excusing condition (functional impairment) than by the underlying disability.[26]

The MPC explicitly lists hypnosis as a condition that should defeat an ascription of voluntariness, but it suggests that unlike the other conditions listed, hypnosis renders behavior involuntary due to dependency rather than due to lack of effort and determination or impaired consciousness.[27] This interpretation seems to suggest that the exculpatory significance of hypnosis rests on a fundamentally different basis than that of the other conditions covered by this section, raising questions about the theoretical consistency of the voluntariness requirement.

The analysis put forth in this chapter, however, would accommodate hypnosis under the same principle that applies to the other conditions listed. Hypnosis, like epilepsy, is not a completely understood and explained phenomenon. On some accounts, however, the hypnotic process is essentially one that alters the focus of the subject's attention in such a manner as to direct his attention toward the hypnotist's voice, and thereby to selected thoughts and experiences. As the subject's attention is directed toward those selected matters, other information and considerations that usually matter may fade from awareness, depriving the subject of the perspective of a broad reality orientation. Consciousness may

---

26 Robinson, *supra* note 2, at sec. 25(b), 161. Note that this claim does not smuggle into the discussion the misguided distinction between sane and insane automatism that was rejected in chapter 3.2. That putative distinction purports to separate defendants on the basis of the presence or lack of a disease of the mind that gives rise to the defect of reason and ignorance of nature, quality, or wrongfulness called for in *M'Naghten*. That distinction fails because a disorder of reason constitutes a disease of the mind as the British courts have interpreted that phrase. The claim here regarding epilepsy, in contrast, addresses different excusing conditions that can occur as part of the epileptic syndrome, rather than supposed differences in the underlying disability.

27 MPC, *supra* note 20, at sec. 2.01 and comments p. 221.

become divided, with some information apparently processed while concealed from awareness.[28]

On this account of hypnosis, the subject's awareness of both his own experiences and of external matters is distorted in the sense that certain beliefs are isolated from their usual context in the broad array of the subject's wants and beliefs. The subject may form and pursue action-plans on the basis of those thoughts and experiences toward which his attention is directed, but he is deprived of the perspective usually provided by the comprehensive set of beliefs that ordinarily informs his understanding of himself, his environment, and the relationship between the two. On this picture of the hypnotic process, the subject's dependency is important not in itself, but due to the resultant lack of access to his comprehensive set of wants and beliefs that normally provides the material for the process of deliberation through which he selects action-plans to pursue.

According to this analysis, both hypnosis and epilepsy may render the subject's behavior involuntary by distorting or limiting his consciousness, depriving him of access to the broad array of wants and beliefs that usually provides the context within which a person's wants and beliefs lead to action through the associative process of deliberation that is characteristic of ordinary human activity. If one understands the voluntary act requirement as addressing the causal process by which an actor's psychological states normally produce action, then voluntariness is defeated when the actor's bodily movements are not the product of his wants and beliefs (as in reflex or convulsion), or when those movements are not produced by his comprehensive set of wants and beliefs in the manner characteristic of ordinary human activity. Automatism is an appropriate defense when clouded consciousness substantially impairs this normal causal process by which the

28 E.R. Hilgard and J.R. Hilgard, Hypnosis in the Relief of Pain 18 (Los Altos, CA: Wm. Kaufman, 1983); P.W. Sheehan and K.M. McConkey, Hypnosis and Experience 252–56 (Hillsdale, NJ: Erlbaum, 1982).

agent's mental processes produce an act-tree.[29] On this interpretation, as long as voluntariness remains an offense element, automatism is a failure-of-proof defense that defeats an ascription of voluntariness.

The allocation of the burden of persuasion has been a problem with the automatism defense. The state generally bears this burden regarding all offense elements, but it may be placed on the defendant for certain affirmative defenses.[30] The burden of proving a particular defense is more likely to be placed on the defendant when the defense involves a matter peculiarly within his knowledge and experience or when the defense turns on a claim that is antecedently improbable.[31] When voluntariness is doubtful due to possible clouding of consciousness, the relevant information regarding the defendant's state of awareness is peculiarly within his experience, and the claim that he did not act voluntarily appears improbable. For these reasons, some courts have placed the burden of persuasion on the defendant.[32] Robin-

---

29 On this account, the automatism defense applies by virtue of the functional impairment of psychological process. Thus, it avoids the confusion encountered by the British courts when they attempted to distinguish sane and insane automatism on the basis of the presence or lack of a disease of the mind. Recall from chapter 3.2 that this approach and the unfortunate internal-external distinction produced cases in which the courts were forced either to deny common usage by calling hypoglycemia a disease of the mind or to deny the apparent causal role of hypoglycemia in the offense.

On the account presented here, neither the sane-insane distinction nor the internal-external distinction applies. The defendant's automatism defense asserts that clouded consciousness substantially impaired the deliberative process, rendering the act involuntary. The success of the defense depends upon the court's conclusion regarding this claim rather than upon the specific event or process that produced the clouding of consciousness. Thus, epilepsy, hypnosis, hypoglycemia, trauma, or any other source of disturbed consciousness can give rise to the defense if the functional impairment affects the defendant's behavior in the described manner.

30 LaFave and Scott, *supra* note 5, at sec. 1.8(b), (c).

31 MPC, *supra* note 20, at sec. 1.12(2), (3); McCormick on Evidence 950–51 (3d ed., St. Paul, MN: West Pub. Co., 1984).

32 State v. Caddell, 287 N.C. 266, 290, 215 S.E.2d 348, 363 (1975); Fulcher v. State, 633 P.2d 142, 147 (Wyo. 1981).

son has argued that this is one reason among several for treating impaired consciousness as an affirmative defense rather than as a failure-of-proof defense with the burden of persuasion on the prosecution.[33]

The analysis here treats automatism as a failure-of-proof defense regarding the voluntariness requirement. Two logically independent questions must be distinguished. First, should automatism be interpreted as a defense that goes to the voluntariness of the actor's conduct? This analysis argues that it should when "voluntary" is understood in the narrow sense in which it is used in the MPC. Second, should the voluntary act requirement be an offense element, or should lack of voluntariness be a general defense? This analysis would be consistent with either answer to this question.

The voluntary act requirement can be understood as the conjunction of two distinct demands that serve two different purposes. The first demand holds that all offenses must include an act in the MPC sense of a bodily movement. This prevents the state from intruding into the individual's mental processes by making mere thoughts illegal and punishing for thoughts alone.[34] By this requirement, the individual must engage in at least some minimal degree of overt activity (or an omission when there is a duty to act) in order to become subject to state coercive force.

Second, that act must be voluntary. This requirement provides Hart's minimal connection between mind and body that renders the act "really" a human action and consequently partially justifies holding the actor responsible for it. According to the analysis presented in Chapter 4, this provision requires that the act arise in the ordinary manner from the actor's relatively comprehensive set of relevant wants and beliefs, justifying attribution of the act to the actor as a prac-

33 Robinson, *supra* note 2, at 171(d), 172.
34 MPC, *supra* note 20, at sec. 2.01 and comments p. 214; LaFave and Scott, *supra* note 5, at sec. 3.2(b); H. Morris, On Guilt and Innocence 1–29 (Berkeley: Univ. of Calif. Press, 1976).

tical reasoner. As such it is a preliminary requirement of culpability.[35]

The MPC currently addresses both of these purposes by requiring a voluntary act as an offense element.[36] When the overt act requirement and voluntariness are combined as a single offense element, and the state carries the burden of proving all offense elements, it becomes inconsistent to place the burden of proving voluntariness on the defendant. Alternately, however, these two components of the voluntary act requirement could be addressed separately in order to more effectively achieve the purpose of each.

The first of these two purposes could be satisfied by requiring an act in the MPC sense of a bodily movement, thus precluding offenses comprised purely of unacceptable thoughts. The second purpose could be addressed by the further requirement that the act be produced by the actor's wants and beliefs in the manner of ordinary human action. This could be treated as part of the general responsibility condition, and thus subject to defeat by a general defense analogous to the insanity defense. Several general defenses, including duress, immaturity, and insanity, exculpate defendants who are not thought to be appropriately held responsible for their behavior despite the fact that they fulfilled all offense elements.[37] Thus, a penal code could sever the voluntariness and act requirements, defining the act requirement as an offense element and the voluntariness provision as a general defense. It would be consistent, therefore, with the purpose of the voluntariness requirement, as well as with the analysis in this book to treat lack of voluntariness as a general defense, with the burden on the defendant.[38]

35 Hart, *supra* note 17, at 107; MPC, *supra* note 20, at sec. 2.01 and comments pp. 215–16.
36 MPC, *supra* note 20, at sec. 2.01.
37 *Id.* at sec. 2.09, 4.10, and 4.01, respectively.
38 This book expresses no preference between the alternatives of treating voluntariness as an offense element or as an affirmative defense. As chapter 6 will demonstrate, the structure of offense elements is not sufficient to achieve its apparent function without additional affirm-

Finally, there is the policy problem regarding disposition that is raised by the British cases. Treating automatism as a voluntariness defeater, whether as a failure-of-proof defense or as a general defense, does not provide the opportunity for confinement of dangerous defendants. There are, however, two avenues open for addressing this concern. First, a general automatism defense could have a provision, similar to that provided with the insanity defense, for compulsory confinement and treatment of the dangerous acquittee.[39] Second, this issue could be addressed according to a public health model, with provisions for confinement and treatment in the least restrictive manner patterned after current statutes regarding contagious diseases.[40]

5.4 CONCLUSION

Chapter 3 reviewed the current state of the automatism defense and concluded that neither the American courts nor their British counterparts have established a satisfactory approach. Chapter 3 also concluded that the current confusion regarding the defense is partially attributable to a similar lack of clarity regarding the structure of offense elements and the relationship of automatism to that structure. Chapter 4 advanced an interpretation of the MPC system of offense elements grounded in action theory. This model interprets the MPC voluntary act and culpability requirements as designed to limit criminal responsibility to actions that can be attributed to the actor as a practical reasoner.

Chapter 5 applied this analysis to automatism and concluded that this defense can consistently be interpreted as a failure-of-proof defense regarding the voluntary act require-

---

ative defenses. The allocation of the voluntariness requirement to either the structure of offense elements or the category of affirmative defenses appears to turn at least partially on issues of evidentiary efficacy that extend beyond the scope of this book.

39 MPC, *supra* note 20, at sec. 4.08.
40 Cal. Health and Safety Code sec. 3114–25 (West 1979).

ment. In order to support the contention that the action theory analysis can provide a generally useful framework for addressing issues involving criminal offenses and defenses, Chapter 6 will apply it to the NGRI defense.

Chapter 6

The insanity defense

6.1.1 Mary. Interviewer (**I**):   Mary, did your lawyer tell you that you have to go back to court?

Mary (**M**):   It wasn't my fault. (speaking very quietly and without apparent emotion throughout the discussion)

I: Do you know why you are going back to court?

M: Because of her, but it wasn't my fault – then I can go home.

I: You expect the court to send you home?

M: They will know it wasn't my fault – I was sick then – I had delusions.

I: Delusions? Tell me what you mean by that, Mary.

M: When you are sick and believe things that aren't true.

I: And you had delusions?

M: I thought they were going to get me.

I: You thought they were going to get you?

M: I was sick then – I thought I had to do it.

I: Did you have to do it?

M: No, but I thought so, I had delusions.

I: Tell me more about what that was like.

M: I thought they were going to kill me, so I had to stab her – so they would think I was bad – like them.

I: You thought the woman you stabbed was going to kill you?

M: No, not her, the other ones.

I: Why did you pick that woman?

160

M: I tried a man, but he was too strong.

I: So then you stabbed the woman?

M: Yes, then – it wasn't my fault – I had to do it.

I: Because they were going to kill you?

M: I thought so.

I: Were they?

M: No, I was sick then; I'm better now.

I: What made you think that they were going to kill you?

M: I heard them say so over the phone.

I: They called you on the phone?

M: No, I heard them plan it when I walked under the telephone wires.

I: You heard them talking on the phone while you were walking on the street?

M: Walking under the lines.

I: Was there any other way you could tell that they wanted to kill you?

M: They watched me on the subway.

I: How could you tell they were watching you?

M: I could feel them, and when I turned around fast, I caught some of them sitting behind me and watching me.

I: How did you know that those people on the subway were part of them?

M: They had to be; they were watching me.

I: Who were they?

M: Bad people, criminals, all in it together.

I: In it?

M: A secret organization; they wanted to kill me because I'm not like them.

I: What were they like?

M: Bad, all criminals – they didn't like me because I'm good – I don't sin like they do.

I: Are you safe now?

M: Yes, now they think I'm like them; they think I'm bad because I stabbed her.

I: Was she one of them?

M: No, she was leaving the church.

I: She was leaving the church?

M: Coming out of the church by my mother's house.

I: Why did you pick her?

M: I was supposed to.

I: You were supposed to stab her?

M: Someone from the church.

I: Why did you think you were supposed to stab someone from the church?

M: I prayed to God to tell me what to do and then I found a dollar that said "In God We Trust," so I knew I was supposed to go to the church.

I: How did you pick that woman?

M: She came out just when I got there, so I knew God wanted me to pick her.

I: You expect the court to let you go home now?

M: Yes, they will let me. I was sick then, but I'm better now.

I: Will it be safe at home?

M: Yes, they won't kill me now; they think I'm bad like them.

I: Will the people who knew her let you come back to the neighborhood?

M: It will be OK; it wasn't my fault. I was sick then, but I'm better now.

I: They won't be afraid or angry?

M: No, I'm better now.

I: And you'll be safe?

M: Yes they think I'm bad – like them.

I: Do they still watch you?

M: Yes, but now they think I'm bad like them – but I'm good – I fooled them.

6.1.2 Bill. Interviewer (**I**): Bill, tell me about the fires.

Bill (**B**): (no response)

I: Why did you light the fires?

B: (angrily) Let me out of here! Send me back to jail!

I: Is jail better than here?

B: You won't let me go!

I: We can't send you back; the court sent you here from jail.

B: I'll burn the whole fucking place down!

I: So we'll send you back to jail?

B: You'll have to.

I: That's not up to us; we can't send you back.

B: I'll kill you too, mother-fucker!

I: Me too? Is someone else dead?

B: Like that fucking rat.

I: The rat? Here?

B: Fucking dead – we killed it.

I: We?

B: Me and Pete.

I: Your brother Pete?

B: Yea, we killed it, we'll kill you fuckers too.

I: Is your brother here?

B: Dead.

I: The rat is dead?

B: Pete! They killed Pete! (increasingly agitated)

I: When did Pete die?

B: When we were kids, after we killed the rat; now we'll kill you all just like that fucking rat. (looking and gesturing toward the floor a few feet from him)

I: That rat? (looking toward the floor) Is the rat here?

B: Yea that fucking rat! (gesturing toward the floor and increasingly agitated)

I: Where is the rat, Bill?

B: Here (holding his stomach): I can feel it eating me away (sounding less angry and more frightened).

I: Is the rat in your stomach, Bill?

B: You fucking doctors know that; you got x-rays. X-rays, ray-guns, praise God; you got Satan in you!

I: But tell me about the rat Bill, can you see it?

B: Yea, right there! (pointing toward the floor a few feet away) Pete killed it with the shovel.

I: Do you think about Pete a lot?

B: He tells me what to do.

I: Is Pete here?

B: He comes; it's none of your business.

I: How did Pete die?

B: Some fucker shot him. (less agitated now)

I: When did he die?

B: We was kids. When can I go back to jail?

I: The court sent you here from jail, Bill. We can't send you back.

B: I'll burn this whole fucking place down. I'll get you all.

6.2 INTRODUCTION AND CONTEXT

Chapter 2 argued that recent developments in the NGRI defense actually constitute a return to the *M'Naghten* test, and further, that this approach does not satisfy its avowed purpose of providing a clear standard that avoids moral mistakes. These recent developments in statutory and case law retain the standing ambiguity regarding the term "wrongfulness," and the arguments supporting the changes do not stand up to careful scrutiny. Perhaps most importantly, the hypothetical cases of X, Y, and Z provided counter-examples to each interpretation of "wrongfulness." Finally, Chapter 2 contended that the historic failure of the search for a satisfactory NGRI test has been partially due to the ongoing lack of clarity regarding the system of offense elements and the relationship of the NGRI defense to that system.

Some theorists might interpret these arguments as supporting volitional standards such as the MPC provision that excuses a defendant who lacks substantial capacity to conform his conduct to the law.[1] Chapter 6, however, will advance the following claims. (1) It will reject volitional standards as they are usually understood. (2) It will argue that although *M'Naghten* is cognitive and inadequate, it is not inadequate because it is cognitive; rather, it is unsatisfactory because it is the wrong kind of cognitive test. (3) One

---

1 American Law Institute, Model Penal Code and Commentaries sec. 4.01(1) (official draft and revised commentaries, 1985).

can understand the NGRI defense more clearly by analyzing the type of functional impairment that actually occurs in major psychopathology and the significance of that impairment for the conceptual framework presented in Chapter 4. (4) The NGRI defense is a *sui generis* specific excuse that exculpates defendants whose acts cannot be attributed to them as competent practical reasoners because they suffer a unique type of impairment in their capacity for practical reasoning. This type of impairment occurs in several forms of major psychopathology, and it is not addressed by the failure-of-proof defenses or by the common excusing conditions of ignorance or coercion.

6.3 VOLITIONAL STANDARDS

Traditionally, volitional standards take the form of an independent "irresistible impulse" test or of a "capacity to conform" clause in a broader provision such as the MPC's. These volitional standards are usually interpreted as addressing the defendant's lack of ability to control his actions, and they are understood as independent of the cognitive provisions in that they excuse defendants who suffer serious psychopathology that is not primarily cognitive in nature.[2] It is difficult to specify what is required of an individual before one can say that he lacked the ability to control his conduct. Douglas Husak explains his control principle in the following manner. "[T]he control principle states that criminal liability is unjust if imposed for a state of affairs over which a person lacks control. . . . The core idea is that S lacks control over a state of affairs if he is unable to prevent it from taking place."[3] Husak relies on the intuitive idea of control rather than analyzing it further than this.

One can distinguish at least two interpretations of the intuitive idea behind the volitional standards. Call them the

2 A. Goldstein, The Insanity Defense 67–79 (1967); M. Moore, Psychiatry and Law 219 (Cambridge: Cambridge Univ. Press, 1984).
3 D. Husak, The Philosophy of the Criminal Law 98 (Totowa, NJ: Rowman & Littlefield, 1987).

literal and the flexible variations. According to the former interpretation, the defendant lacked the ability to control his act if he were physically unable to direct his movement (or lack thereof) through decision. Some behavior that causes harm appears to be appropriately excused for this reason. Suppose Diane kills another person by running the victim over with her car because she has suffered an unpredictable stroke while driving. She may remain conscious and know that she is running over the victim, yet she is unable to control the car or even to lift her foot from the accelerator because her paralysis prevents her from directing her limbs. In this case, Diane knowingly causes bodily injury to another, but she is clearly not culpable because she cannot control the bodily movements that caused the harm. She cannot do even what she decides to do.

While Diane appears to be an obvious candidate for exculpation due to her inability to control her movements, two problems remain for the literal interpretation. First, on this understanding the NGRI defense is superfluous. Diane, or any other defendant who qualifies for the volitional clause of the NGRI defense under this interpretation, can avoid liability through a failure-of-proof defense addressing the voluntary act requirement. Second, most NGRI defendants do not behave in this manner. Many plausible NGRI defendants raise this defense in order to avoid liability for conduct performed in a directed, organized, and apparently controlled manner. In many cases, they acted for the purpose of performing the offense with which they are charged.

Recall, for example, Skinner, who purposefully killed his wife in a goal-directed manner that he considered justified.[4] Skinner's delusions included him under the ignorance clause of *M'Naghten*, but the hypothetical cases of X, Y, and Z in Chapter 2 do not fall within the scope of these ignorance provisions, nor do Mary and Bill as represented in the prologue. Yet, all of these actors are intuitively plausible candidates for the NGRI defense who acted in a controlled,

4 *See supra*, chapter 2.1.1.

directed, and apparently purposeful manner. In short, the literal variation seems to apply only when it is not needed.

At least at first glance, a more flexible interpretation of the volitional standard intuitively seems to be more appropriate. Husak contends that control admits of degrees. "The test to be applied is a normative standard of what is reasonable to expect from a defendant in his particular circumstances."[5] This flexible volitional standard, then, exculpates the defendant who lacked the ability to control his behavior, and he lacks that ability just in case it would be unreasonable to expect him to perform (or refrain from performing) that act under those circumstances. If it would be unreasonable to expect him to perform (or refrain from performing) a certain act, then the criminal justice system could not reasonably hold him responsible and liable to criminal punishment and condemnation. Although Husak does not attempt to define the parameters of reasonable expectations, he suggests that case law regarding duress or diminished capacity might provide some guidance.[6]

Husak addresses the control principle in his discussion of the physical component of the crime, which generally corresponds to the MPC's voluntary act requirement. The MPC includes a volitional clause in its insanity defense that is similar to Husak's flexible control principle in that this provision exculpates those who lack substantial capacity to conform to the law.[7] This similarity seems to suggest that Husak's flexible control principle provides a reasonable interpretation of the MPC's volitional provision. As indicated in Chapter 2, however, volitional clauses such as the MPC's have recently been subjected to considerable criticism as failing to provide a clear standard and as leading to moral mistakes. In order to evaluate these criticisms, consider the structure of the NGRI defense.

Robinson contends that all excuses conform to a structure

5 Husak, *supra* note 3, at 98–99.
6 *Id.* at 99.
7 MPC, *supra* note 1, at sec. 4.01(1).

consisting of a disability that causes one of four excusing conditions. The excusing condition is some type of functional impairment that renders the actor blameless for the offense and provides the central reason for exculpation. The disability clause identifies some abnormal condition that existed at the time of the act constituting the offense. The disability must be observable in some manner that is independent of the offense, and its role is largely evidentiary in that it clearly differentiates the defendant from the general population and it provides reason to believe that the excusing condition actually obtained.[8]

The *M'Naghten* and MPC NGRI defenses can be analyzed into three components in a manner consistent with Robinson's structure of excuses.

1. **M'Naghten**
   a. "To establish a defense on the ground of insanity, it must be clearly proved that . . . "
   b. "the party accused was labouring under such a defect of reason, from disease of the mind . . . "
   c. "as not to know the nature and quality of the act he was doing; or if he did know it, that he did not know he was doing what was wrong."[9]

2. **MPC**
   a. "A person is not responsible for criminal conduct . . . "
   b. "as a result of mental disease or defect . . . "
   c. "he lacks substantial capacity either to appreciate the criminality [wrongfulness] of his conduct or to conform his conduct to the requirements of the law."[10]

---

8 P.H. Robinson, Criminal Law Defenses sec. 25(b), (c) (St. Paul, MN: West Pub. Co., 1984) *see supra*, chapter 1.2.
9 M'Naghten's Case, 8 Eng. Rep. 718, 722 (1843).
10 MPC, *supra* note 1, at sec. 4.01(1).

Both tests have three types of clauses that are related to each other in a manner that is consistent with Robinson's structure.

    a. **Exculpatory conclusion.** This clause asserts that certain defendants are not appropriately held blameworthy or responsible for specified conduct.
    b. **Disability clause.** This clause identifies the abnormal condition that underlies the excusing clause that provides the justification for clause a.
    c. **Excusing clause.** This clause identifies the functional impairment that renders the defendant blameless and, thus, inappropriate for punishment or condemnation. It provides the principle justification for clause a.

The exculpatory conclusion states the significance of the defense, which is that the defendant is not blameworthy or appropriately subject to punishment or condemnation. This clause does not, in itself, provide an explication of the excuse or a rationale for it. The other two clauses, however, serve somewhat more complex functions. Both the excusing and disability clauses fulfill epistemic and justificatory roles.

A clause serves an epistemic function insofar as it provides selection criteria that the court can use in identifying those defendants who appropriately fall within the scope of the defense. The excusing clause serves its epistemic function by describing some property of the appropriate NGRI defendant that enables the court to accurately differentiate those persons from the candidates who should not be excused through the NGRI defense. Ideally this property should be one that we can identify through some process other than merely inferring it from the conduct that constitutes the offense.

The primary function of the disability clause is to augment this epistemic role of the excusing clause. Suppose, for example, that the excusing clause exculpates those defendants who are ignorant of the nature, quality, or wrongfulness of their acts, and that this defendant has beaten his child with sufficient severity to constitute an assault. The excusing clause tells the court to look for evidence that supports or undermines the contention that the defendant did not know that such conduct was harmful or wrongful. Ideally, this evidence would be independent of the offense itself. It might consist of statements or actions in other contexts that suggest that the defendant did not know that his actions were harmful or wrongful.

Generally, most people would be unlikely to believe that a parent did not know that it was harmful and wrongful to severely beat their child. The claim becomes more plausible, however, when there is clear evidence that this defendant did so in response to an hallucinatory command from God and that he believed he was driving away a devil that had possessed the child. The claim becomes yet more believable if there is further evidence, independent of the conduct in question, that the defendant suffers a major disorder such as psychosis. In this manner, evidence establishing the presence of an appropriate disability, such as mental disorder of psychotic proportion, augments the epistemic function of the excusing clause.

In many cases, the disability may be more amenable than the excusing condition to independent verification. For example, retardation or a chronic psychotic condition that preexisted the offense and continues after it may be verifiable through examination of the defendant and of the relevant records. In such cases, the disability clause may fulfill the epistemic role more effectively than does the excusing clause.

The excusing clause, however, provides the primary justificatory force. It identifies the functional impairment that renders the defendant immune from blame, punishment, and condemnation. It does so by providing justificatory reasons that support the exculpatory conclusion by appealing, at least implicitly, to some theory of personal responsibility. In the example described earlier, the excusing clause appeals to the implicit principle that a person can justly be held responsible for the harmful effects of his actions only if he knew that they were harmful and wrongful.

170

The disability clause plays a qualifying role regarding this justificatory function by limiting the exculpatory force of the excusing condition to those defendants who are not appropriately held responsible for their own ignorance of harmfulness or of wrongfulness. The defendant who is excused by virtue of ignorance of harmfulness or wrongfulness that arises from his retardation or psychosis, for example, is unlikely to be culpable for his own excusing condition. The drunken defendant, in contrast, may be held liable for his actions despite the presence of an excusing condition because he may be considered responsible for that condition.

In summary, an NGRI provision exculpates certain defendants, and it supports that exculpatory conclusion with excusing and disability clauses that serve justificatory and epistemic roles. One can evaluate the adequacy of any particular NGRI standard, at least partially, by determining whether it satisfactorily fulfills the epistemic and justificatory roles. The *M'Naghten* and MPC NGRI standards both reflect this structure.

The *M'Naghten* standard addresses the epistemic and justificatory functions in the manner illustrated by the child-beating case just described. It serves the epistemic function by directing the court to look for evidence that either supports or undermines the contention that the defendant suffered a defect of reason from a disease of the mind that prevented him from knowing the nature or quality of his act or that it was wrongful. These claims might be supported by direct evidence of relevant false beliefs (excusing clause) or by other indications that the defendant suffered the appropriate type of psychopathology (disability clause). The *M'Naghten* test addresses the justificatory function by implicitly appealing to the intuitively plausible principle that holds that a person can justifiably be held responsible for his actions only if he knew, or with proper care would have known, what he was doing and that it was both harmful and wrongful. The excusing clause represents the basic justificatory principle, whereas the disability clause limits the excuse to those who

171

suffer some disorder that produces the required ignorance without fault by the actor.[11]

The MPC NGRI provision employs the term "appreciate" in place of *M'Naghten*'s "know." The analysis in Chapter 2 demonstrates, however, that these terms do not differ substantially unless "appreciate" is understood as requiring knowledge fused with affect, and that this affective interpretation produces counter-examples involving both the cold or vicious criminal and the average citizen under certain conditions. When one interprets "know" and "appreciate" interchangeably, the analysis of the epistemic and justificatory functions of the ignorance clause in the MPC standard corresponds to that described earlier for the *M'Naghten* test. The MPC ignorance provision is actually a bit less inclusive than *M'Naghten* because it discards the nature and quality conditions, addressing only ignorance of wrongfulness.

The MPC's volitional standard adds a dimension that is not addressed at all by *M'Naghten*. The manner in which this clause fulfills the epistemic and justificatory functions of the NGRI defense differs for the literal and flexible variations. Unfortunately, however, neither interpretation is satisfactory. The literal variation would add an appeal to an implicit moral theory holding that a person should be held responsible for his behavior only if he had control of his behavior in the sense that he was able to direct his bodily movements according to his decisions. It would serve the epistemic function by directing the court to seek evidence of some disorder such as a stroke or seizure that impaired this ability. Although the literal interpretation provides an intuitively plausible account of the epistemic and justificatory functions of a volitional clause, it is unsatisfactory for the reasons identified earlier; it merely provides a redundant defense for those defendants to whom it applies, and it fails to address most plausible NGRI candidates.

---

11 The claim here is only that the *M'Naghten* test addresses both functions, not that it does so satisfactorily. This standard is inadequate for the reasons given in chapter 2.

The flexible variation of the volitional clause is more consistent with the wording of the MPC provision and with Husak's formulation. It is a normative standard that exculpates a defendant if it would be unreasonable to hold that person responsible for failing to conform to the law under the circumstances. Although this seems to be an intuitively plausible standard, it provides no guidance regarding the epistemic function. It directs the court to exculpate defendants when it is reasonable to do so, but the flexible variation tells the court nothing about what properties it should look for in order to identify the exculpable actors. The standard describes neither functional impairments, underlying disabilities, nor any other characteristic of defendants or situations that a court can seek evidence to confirm or deny.

The flexible variation of the control principle also fails to address the justificatory function. It merely states as an excusing condition that the defendant could not reasonably have been expected to conform to the law, offering no explanation of the characteristics of the person or the situation that render it unreasonable to expect conformity. Thus, it provides no justifying reasons for exculpating any defendant, and it appeals to no explicit or implicit moral theory of personal responsibility.

The exculpatory conclusion of an NGRI provision states that a person is not responsible for criminal conduct performed under certain conditions. The excusing and disability clauses fulfill the epistemic and justificatory functions by describing those conditions. The exculpatory conclusion exempts certain defendants from responsibility in the sense that it identifies them as inappropriate subjects for blame, punishment, or condemnation for the act in question. When the volitional excusing clause in an NGRI standard such as the MPC's is interpreted according to the flexible control principle, it merely restates the exculpatory conclusion. That is, on the flexible interpretation, the MPC's volitional clause makes the vacuous claim that the defendant cannot reasonably be held responsible for his conduct if it would not be reasonable to hold him responsible for it.

In short, volitional clauses such as the MPC's provide unsatisfactory NGRI standards because they are either unnecessary and irrelevant or they are vacuous. They are unnecessary and irrelevant when they are interpreted in the literal manner. The flexible variation, in contrast, seems intuitively reasonable, but it adds nothing to the exculpatory conclusion, failing to address either the epistemic or the justificatory functions. If neither ignorance standards such as *M'Naghten* nor volitional tests such as the MPC's offer an adequate formulation of the NGRI defense, some would suggest that we abandon the search for a satisfactory explication of the defense and rely on the intuitive understanding of the jury.

Some writers who view the NGRI defense as a status excuse would simply instruct the jury to excuse a defendant who is sufficiently crazy. Moore suggests that we ask the jury, "Is the accused so irrational as to be nonresponsible?"[12] Similarly, Morse proposes the following charge to the jury: "A defendant is not guilty by reason of insanity if, at the time of the offense, the defendant was so extremely crazy and the craziness so substantially affected the criminal behavior that the defendant does not deserve to be punished."[13] Both of these approaches rely on the jury's intuitive understanding of "crazy" and "irrational" and of the significance of these notions for moral responsibility. In effect, these proposals suppose that the jury has a better intuitive grasp of the epistemic and justificatory functions of the NGRI defense than we are likely to be able to formulate in a formal analysis. They advocate, therefore, that we abandon the attempt to develop a clear formulation of the NGRI defense and rely on the moral intuitions of the jury.

These proposals may accurately represent the approach that juries actually take regardless of the formal standard with which they are charged. That is, juries may currently

---

12 Moore, *supra* note 2, at 245.
13 Morse, *Excusing the Crazy: The Insanity Defense Reconsidered*, 58 S. Cal. L. Rev. 777, 820 (1985).

decide cases on the basis of their moral intuitions rather than by systematically applying the official instructions they are given.[14] Furthermore, juries may achieve morally correct results through this process as often as they would if they attempted to apply the formal standard.[15]

Facilitating practical deliberation is not, however, the only purpose served by ongoing attempts to develop an adequate formulation of the NGRI defense. Continued pursuit of a satisfactory formulation of the defense remains important precisely because the excusing and disability clauses play a justificatory role. A fully formulated NGRI standard, including an explication of the justificatory function, would facilitate the larger project of articulating the implicit notions of personal responsibility that underlie the broad system of offense elements and defenses that provide the framework of the criminal law.

Perhaps, therefore, before resorting to the intuitive wisdom of juries, we ought to reconsider the role of the NGRI defense in light of the conceptual framework presented in Chapter 4 and the types of impairment that people suffering major psychopathology actually manifest. That is, if many people share the intuitive idea that extremely crazy defendants ought to be excused, perhaps we should attempt to understand the basis of that excuse by considering the types of pathology that these highly pathological defendants suffer. Chapter 4 interpreted the MPC system of offense ele-

14 Some empirical research supports this speculation. *See, for example,* Finkel, *De Facto Departures from Insanity Instructions,* 14 Law and Hum. Behav. 105, 112–13 (1990).
15 If juries tend to achieve morally defensible results through intuitive evaluations of each case, then a vacuous standard such as the flexible variation of the MPC volitional clause may serve some positive purpose by providing jurors with a "wild-card" they can use as an opportunity to apply these intuitive evaluations. Note, however, that this function is a positive one only if we have some reason to believe that the results are generally morally defensible. Furthermore, if we want jurors to apply an open-ended intuitive analysis, instructions explicitly communicating that role would have the virtue of honesty and would be less likely to confuse or mislead the jurors with illusory criteria.

ments as intended to restrict criminal liability to those actions that could appropriately be attributed to the actor as a practical reasoner. In what manner does the kind of impairment associated with major psychopathology affect this attribution?

6.4 PSYCHOPATHOLOGY AND THE NGRI DEFENSE

Recall the cases of Mary and Bill from the prologue. Both are clearly crazy in the intuitive sense in which we ordinarily use that term, and both are psychotic in that they suffer gross distortion of reality relatedness including delusions, hallucinations, and disturbances of language, thought, judgment, and interpretation of perceptions.[16] In addition, both are clearly plausible NGRI candidates. Whether they ought to be exculpated may be controversial, but they are plausible candidates in that either could present a nonfrivolous argument in support of the defense. If one thinks that anyone ought to be exculpated under an NGRI defense, then Mary and Bill are reasonable candidates for that status.

Although both are delusional, neither revealed delusional content that would satisfy the ignorance clauses regarding the nature, quality, or wrongfulness of the act. Mary's delusional thoughts included false beliefs regarding the offense. For example, she believed that there was a conspiracy against her by some group of bad people who wanted to kill her because she was good and that she could protect herself by convincing them that she was bad. She knew, however, what she was doing when she stabbed her victim, that the stabbing was harmful, and that it was both illegal and contrary to socially accepted moral standards. In fact, she stabbed the victim just because she wanted to do something bad in order to convince the conspirators that she was like them. That is,

16 American Psychiatric Association, Diagnostic and Statistical Manual of Mental Disorders 404 (3d ed. rev., Washington, DC: Am. Psychiatric Assn., 1987); L. Hinsie and R. Campbell, Psychiatric Dictionary 620 (4th ed., New York: Oxford Univ. Press, 1970).

the act was wrongful by Mary's personal standard as well as by the social moral standard.

Bill is also delusional, but he has no false beliefs regarding the offense at all. He knew that he was setting fires and that doing so was harmful, illegal, and socially regarded as wrongful. He set them because he was mad at the people running the mental health institution and he hoped to convince them to send him back to jail. He, like Mary, performed the conduct constituting the offense partially because he wanted to do something illegal as well as wrongful by accepted social standards.

Neither person had delusions that if true would establish exculpation under other defenses. These are not cases in which mental disorder causes a nonculpable mistake regarding justification. Mary believed that killing her victim would protect her from the bad people. This would not qualify under the usual formulations of the general justification defense known as "choice of evils" because that defense requires that the evil avoided through criminal conduct be greater than the evil caused.[17] Mary, however, caused an evil as great as the one she attempted to avoid. Self-defense (as well as mistake regarding self-defense) does not apply because this form of justification applies only when the force exerted in defense of oneself is directed toward the threatening party.[18]

Duress would not apply, even if Mary's delusional beliefs had been true, for two reasons. First, in many jurisdictions, duress does not apply to homicide.[19] Other jurisdictions do not limit the defense in this way, but duress exculpates the actor who performed the proscribed conduct, "because he was coerced to do so by the use of, or a threat to use, unlawful force against his person or the person of another, which a person of reasonable firmness in his situation would have been unable to resist."[20]

17 MPC, *supra* note 1, at sec. 3.02(1).
18 *Id.* at sec. 3.04(1).
19 *See, for example,* Arizona Revised Statutes, sec. 13–412(c) (1988).
20 MPC, *supra* note 1, at sec. 2.09(1). I will not address the usual concern

Mary's delusions did not include any belief that the actual use of force or threats of force had occurred. Neither did her delusional beliefs provide any reason to think that the danger was imminent. She took no less drastic action such as going to the police. If Mary's pathology were relevant only by virtue of the delusional content of her beliefs as a source of duress, she would not be excused. It is unlikely that a court would accept a claim of duress from an intact person who killed an innocent party in order to avoid danger to himself when that danger was not imminent, and the defendant attempted no less drastic form of self-protection. Intuitively, it seems likely that many people would hold such an actor morally blame-worthy, if that person were psychologically intact.

In short, if Mary's delusions have exculpatory force, this cannot be due merely to the content of her beliefs. Her delusional belief content, if true, would not exculpate a psychologically intact person. This conclusion holds true even more clearly for Bill, who was not trying to protect himself or another. Bill acted in order to get even with people he was angry at and in order to convince them to do what he wanted them to.

In summary, Mary and Bill are both clearly psychotic and plausible NGRI candidates. Equally clearly, however, neither is covered by the ignorance clauses regarding the nature, quality, or wrongfulness of their acts, and substituting "appreciate" for "know" does not change this for the reasons given in Chapter 2. Volitional clauses do not address these cases because the literal variation does not apply to these defendants, and the flexible variation is vacuous. The standard NGRI tests do not apply because they do not address the kind of pathology that these defendants actually suffer. Both are psychotic and plausible NGRI candidates by virtue of cognitive disorder, but the usual NGRI tests address the

regarding the mixture of excusing and justificatory elements in this defense because an analysis of the duress defense would take us too far afield from the immediate question.

content of the defendants' beliefs, whereas the core of their pathology lies in the disorder of cognitive *process.*

Three types of disordered cognitive process stand out most obviously. First, both parties experience hallucinations that distort their perception of the external world and their place in it. Second, they both hold blatantly contradictory beliefs. Third, they draw unwarranted conclusions about the significance of events, often basing those conclusions on little or no evidence, and these unwarranted conclusions sometimes lead to action-plans. Their hallucinations include Bill's visits from his dead brother and the presence of the long-dead rat. Mary hears phone conversations among the conspirators when she walks under the telephone wires on the street.

Bill holds the contradictory beliefs that his brother is dead and that this same brother visits him and will help him burn the hospital. He also believes simultaneously that he killed the rat a long time ago in another location, that it is present in his stomach, and that he can see it outside of his body in the room. Mary's contradictory beliefs are somewhat more subtle, but they are contradictory no less. She believes that killing an innocent person will demonstrate that she is bad, but that she will remain good while doing it. She believes that others are bad because they kill, but that she is good despite her killing an innocent party. She also holds that her prior belief in the conspiracy was a delusion and that the conspiracy continues. Finally, she believes simultaneously that her prior belief that she had to kill the victim in order to protect herself was false and that she had to do it in order to protect herself.

Many people may hold contradictory beliefs yet never confront the inconsistency because those beliefs arise at different times or address relatively insulated aspects of their lives. Mary and Bill, in contrast, hold blatantly contradictory beliefs about the same set of circumstances, and they maintain them simultaneously, with no apparent attempt to reconcile them.

A bigot may continue to claim that all members of some minority group are stupid when confronted with a brilliant member of that group. Usually, however, he will attempt to explain away the contradiction by arguing that this particular person actually has mixed heritage, or that this person's apparent achievements are illusory. Alternately, he might qualify his belief somewhat by accepting this individual as a rare exception to the general pattern. Generally, however, he will make some attempt to resolve the inconsistency, and he is likely to recognize that there is some embarrassment in holding contradictory beliefs. Mary and Bill, in contrast, just assert blatantly contradictory beliefs with no attempt to reconcile them and no apparent recognition that this is awkward or problematic.

Mary provides the most obvious example of the third category of disordered cognitive process. She draws clearly unwarranted conclusions from her observation that people sitting behind her in the subway are looking toward her when she concludes that they are watching her, and further, that this supports her belief in the conspiracy. She draws a less extreme but still unwarranted conclusion when she decides that the people in the neighborhood in which she committed the homicide will not object to her return because she was sick at the time of the act. Finally, she vests great significance in the motto on the dollar bill and on the fact that her victim was leaving the church when she arrived.

Bill may exemplify the same type of process, although it is difficult to be certain without further information. If he has derived his belief that the rat is in his stomach from some physical sensation in his stomach, he has drawn a wildly unwarranted conclusion from a minimal sensation. Unfortunately, we have no indication what Bill based his belief on. The point here is not, of course, that any instance in which a person draws unwarranted conclusions is evidence of major psychopathology. Rather, the claim is only that people who suffer major psychopathology demonstrate several types of disordered cognitive process, and therefore one ought to consider these types of dysfunction when searching for an adequate formulation of the NGRI defense.

Mary and Bill demonstrate the fundamental shortcoming

of the usual cognitive NGRI standards. NGRI tests such as *M'Naghten* or the MPC provision frame the excusing clause in terms of belief content by excusing those who acted in ignorance regarding specified issues such as wrongfulness. The cognitive disorder involved in major psychopathology, however, is manifested primarily by distortion of cognitive process rather than by erroneous content. For example, thought blocking is a pattern of disruption of reasoning in which the cognitive processes come to a sudden halt, apparently leaving the individual completely devoid of thought. There are several other patterns of disordered thought process. Each is defined in terms of disruption in the ordinary processes of thinking rather than with reference to thought content.[21]

Some aspects of psychopathology, such as delusions, are defined partially in terms of thought content. The pathological significance of delusions, however, lies primarily in the disordered process that supports the misguided belief content. A delusion is "[a] false belief, born of morbidity... engendered without appropriate external stimulation.... [they] are condensations of perceptions, thoughts, and memories."[22] A delusion is also defined as "a false personal belief based on incorrect inference."[23] Delusions, which are usually classified as disorders of thought content, are defined partially by the distorted processes that underlie them.

Consider a paranoid individual named Paul who believes that the FBI is watching him. He developed this belief because he found the lights on when he entered his apartment and the first TV show he saw the next night involved a fugitive named Paul. He interprets this sequence of events as a special warning directed to him by the FBI. Clearly, Paul

21 L. Kolb, Modern Clinical Psychiatry 102–07 (8th ed., Philadelphia: Saunders, 1973); Nicholi, Jr., History and Mental Status 34–35, in The Harvard Guide to Modern Psychiatry (A. Nicholi, Jr., ed., Cambridge, MA: Harvard Univ. Press, 1978). These common patterns of disordered thought process will be discussed more thoroughly in the context of schizophrenia.
22 Hinsie and Campbell, *supra* note 16, at 191.
23 American Psychiatric Association, *supra* note 16, at 395.

is delusional. Now suppose that the FBI really is watching him because the president is coming to town, and Paul has been identified as a suspicious character who lives along the route from the airport. Paul, however, knows nothing about these facts. Paul's belief that the FBI is watching him is true, but does that mean he is not delusional? No – Paul is delusional, despite the fact that his belief is incidentally true, because his belief is a product of pathological process.

Some critics might argue that Paul is pathological but not delusional just because the belief is true. They might contend that falsity is a necessary condition for a belief to qualify as delusional, and therefore no true belief can be delusional regardless of the pathological processes that underlie it.

Consider the following variation of Paul's story. Suppose that Paul forms his belief in the manner described but that the FBI is completely unaware of him. Paul then begins writing angry and disorganized letters to the TV station, which forwards them to the FBI without Paul's knowledge. The FBI then watches him for a while, concludes that he is harmless, and discontinues the surveillance. Paul held the same beliefs for the same pathological reasons throughout, but if falsity is a necessary condition for delusions, then he was delusional initially, ceased being delusional while the FBI watched him, and then became delusional again when the surveillance ended. Paul's pathology remained constant, but other people's actions varied. If an individual's status as delusional can fluctuate as a result of the fortuitous truth of his belief content due to external events of which he is unaware, then delusional status is irrelevant to pathology. Yet, delusions are important just because they indicate serious psychological disorder. In short, delusions almost always involve false beliefs, but they are seriously pathological because they are produced and maintained by distorted cognitive process, not merely because they are false.

On this account, delusional thought lacks epistemic justification. Epistemically justified beliefs are, roughly, those that the believer should believe because they are supported by epistemically correct processes.[24] The correct conception of epistemic justification remains controversial, but delusional beliefs lack justification, according to the major competing theories. Internalist theories contend that epistemic justification depends only on internal states of the believer, whereas externalist theories hold that both the internal states of the believer and factors external to the actor enter into epistemic justification. Reliabilism, for example, is an externalist theory according to which beliefs are justified if and only if they are produced by cognitive processes that reliably produce true beliefs.[25] Reliabilists would contend that delusional beliefs are unjustified because they are the product of delusional thought processes that usually do not generate true beliefs.

Internalist theories of epistemic justification hold that beliefs are justified if they are the product of correct cognitive processes, where the correctness of these foundations for beliefs are inherent features of the cognitive processes involved.[26] A belief can be justified either subjectively or objectively. A belief is subjectively justified if it is one that the believer epistemically ought to believe given the other beliefs he holds, while it is objectively justified if it is subjectively justified and it would remain so if the believer held all relevant true beliefs.[27]

A delusional person such as Paul lacks subjective justification because his other beliefs do not provide good reasons to hold his delusional beliefs. Thus, Paul's delusional beliefs are not ones that he epistemically ought to derive from his other beliefs. Paul also lacks objective justification for his delusional beliefs because subjective justification constitutes

24 J.L. Pollock, Contemporary Theories of Knowledge 7–10 (Savage, MD: Rowman & Littlefield, 1986).
25 *Id.* at 21–24. This discussion of epistemic justification will provide only rough statements of very complex theories. A sophisticated treatment of these issues and theories would extend well beyond the scope of this book.
26 *Id.* at 21–22.
27 *Id.* at 183–85.

one component of objective justification, and he lacks that component.

Because delusional thought processes do not provide epistemic justification, they will usually generate false beliefs. In some cases, however, delusional thought processes may produce beliefs that are coincidentally true. Paul's delusional beliefs, for example, were true during the period that the FBI actually watched him. These beliefs remained unjustified, however, because they were produced by unreliable processes, and Paul's other beliefs did not provide good reasons to accept the delusional ones.

In a few cases, a person might even hold true delusional beliefs while holding other beliefs that provide good reasons to hold the delusional beliefs. Suppose both that Paul had acquired documents confirming his belief that the FBI watched him during the second period described above and that Paul accurately believes that these documents are authentic FBI materials. Then Paul's belief that the FBI watched him is true, and he holds other true beliefs that provide good reasons to believe it. Paul, however, continues to hold his delusional belief for the same delusional reasons that he initially formed it. Paul's delusional belief is epistemically justifiable both subjectively and objectively, but Paul is not justified in holding it because he does not hold it for the reasons that justify it. Although the belief that Paul holds could be justified by reasons that Paul has available, Paul's believing it remains unjustified and delusional because he believes it through delusional process rather than as a result of those good reasons.

In short, delusional beliefs are usually false and epistemically unjustified. Occasionally, they might be true, and they might even be justifiable in the sense that there are good reasons available for believing them. The delusional person, however, remains unjustified in holding those delusional beliefs.

Delusions occur in several types of major psychological disorder. Perhaps the most common type of disorder that might give rise to the NGRI defense is schizophrenia. Schizophrenia is a clinical syndrome that includes delusions, hallucinations, incoherence or marked loosening of associations, catatonic behavior, and flat or grossly inappropriate affect. Under the most common diagnostic criteria, the course of the disorder must include at least one period of psychotic disturbance.[28] Major cognitive disturbance in schizophrenia includes distortion of thought process and reality relatedness.

Major disorder of thought process involves disturbances in cognitive focus, reasoning, and concept formation.[29] Cognitive focus involves the normal ability to "scan information selectively, attending to essential and ignoring irrelevant stimuli."[30] Schizophrenics who suffer impaired cognitive focusing are unable to effectively select relevant aspects of a stimuli field or to adjust attention in response to changing situations. Schizophrenics manifest impairment of cognitive focus in several forms of thought disturbance including "perseveration," which involves repetition of previously appropriate responses in circumstances in which they are no longer relevant; "clang associations," in which the individual responds to a word or question with an association to the sound of that word or question rather than to the meaning; or "thought blocking," which occurs when an individual's associative activity comes to a complete halt. Thought blocking is sometimes described as "thought deprivation," and it differs from the common experience of losing one's train of

28 American Psychiatric Association, *supra* note 16, at 188–94. I do not claim that all and only schizophrenics are appropriate for the NGRI defense. The syndrome serves as an example of one type of major disorder that gives rise to the NGRI defense. This discussion addresses schizophrenia as a clinical syndrome without taking any position regarding the status of the disorder as an illness or disease.

29 I. Weiner, Psychodiagnosis in Schizophrenia 16–102 (New York: Wiley, 1968). The following account of cognitive disorder in schizophrenia is drawn primarily from chapters 4–8 in this work. Other writers may classify thought disorder differently or interpret certain examples as representing different categories. Weiner is representative, however, insofar as he analyzes schizophrenic thought disorder as disrupted process.

30 *Id.* at 16, 27, *see, generally,* at 27–48 regarding cognitive focus.

thought in that the ordinary thinker usually experiences the latter process as one of distraction in which he loses track of the specific point he was about to make due to the intrusion of some other association or perception. Schizophrenic thought blocking, in contrast, apparently involves a complete halt to the associative process resulting in an absence of thought content for a brief period.

Various types of distortion of cognitive focus can occur separately or in combination with other types of thought disorder. Neither Mary nor Bill demonstrated perseveration or thought blocking, but Bill engaged in clang associations when was asked about the rat in his stomach. His initial response included a reference to x-rays, but his following associations were to the sound of the words rather than to the meaning. He associated from x-*rays* to *ray* guns and then to *praise* God rather than to further information about the location of the rat in his stomach.

In this context, reasoning is the normal ability "to draw logical inferences about the relationships between objects and events."[31] Schizophrenics often manifest several characteristic types of disturbed reasoning including overgeneralized or combinative thinking. A person demonstrates overgeneralized thinking when he draws conclusions without evidence or vests experiences with elaborate meaning that is not supported by the experience. Mary, for example, noticed that some of the people sitting behind her in the subway were looking toward her (probably because their seats, like hers, were facing forward), and she concluded from this that they were watching her. Combinative thinking involves the inappropriate condensation of impressions and ideas into beliefs and conclusions that violate realistic boundaries. Bill, for example, concluded that the rat was both in his stomach and outside of him in the room, and he believed

---

31 *Id*. at 16. The term "logical" does not refer in this case to formal logic. Rather, it refers to the conclusions that a reasonable, unimpaired person would draw from the available information.

that both Pete and the rat were alive although he was aware that they had died long ago.[32]

The normal capacity of concept formation involves the ability "to interpret experiences at appropriate level of abstraction."[33] Schizophrenics often interpret events at an over-inclusive level of abstraction, misinterpreting salient aspects of a situation and inappropriately enlarging conceptual categories. This process leads to idiosyncratic generalizations and symbolism that other people find difficult or impossible to understand.[34] Mary demonstrated this type of distortion when she interpreted the words "In God We Trust" on the dollar bill she found as a symbolic message that few others would understand.

Reality relatedness is the capacity to accurately perceive the external world (reality testing) and the individual's relationship to it (reality sense). Schizophrenics' perceptions of the external world tend to be only loosely tied to the external stimuli that elicit those perceptions. Thus, they tend to perceive and evaluate situations inaccurately, and as a result they often exhibit poor judgment and maladaptive responses.[35] Bill demonstrates impaired reality testing about the external world when he perceives his dead brother and the previously killed rat and believes that both are simultaneously dead and alive. Whereas reality testing refers to the ability to accurately perceive the external world, reality sense involves one's perception of oneself and one's relation to the external world. Schizophrenics sometimes do not successfully identify the boundaries between themselves and others or between themselves and the external world.[36] Bill, for example, sees the rat outside of his body in the room, but he also believes that it is inside his stomach.

---

32 *See, generally, id.* at 60–84 for an account of disturbances of reasoning in schizophrenia.
33 *Id.* at 16.
34 *Id.* at 92–94.
35 *Id.* at 16, 104–16.
36 *Id.* at 16, 125.

In summary, the schizophrenic suffers cognitive impairment manifested as distortion in cognitive focus, reasoning, concept formation, and reality relatedness. Impairment in these areas disrupts the schizophrenic's ability to accurately perceive, evaluate, and plan for external events and understand his own relationship to those events. Consequently, his understanding, reasoning, judgment, and actions tend to be idiosyncratic and often maladaptive.

The categories of cognitive disorder described here are not as clearly defined as one would like. They often overlap in that a particular sample of schizophrenic thinking may be interpretable as an example of more than one category. They are neither exhaustive nor mutually exclusive. One common characteristic of these various types of disorder, however, is that they are distortions of cognitive process rather than merely of belief content. An NGRI defense that satisfactorily accommodates the kinds of cognitive impairment suffered by seriously disturbed individuals such as schizophrenics must address impaired process and not merely belief content. Section 6.5 will discuss the significance of this kind of impairment for practical reasoning and criminal liability.

6.5 PSYCHOPATHOLOGY AND PRACTICAL REASONING

6.5.1 Practical reasoning. Chapter 4 discussed practical reasoning as a process by which the individual reasons from wants and beliefs about the acts that will serve as means to fulfilling those wants to a conclusion that takes the form of a want or decision to perform those acts. Deliberation is the associative process through which the reasoner considers alternative acts in light of his comprehensive network of wants and beliefs. In reasoning to a satisfactory means to fulfilling a particular want, the competent practical reasoner will become aware of other standing wants and beliefs that are relevant to those being considered. Thus, the associative process enables the reasoner to select an act that is likely to promote his target want without frustrating other important wants. When no available act will satisfy the target want without frustrating other important wants, effective deliberation enables the reasoner to select the act most likely to promote the best net satisfaction of the comprehensive set of wants.

Effective practical reasoning requires at least three types of cognitive competency. First, the actor must be able to form accurate beliefs about the relevant wants and circumstances. Second, the actor must engage in an efficient associative process through which those wants and beliefs that are occurrent during the reasoning process elicit awareness of relevant standing wants and beliefs. Finally, the actor needs an accurate reasoning process that allows him to draw warranted conclusions about the probable relationships among various wants, acts, and consequences. Although severe psychopathology can impair any of these three types of competency, major thought disorder is particularly relevant to the reasoning process that the reasoner employs in order to select action plans in light of his wants and the anticipated consequences.

The relationship between practical reasoning and traditional logic is controversial. Richard Hare argues that practical reasoning is an application of traditional logic in which the actor reasons to acts that provide necessary or sufficient conditions for fulfilling his wants.[37] In contrast, Gilbert Harman denies that formal logic has any special significance for practical reasoning. He argues that the reasoner depends on basic dispositions to recognize that certain propositions immediately imply others and that some propositions are immediately inconsistent with others.[38] These dispositions do not require awareness of the formal principles of implication or consistency. Harman apparently intends these dispositions to be understood as psychological propensities to accept

---

37 R.M. Hare, Practical Inference 59–73 (Berkeley: Univ. of Calif. Press, 1972).
38 G. Harman, Change in View 11–20 Cambridge, MA: MIT Press, 1986).

intuitively that if one recognizes that one's beliefs imply another belief, then that is a good reason to accept that proposition also and, similarly, that if one's beliefs are inconsistent with another belief, then that is a good reason to reject that additional proposition.

Harman also contends that coherence plays an important role in reasoning in that the effective reasoner reasons to a view that provides the most coherent and intelligible explanation of the evidence. The role of coherence is also evident in his principle of positive undermining, which states that the effective reasoner gives up a particular belief when he believes that his reasons for believing that proposition have been undermined.[39]

Hare and Harman agree that practical reasoning does not require knowledge of formal logic and that the effective practical reasoner must be able to reason accurately to necessary and sufficient conditions for satisfying his wants in light of his comprehensive network of beliefs and wants. This process requires the ability to intuitively recognize immediate implication and immediate inconsistency, and to reject inconsistent sets of beliefs or propositions that conflict with the reasoner's broader network of beliefs. In addition to these capacities, the practical reasoner needs the abilities to accurately appraise external circumstances and his own wants and to engage in an efficient associative process. If these capacities are necessary to effective practical reasoning, and if criminal liability is limited to those acts that are appropriately attributed to the actor as a competent practical reasoner, then psychopathology that substantially impairs these processes should exculpate.

6.5.2 Psychopathology, criminal liability, and practical reasoning. Chapter 4 advanced an interpretation of the MPC system of offense elements as intended to restrict criminal liability to acts that are accurately attributable to the defendant as a practical reasoner. The actor acts as a practical reasoner when

39   *Id.* at 29–42, 65–75.

he deliberates regarding possible action-plans in light of his comprehensive network of wants and beliefs, selects an action-plan intended to maximize his want satisfaction, and acts according to his action-plan in a manner such that his acts are caused by his wants and beliefs according to the usual causal process.

The failure-of-proof defense regarding the voluntary act requirement precludes guilt when the act cannot be attributed to the actor as a practical reasoner because his wants and beliefs did not cause the act-tree in the ordinary manner. This causal process may be disrupted when the defendant's movements are not caused by his wants and beliefs or when the movements are caused by certain wants and beliefs while the individual is deprived of access to his broader set of wants and beliefs. The former conditions occur during convulsions, whereas the latter pattern reflects impaired consciousness that gives rise to the automatism defense. In the latter case, the action-plan may cause the behavior in the ordinary way that action-plans cause conduct, but the action-plan is not developed through the usual associative process of deliberation that allows consideration of relevant standing wants and beliefs. Thus, the usual pattern of causal relationships among the behavior, the action-plan, and the more comprehensive set of wants and beliefs is significantly distorted.

The failure-of-proof defense regarding the culpability element precludes guilt when the conduct constituting the objective elements of the offense does not stand in the required relation to the action-plan, and thus does not represent the wants and beliefs of the actor in the appropriate manner. In these cases, the act-tree can be attributed to the actor as a practical reasoner, but this particular act on the tree does not bear a sufficiently close relationship to the actor's wants and beliefs to constitute the offense as defined in the code.

The failure-of-proof defenses regarding the culpability and voluntary act requirements address two different ways in which the offense can fail to be appropriately attributable to the actor as a practical reasoner. The commentaries to the MPC describe these two provisions as necessary conditions for the justifiable imposition of criminal conviction and penal sanctions.[40] Similarly, H.L.A. Hart interprets the voluntariness requirement as providing the minimal link between mind and body that is required for responsibility, and he contends that responsibility is a necessary condition for justified punishment.[41] Moore argues that the legal and moral conception of a person is that of a practical reasoner, and, further, that only persons in this sense are appropriately subject to moral blame and criminal liability.[42]

Interpreted collectively, the MPC and these commentators contend that the state can justifiably convict and punish only those who commit illegal acts under certain minimal conditions of personal responsibility, and that these conditions are not met when a failure-of-proof defense precludes attribution of the offense to the actor as a practical reasoner. Although these two offense elements provide plausible necessary conditions for justifiable criminal liability, they do not constitute jointly sufficient conditions because these requirements for attribution of an act to an actor as a practical reasoner are minimal. Any agent capable of selecting an act expected to satisfy some want in light of the relatively comprehensive set of wants can be understood as exercising some level of practical reasoning. Certain agents, including very young children and seriously retarded adults, are capable of engaging in some level of practical reasoning, although they are not usually considered appropriate subjects of moral blame or criminal culpability.

Although these agents may qualify as practical reasoners at some minimal level, effective practical inference involves reasoning from wants and beliefs to necessary and sufficient conditions for satisfying those wants. Such reasoning requires at least some unspecified degree of competence at

40 MPC, *supra* note 1, at sec. 2.01 commentaries pp. 214–16, sec. 2.02 commentaries p. 229.
41 H.L.A. Hart, Punishment and Responsibility 99, 181–83, Oxford: Oxford Univ. Press, 1968).
42 *See supra*, chapter 4.3.1.

recognizing intuitive implication and inconsistency.[43] A competent practical reasoner, then, is one who has the capacities necessary to engage in practical inference at a level of effectiveness sufficient for some identified purpose; in the context of criminal liability, this purpose is the justification of conviction and punishment. On this account, the failure-of-proof defenses are part of a complex system intended to limit criminal liability to acts that are appropriately attributable to the actor as a competent practical reasoner, where competence is defined in terms of the level of effective practical reasoning required to justify criminal conviction and punishment.

Admittedly, it is difficult to specify the type and level of competence that is required to justify liability to criminal sanctions. Traditionally, however, infants and those who suffer serious mental retardation or psychological dysfunction have not been considered subject to such liability. The MPC's NGRI provision is intended to excuse certain agents who, by virtue of psychological defect or disorder, are not appropriately subject to conviction or reprobation.[44] Certain defendants fulfill all offense elements yet fail to act as competent practical reasoners because they suffer a defect in their capacity for deliberation and practical inference that is not addressed by either failure-of-proof defense. These defendants lack the capacities of comprehension and reasoning that competent practical reasoners possess.

Whereas the voluntary act requirement addresses the availability of the actor's relatively comprehensive set of wants and beliefs to the process of action-plan selection, the current concern involves the processes by which the actor reasons from his wants and beliefs to an action-plan. Actors with unimpaired consciousness may have ordinary access to their own wants and beliefs yet lack the normal ability to reason accurately from them to action-plans. Nothing in the MPC structure of offense elements addresses this concern. Thus,

---

43 *See supra,* chapter 6.5.1.
44 MPC, *supra* note 1, at sec. 4.01 commentaries pp. 164–65.

in order to limit criminal liability to acts appropriately attributable to the actor as a competent practical reasoner, the complete system of offenses and defenses requires a general defense that precludes conviction of defendants who lacked the competent practical reasoner's capacity to derive action plans through unimpaired reasoning.

The NGRI defense uniquely addresses this need in the comprehensive system. It exculpates those defendants who lacked the capacity to select their action-plans through the unimpaired process of practical reasoning. Psychological disorder may give rise to a failure-of-proof defense if it produces ignorance or mistake that negates the culpability element or when it constitutes a nonculpable mistake regarding justification. For example, a psychotic defendant may not have known that he was taking another's property because he believed that God just gave the item to him, or the psychotic defendant might have taken the property because he thought that the owner was using it to direct harmful laser beams at him. In these cases, however, the disorder would have exculpated the defendant in jurisdictions without the NGRI defense. The unique function of the NGRI defense involves those cases in which the defendant deserves exculpation by virtue of a disorder of psychological process rather than due to mistaken belief content.[45]

The competent practical reasoner must select an action-plan through an associative process of deliberation that elicits

---

45 Although the *M'Naghten* standard is usually formulated and interpreted as an ignorance test as to excusing condition, there is some reason to think that the opinion may have been written with some awareness of the content/process concern. The traditional *M'Naghten* test requires a defect of reason, and a separate provision addressing defendants who suffer insane delusions as to existing facts but who are not in other respects insane holds these defendants responsible as they would have been had the delusional beliefs been true. *M'Naghten's Case*, 8 Eng. Rep. 718, 723 (1843).

These passages suggest that false belief content was not contemplated as the sole determinant of exculpation under the primary test. It was a necessary condition, however, and it appears to have been the condition that carried the exculpatory force. As such, the *M'Naghten* standard differs markedly from the interpretation advanced here.

awareness of relevant wants and beliefs, enabling him to reason from the comprehensive set of wants and beliefs to acts that will provide sufficient or necessary conditions for satisfying the comprehensive network of wants. As discussed in Chapter 5, the automatism defense applies to those defendants who suffer impaired consciousness that prevents access to their own complex set of wants and beliefs. An effective process of practical reasoning requires not only access to the relevant wants and beliefs, however, but also intact capacities of concept formation, comprehension, and reasoning for selecting the action-plan likely to promote the set of wants. In order to be effective, the action-plan selection process requires at least the capacities to recognize intuitive implication and inconsistency and to maintain a set of beliefs with a satisfactory degree of coherence.

Consider the significance of the various types of schizophrenic thought disorder for this practical reasoning process. The schizophrenic who suffers impaired cognitive focus may attend to peripheral rather than central features of an event or situation, and thus fail to register implications, inconsistencies, or the significance of an act for his other wants. Such an actor may select an action-plan due to some relatively secondary characteristic of the plan while failing to attend to more central considerations. If an actor who is selecting an action-plan becomes sidetracked by clang association – as Bill did, for example – he may be unable to direct his focus toward the central aspects of his situation. One who experiences thought blocking will not be able to pursue the selection process at all, and thus will be likely to act impulsively with no organized plan.

Impaired reasoning may produce an action-plan that is based on some unwarranted interpretation of the situation. Such plans are likely to be irrelevant to the actual circumstances or counter-productive. Mary, for example, based her decision to stab her victim on the significance she attributed to people looking toward her on the subway, the motto on the dollar bill, and the fact that the woman was leaving the church when she arrived.

Bill's combinative thinking also distorted his action-plan selection. Bill decided to attempt to get transferred from the treatment center to the jail by setting a series of fires, and he selected this plan partially on the basis of his belief that Pete would assist him, although he knew that Pete had been killed long ago. The point here is not merely that Bill decided to set the fires while holding these particular inconsistent beliefs; more importantly, he selected his action-plan through the exercise of cognitive processes that allowed him to hold that both Pete and the rat were simultaneously dead and alive. This strongly supports the claim that Bill's capacity to recognize intuitive inconsistency was impaired. The thought disorders that allowed Mary and Bill to hold blatantly inconsistent beliefs prevented them from responding appropriately to the immediate implications and inconsistencies in their thinking about their conduct that constituted the offenses. Mary, for example, believed that she had to kill her victim in order to avoid being killed eventually by the bad people, and that this belief was a delusion.

Those who suffer marked impairment in their capacity for concept formation are vulnerable to at least two different types of distorted thought. First, abstract concepts, including moral ones, may have no meaning to them, or they may not be able to accurately apply those concepts to concrete events. Thus, Mary believed that the other people who committed crimes were bad, but this belief did not lead her to wonder how she could stab someone yet remain good. Second, idiosyncratic interpretations and symbolism can lead one to vest events with inappropriate significance in one's planning. Mary, for example, based her decision partially on the meaning that she attributed to the motto on the dollar bill and the effects of the seating arrangements on the subway.

Impaired reality relatedness involving inaccurate perceptions of events can generate misinterpretations of the significance of those events, and thus poor judgment and maladaptive responses. At first glance, distorted reality testing may appear to be a matter of belief content rather than cognitive process. Mary's hallucinatory voices, for example, may seem to be important by virtue of what they said.

Imagine, however, how a psychologically intact person would respond to a mere perceptual aberration. If such a person heard voices with no apparent source, he would probably seek a reasonable explanation, try to find out if others heard them, or even worry that he might be going crazy. Intact persons who hallucinate due to sleep deprivation or chemicals tend to interpret these experiences as unrealistic.[46] In contrast, hallucinations that occur as part of psychopathological process are the product of condensations of perceptions, thoughts, and memories. They are often associated with delusional thought process.[47] Hallucinations as false sensory experience only indicate psychosis when they are combined with gross impairment of reality testing that reflects severely disturbed cognitive processes because it is only in these cases that they are interpreted unrealistically as actual events independent of the perceiver's sensory processes.

This distinction between mere perceptual aberrations and hallucinations embedded in major cognitive dysfunction is central to the exculpatory significance of the embedded hallucinations. They are not mere mistakes about the environment. They occur as part of a pattern of pathological cognitive functioning in which the person's distorted cognitive processes allow him to accept these perceptual and cognitive distortions as accurate representations of the world and to interpret his other experiences in light of them. Recall that neither Mary's hallucinatory phone calls nor Bill's hallucinatory rat provided belief content that if true would justify their behavior. The diagnostic and exculpatory significance of these perceptions lies in the fact that they were embedded in impaired cognitive processes through which Mary and Bill incorporated these perceptual experiences into their interpretations of the world and of their place in that world.

46 Kolb, *supra* note 21, at 101.
47 Hinsie and Campbell, *supra* note 16, at 191; Kolb, *supra* note 21, at 101.

In conclusion, cognitive disfunction of the type that schizophrenics actually experience precludes attribution of some acts to the actors as competent practical reasoners because these actors lack the capacity to generate action-plans through the normal process of practical inference. This type of defect is fundamentally different than those addressed by the failure-of-proof defenses or by the defenses based on ignorance or mistake. It is a type of defect that specifically arises for those who are intuitively considered to be crazy and who are clinically diagnosed as psychotic by virtue of a major cognitive disorder. Hence, the NGRI defense is a *sui generis* one, rather than an application of the more common excusing conditions of ignorance or coercion.

This interpretation does not require that one accept the nomenclature or specific categories of cognitive disorder described above. Indeed, several of these types of cognitive malfunction are described in a vague and overlapping manner. An information processing model of cognitive operations supports the same point. On this account, external stimuli are briefly represented by an internal sensory image known as an icon. Information from the icon is encoded in memory and assorted into categories called assemblies, which are, in turn, combined with other assemblies into schemata. Once established, assemblies and schemata can affect future encoding because new icons are encoded largely into existing categories.

Research indicates that schizophrenics differ from normals in that they use inefficient encoding strategies for the task at hand. Their recognition memory is intact for tasks that require minimal associative activity, but they demonstrate impaired recall that apparently reflects defective assemblies of associations. Schizophrenics form loose conceptual associations and idiosyncratic assemblies. Paranoid schizophrenics tend to organize ambiguous stimuli in an unusually rigid, stereotypical manner, and delusions might represent extreme cases of rigidly and inaccurately categorized events. In short, schizophrenics encode and categorize information in a manner that makes it particularly difficult to understand the external world accurately and reason about it effectively.[48]

Both the clinical model described initially and the information processing account support the contention that schizophrenics engage in defective cognitive processing. They tend to organize information according to idiosyncratic categories and concepts, reason poorly, and draw erroneous conclusions from information due to loose or stereotypically rigid associations. On either account, the schizophrenic may form false belief content, but the prototypical type of schizophrenic dysfunction is distorted cognitive *process*, and that defective process produces maladaptive reasoning. This impairment prevents the individual from deriving action-plans from his wants and beliefs through the same processes of practical reasoning that are available to the unimpaired adult. The usual capacities to intuitively recognize coherence and immediate implication and inconsistency are adversely affected, and thus neither the action-plan nor the resultant act represents the actor as a competent practical reasoner.

On this interpretation, the defendant is an appropriate candidate for the NGRI defense if and only if the conduct constituting the objective elements of the offense were the product of an action-plan selected through the exercise of substantially impaired cognitive processes that prevented the defendant from engaging in the ordinary process of practical inference from his wants and beliefs to an action-plan. Major cognitive disorder, including gross disturbance of cognitive focus, reasoning, concept formation, or reality relatedness, constitutes impairment sufficient to substantially impair the action-plan selection process.

This interpretation of the NGRI defense, like all the others that have been advanced, fails to provide a mechanical test that eliminates hard cases. The jury would still have to exercise judgment in deciding whether the type and degree of

48 Magaro, *Schizophrenia* 164–72, in Adult Psychopathology and Diagnosis (S. Turner and M. Hersen, eds, New York: Wiley, 1984).

distortion of cognitive process suffered by this defendant was sufficient to defeat culpability. On this interpretation, the defense would present evidence to support the contention that the defendant selected the action-plan that produced the conduct constituting the offense through the exercise of substantially impaired cognitive processes. This evidence could take the form of testimony about the defendant's acts or words at the time of the offense from which the jury might infer impaired practical reasoning. Additionally, professional witnesses might testify regarding their evaluations of the defendant's cognitive impairment before or after the act in question. In the latter case, the jury would have to infer the presence of impairment at the time of the offense from evidence of impairment before or after the offense. That problem, however, arises with testimony regarding pre- or post-offense evaluation, regardless of the standard applied.

Some critics might question whether mental health professionals have sufficient expertise to testify regarding these matters. Perhaps most commentators would agree that current understanding of psychopathology is not as precise as they would like it to be. This interpretation of the NGRI defense, however, calls for information from mental health professionals that is more compatible with their ordinary clinical practice and expertise than is the information required by either the *M'Naghten* or MPC standards.

Clinicians routinely diagnose and treat people who suffer disordered psychological process. Although the diagnostic methods and instruments may not be as reliable as the clinicians or commentators would like, those methods and instruments play a central role in the clinicians' practice.[49] The clinician called upon to testify regarding the NGRI defense as interpreted in this chapter would be asked to describe the defendant's psychological processes and any identified dis-

---

49   *See, for example,* Weiner, *supra* note 29; Clinical Diagnosis of Mental Disorders (B. Wolman, ed., New York: Plenum, 1978). Both works present detailed accounts of the manner in which various clinical methods and instruments are used to identify and describe various patterns of psychopathological process.

tortion of those processes. That is, the clinician would be asked to testify regarding the ordinary clinical diagnostic practices as performed with this defendant.

The jury would have to decide whether the defendant's disordered psychological process directly affected the decision to perform the act constituting the offense. Thus, the expert would testify regarding the presence or lack of the kind of dysfunction that clinicians ordinarily evaluate in practice, and the jury would determine the significance of that testimony for this particular set of facts.

Under the cognitive clauses of the *M'Naghten* and MPC tests, in contrast, the central issue is not disordered process but mistaken belief content. Clinicians, however, diagnose and treat psychopathology that takes the form of disordered psychological process, not false belief content. Clinicians gather information about false belief content in the same manner that others do; that is, they ask the defendant what he believed, or they infer beliefs from the defendant's statements and actions. In short, NGRI standards that attach primary significance to ignorance do not directly involve the mental health practitioner's area of expertise, but NGRI provisions that address disordered psychological process do.

6.6 ISSUES REGARDING CLASSIFICATION

6.6.1 Volition and the causal model. I have argued in Section 6.3 that volitional NGRI tests are unsatisfactory because they are unnecessary and irrelevant if they take the literal form, whereas they are vacuous if they take the flexible form. Traditionally, volitional clauses have been advanced as substitutes for cognitive ones or as alternative grounds for exculpation. The MPC NGRI standard, for example, contains cognitive and volitional clauses that provide alternative excusing conditions.[50] The traditional pattern of drafting NGRI tests with cognitive clauses, volitional ones, or both as al-

50 MPC, *supra* note 1, at sec. 4.01.

ternative grounds for exculpation suggests that cognition and volition constitute two independent processes, either of which can independently provide grounds for excuse. It is not clear, however, that this is an accurate picture of the relationship between cognition and volition.

Volition is "[a]n act of willing or resolving; a decision or choice made after due consideration or deliberation . . . [t]he power or faculty of willing." The will is "that faculty or function which is directed to conscious and intentional action."[51] Volition, then, is an exercise of the faculty or function by which one engages in conscious and intentional action as a result of decision or choice through deliberation. A volitional impairment would involve some disorder of the capacities by which one engages in conscious and intentional action in response to deliberation and choice.

According to the action theory interpretation of the MPC structure of offense requirements advanced in Chapter 4, an actor chooses an action-plan that produces an act-tree. The actor's reasons serve as structuring causes of the selected act through the process of deliberation among various potential action-plans. A volitional impairment would be some disruption of the process through which the actor selects the action-plan and translates that action-plan into action. The literal form of the volitional clause would apply to certain types of impairment that would constitute such a disruption, but as that discussion indicated, this sort of disability grounds a failure-of-proof defense. Severe cognitive dysfunction, such as that found in schizophrenia and described in Section 6.5, constitutes another form of disruption of the processes by which one chooses through deliberation to engage in conscious and intentional action. Severe cognitive psychopathology distorts the process of action-plan selection through which the actor decides which conscious action he will engage in. Major cognitive psychopathology, therefore,

---

51 II Oxford English Dictionary (compact ed., Oxford: Oxford Univ. Press, 1971).

disrupts the volitional process by distorting the causal process through which the actor's reasons for acting serve as
structuring causes for his decision to perform the act he
selects.

In short, major cognitive dysfunction constitutes the type
of volitional disorder that gives rise to the NGRI defense.
Traditional volitional standards have been misguided because they have sought a volitional basis for exculpation that
stands separately from the cognitive one. A cognitive interpretation of the NGRI defense that addresses distortion of
cognitive process, rather than content, provides an accurate
account of both the cognitive and the volitional aspects of
major psychopathology. Major disruption of cognitive process substantially impairs the deliberative process through
which an individual selects an action-plan for intentional
action, and this cognitive disorder constitutes the type of
volitional impairment that is relevant to the NGRI defense.

On this account, the NGRI defense exculpates individuals
whose acts cannot be attributed to them as competent practical reasoners because their cognitive disorders prevented
them from selecting an action-plan through the ordinary process of deliberation. According to Chapter 4, deliberation is
an associative process during which the practical reasoner
considers various acts as means to his ends. Review of potential acts as means to secure satisfaction of occurrent wants
causes the reasoner to become aware of associated standing
wants and beliefs. The actor's network of wants and beliefs
provides a structuring cause of his action; that is, his wants
and beliefs provide reasons that cause him to act in the manner that he does. Thus, an NGRI defense that exculpates
defendants due to impairment of the cognitive capacities that
ordinarily allow selection of an action-plan through the deliberative process provides an excuse that addresses dysfunction in the causal process of act selection. That is, it
exculpates due to distortion of the causal relationship between the actor's reasons and the action-plan he selects.

Moore has argued forcefully against the causal theory of

excuses.[52] One can distinguish, however, two types of causal theories of excuse. The first is the categorical causal theory, which contends that acts are appropriately excused if they are caused by some factor outside of the agent's control. These theories are categorical in the sense that they claim that acts should be excused if and only if they are caused by such factors. These theories encounter difficulty because they do not seem to accommodate the types of excuses that are often accepted as justified, and if one accepts determinism, this approach arguably leads to the conclusion that all acts are appropriately excused. In addition, it is very difficult to develop a satisfactory conception of control.

The second type of causal theory of excuse is the selective causal theory. Selective causal theories contend that an act should be excused if the actor produces his act under conditions that distort the usual causal processes by which actors cause their acts. Theories of this type must specify the type of causal distortion that exculpates, and they must justify the exculpatory force of that type of distortion.

Moore correctly rejects categorical causal theories, but he does not address selective theories. The interpretation of the NGRI defense advanced here, however, is a selective causal theory in that it identifies a particular type of distortion in the process by which the actor's reasons cause his acts as the core of the excuse. On this account, major cognitive disorder distorts the process by which actors' wants and beliefs serve as structuring causes for their actions because these actors lack the capacity to process their wants and beliefs in the ordinary manner that allows intact actors to derive action-plans in light of their network of wants and beliefs.

6.6.2 *Mood disorders.* I have argued that a satisfactory NGRI defense exculpates those who select action-plans through a process of practical reasoning that is distorted by cognitive impairment of the type manifested by those suffering from some major psychological disorders such as schizophrenia.

52   Moore, *Causation and the Excuses,* 73 Calif. L. Rev. 1091 (1985).

In addition, I have argued that such cognitive disorder constitutes the relevant type of volitional impairment, but I have not addressed the appropriate place of mood disorders in an account of the NGRI defense. Should the NGRI defense exculpate those who suffer psychopathology of a primarily affective type?

Major mood disorders can adversely affect one's effort to conform to the law in at least two different ways. First, the mood itself can make it very difficult to direct one's behavior according to the law. For example, a very depressed person with a legal duty to act may find it unusually difficult to meet that duty. Second, the major mood disorder can include psychotic disturbance of cognition, including hallucinations or delusions.[53] The psychotic depressive identified as Z in Chapter 2 illustrates this second pattern in that Z's depressive disorder included delusional thought processes, and these cognitive distortions directly influenced his selection of the action-plan that included strangling his children. Psychotic depressives such as Z would clearly fall within the scope of the cognitive interpretation of the NGRI defense advanced in this chapter. Psychotic depressives, like schizophrenics, suffer major cognitive dysfunction that distorts the deliberative processes by which they select their action-plans.[54] Thus, Z's act of strangling his children cannot be attributed to him as a competent practical reasoner.

Consider, however, the case of George, who is a seriously depressed nurse on a cardiac ward. George suffers from

53 American Psychiatric Association, *supra* note 16, at 222–23. Major depressive disorder, for example, is diagnosed on the basis of depressed mood and a variety of symptoms that constitute the clinical depressive syndrome. Although this syndrome may include psychotic disturbance of cognition, it more often does not. That is, many people suffer major depressive disorder without substantial distortion of cognitive functioning.

54 More precisely, both psychotic depressives and schizophrenics suffer the major cognitive dysfunction that can distort the deliberative process through which they select action-plans. It is at least logically possible that persons suffering these disorders select many of their action-plans through processes that are not adversely affected by their disorder. I will not address this issue here.

deeply depressed mood, loss of energy, and sleep disturbance. All of life's little pleasures have lost their appeal to
him, and it requires great effort to perform ordinary tasks.
He does not, however, suffer any major disturbance of perception or thought. He continues to accurately perceive the
world about him and his place in it, and he can process
information through the usual cognitive processes. George
suffers a major depressive disorder without substantial distortion of cognitive functioning. One night, he decides to lie
down in an empty room instead of monitoring the equipment
as he is supposed to. While he is away from his station, a
patient suffers a heart attack and dies because no one is
monitoring the equipment that would have alerted the emer-
gency team to intervene. George would not be exculpated
on the interpretation of the NGRI defense advanced in this
chapter because, by hypothesis, he did not suffer any major
impairment of the cognitive capacities used to select action-
plans.

Why exculpate Z but not George? In order to understand
the relevant difference between the two, one must consider
the difference between psychotic depression, which includes
major distortion of cognitive process, and major but non-
psychotic depression, which does not involve severe cognitive dysfunction, in light of the analysis in Chapter 4. When
the depressive syndrome includes major cognitive disorder,
the depressed person selects action-plans through a qualitatively distorted process of deliberation, and as a result the
act cannot be attributed to him as a competent practical reasoner for exactly the same reasons that the corresponding
attribution cannot be made regarding a schizophrenic.[55]
Neither psychotic depressives nor schizophrenics function
as competent practical reasoners when they select action-
plans through the use of distorted cognitive processes.

55 The claim here is not that schizophrenia and psychotic depression are
    identical. Rather, the point is that both schizophrenics and psychotic
    depressives suffer severe distortion of cognitive process that prevents
    them from selecting action-plans through the ordinary processes of
    deliberation and practical reasoning.

George, in contrast, does select his action-plan through the same processes that ordinary practical reasoners do. Although George and ordinary practical reasoners employ the same type of deliberative capacities, George experiences seriously depressed mood, which provides him with an unusually strong want to isolate rather than fulfill his responsibilities. Conforming to the requirements of his job is therefore a much more difficult task for George than it is for nondepressed nurses in the same circumstances. The causal deliberative process, however, is not distorted. George selects his action-plan as a competent practical reasoner because he possesses the same cognitive processes of practical reasoning that other competent practical reasoners do. The distinctive characteristic of George's situation is that his dysphoric mood renders the decision to conform to his responsibilities much more difficult than the same choice is for most others. That is, George's deliberative process differs from that of the ordinary practical reasoner in a quantitative manner, not a qualitative one. The NGRI defense, however, exculpates defendants because their acts cannot be attributed to them as competent practical reasoners, not because the choice they faced as practical reasoners was unusually difficult.

Some critics will object that it would be unreasonable, unfair, or just plain futile to subject George to criminal punishment. They may well be right. There might be several good reasons for treating George differently than the average criminal. Punishment might be futile from the perspective of the usual preventive purposes of the criminal justice system, and treatment might promote these purposes much more effectively. Benevolence or mercy might lead us to approach George with sympathy rather than with condemnation. Although these considerations provide good reason to think that the criminal justice system should respond to George differently than it does to the average criminal, it does not necessarily follow that the NGRI defense is the appropriate vehicle for this concern.

Unfortunately, it is easy to forget that the NGRI defense

serves only to add a special excuse for those defendants who suffer certain forms of psychopathology; it does not exhaust the variety of exculpatory or mitigating claims open to them. For example, psychological disorder can give rise to a failure-of-proof defense if it prevents the defendant from fulfilling the culpability requirement. It can also exculpate due to mistake regarding justification in those jurisdictions that do not require such mistakes to be reasonable. In addition, defenses such as duress, justification, and mitigation all apply to psychologically disordered defendants just as they do to an accused person who does not suffer psychological disturbance. Compare George's situation with Harvey's.

Harvey lacks any psychological disorder of clinical proportions, and he has no history of any criminal behavior. He is a factory worker who provides the sole financial support for his small children. His income barely covers expenses, so he has virtually no savings. One day, Harvey fails to make his production quota because his machine breaks down through no fault of his own. The foreman knows that the problem is not Harvey's fault, but he does not like Harvey, so he reports to the owner that the failure was due to Harvey's carelessness, and the owner fires Harvey. As Harvey walks out of the factory, worrying about how he will feed his kids, the foreman insults him, and Harvey responds by punching the foreman. The foreman suffers a broken nose, and Harvey is charged with assault.

Harvey's act clearly constitutes assault; he has purposefully caused bodily injury to another.[56] By hypothesis, Harvey suffers no psychopathology; he was just frustrated, worried, and angry. Although many of us might feel inclined to say that the foreman deserved it, Harvey was not legally justified. No exculpatory defenses apply, yet it seems obvious that it would be unreasonable, unfair, and just plain futile to punish Harvey. It seems quite unlikely that most courts would fine or imprison him. Rather, the court would probably convict him of the minimum applicable charge, sus-

56 MPC, *supra* note 1, at sec. 211.1.

pend his sentence, and place him on probation. The MPC provides several grounds for this approach to cases like Harvey's. Among the reasons for suspending sentence: The defendant was provoked; there were substantial grounds tending to excuse, but insufficient to establish a defense; the defendant has a law-abiding history with no previous offenses; the crime is unlikely to recur; and the defendant is likely to respond to probation.[57]

Ordinarily, punishment is suspended or decreased due to mitigating circumstances such as those just listed because these considerations suggest that punishment would be counter-productive or because the individual is less blameworthy than the average defendant convicted of this crime. Harvey was less blameworthy than the average defendant who is convicted of assault because the particular circumstances rendered conformity to the law unusually difficult. Although Harvey is guilty of an offense, the fact that he is less blameworthy than most offenders who perform similar offenses renders it appropriate that he receive correspondingly less punishment. Because the conditions in this case were extreme, Harvey receives little or no substantive punishment. The official condemnation of the act through conviction and suspended sentence suffices.

George's depression, like Harvey's provocation, worry, and anger, rendered conformity to the law unusually difficult. George's depression provided him with a very strong want to isolate rather than monitor the equipment, and Harvey's worry and anger provided him with a very strong want to strike the foreman. Neither George nor Harvey was responsible for causing the conditions that rendered their situations unusually difficult. Neither one, however, suffered impairment of their cognitive processes that prevented them from selecting action-plans through the same cognitive processes that competent practical reasoners employ. Rather,

---

57 MPC, *supra* note 1, at sec. 7.01(2). Traditionally, these considerations have been addressed as mitigating factors. Some penal codes include them as factors for the court to consider at sentencing. *See, for example,* Arizona Revised Statutes, sec. 13–702 (1988).

PSYCHOLOGY OF CRIMINAL RESPONSIBILITY

both took action as practical reasoners under circumstances that forced them to decide on an action-plan while faced with a very strong want that made conformity with the applicable norms extremely difficult.

The intuitive inclination to say that it would be unreasonable, unfair, and futile to punish either George or Harvey seems to be well founded. The reasons that support that response, however, are not the same considerations that ground exculpation of severely cognitively disturbed persons through the NGRI defense. The latter group are excused because their impairment prevents attribution of their act to them as competent practical reasoners, whereas George and Harvey deserve special consideration because they exercised their capacities for practical reasoning under very difficult circumstances.

Major mood disorder appropriately exculpates through the NGRI defense when it includes severe cognitive impairment that prevents attribution of the act to the actor as a competent practical reasoner. Major mood disorder that does not include severe cognitive impairment should not exculpate under the NGRI defense because this type of psychopathology does not prevent attribution of the act to the actor as a competent practical reasoner. Such pathology might, however, justify special consideration for the defendant. That special treatment would be motivated by benevolence, mercy, justice in light of the defendant's lesser blameworthiness, or recognition of the futility of punishment. The law accommodates such concerns through mitigation, probation, or suspended sentences.

6.6.3 NGRI: Specific excuse or status offense? As defined in Chapter 1, a specific excuse exculpates a defendant who satisfies an identifiable excusing condition that renders him blameless for that particular act. In contrast, a status defense exculpates by virtue of some general status such as age without reference to specific excusing conditions regarding the particular act in question. Robinson identified four socially accepted excusing conditions: lack of voluntary act, ignorance regarding the physical characteristics or consequences of the act, ignorance regarding the illegality or wrongfulness of the act, and inability to control one's conduct.

Chapter 1 also listed four plausible interpretations of status defenses in the system of defenses described in that chapter. Status defenses might be understood as nonexculpatory exemptions from punishment, defenses that identify groups for whom there is a strong presumption of a standard excusing condition, defenses that can be subsumed under the category of specific excuses when suitable excusing conditions are added to the four listed, or a distinct category of defense based on class membership.[58]

On the interpretation advanced in this chapter, the NGRI defense addresses a specific type of psychological impairment that distorts the process by which the actor selects the action-plan that generates the act-tree that includes the conduct constituting the objective elements of the offense. On this account, the NGRI defense exculpates the actor from liability for this act due to the actor's lack of ordinary capacities with which to select the action-plan that gave rise to the act constituting the offense. Thus, the NGRI defense is a specific excuse regarding a particular act and based upon a specified type of excusing condition. This excusing condition, however, is not one of the four listed. Rather, the defendant is excused because he suffers a severe disturbance of the cognitive processes – such as cognitive focusing, reasoning, concept formation, or reality relatedness – that prevents him from selecting an action-plan for this act through the ordinary process of practical reasoning.

A critic might argue that this excusing condition can be subsumed under Robinson's fourth condition that addresses the actor's ability to control his conduct. This critic would contend that the fourth condition is intended to include the general class of volitional defects and that I have argued that the cognitive formulation of the NGRI defense advanced in this chapter constitutes the relevant form of volitional

58 *See supra*, chapter 1.2.

defense. Therefore, the critic would claim, the cognitive formulation advanced in this chapter is one type of condition covered by this fourth category.

I understand the interpretation of the NGRI defense advanced in this chapter as requiring a fifth type of excusing condition because Robinson's fourth category seems to contemplate the more traditional sorts of volitional standards that are thought to be independent of cognitive dysfunction and that I have rejected as either irrelevant to the NGRI defense or vacuous. If one is convinced by the arguments supporting the interpretation of the NGRI defense advanced in this chapter, however, it is not important whether one understands it as requiring a fifth excusing condition or as identifying a special subtype of the fourth. In either case, it constitutes a *sui generis* specific excuse insofar as it exculpates those who suffer certain types of cognitive dysfunction for reasons that are unique to this defense. It is not an application of the failure-of-proof defenses or of the more common excusing conditions of ignorance or coercion.

Finally, some critics might argue that the formulation advanced here is actually indistinguishable from a status defense. They might contend that to say that a person suffers major cognitive impairment that prevents him from selecting action-plans as a competent practical reasoner is just to say that he is crazy or irrational. Therefore, they would conclude, this proposal is no different from those that advocate excusing defendants on the basis of their membership in the class of crazy or irrational people.

Those who argue that an NGRI defense excuses the crazy because they are crazy could intend any of several different theses. First, they could mean that the NGRI defense excuses all defendants who suffer any psychopathology just because they suffer some form of psychological disorder. This thesis would clearly differ from the proposal endorsed in this chapter that selects certain sorts of impairment because these types of impairment prevent selection of an action-plan through the ordinary processes of practical reasoning. Second, they could mean that the NGRI defense excuses all defendants who suffer certain types of psychopathology just because they suffer these forms of psychological disorder.

The second thesis is more plausible than the first, but it naturally leads one to ask how and why we select the appropriate types of pathology to include. If the proponent responds that there is no particular reason, we just do, then this proposal certainly differs markedly from the one in this chapter, although it is not clear why anyone would endorse it. If the proponent responds that we select those types of pathology that involve certain important functional disabilities, and if the disabilities cited are the same as the cognitive impairments identified in this chapter, then this type of "status excuse" might be identical to the formulation advanced here, but it also reduces to a specific excuse. Finally, if the proponent were to provide reasons that were independent of functional impairments that serve as excusing conditions and did not constitute the sort of policy considerations that ground nonexculpatory defenses, then this proposal might take the form of a true status excuse, but it would also differ markedly from the one advanced here.[59]

6.7 CONCLUSIONS

In summary, neither the traditional cognitive tests nor the traditional volitional standards provide satisfactory interpretations of the NGRI defense. Those who suffer the relevant forms of psychopathology manifest major cognitive disorder that prevents them from reasoning effectively from their wants to appropriate action-plans and, thus, from selecting action-plans through the ordinary processes

---

59 The most recent and influential interpretations of the NGRI defense as a status excuse have been advanced by Moore and Morse. *See supra,* notes 2 and 13 respectively. Neither of these proposals, as I understand them, would be inconsistent in principle with the interpretation I am advancing in this chapter, although I am proposing a specific excuse formulation that articulates more precisely the grounds for exculpation. In addition, this formulation places the NGRI excuse in the context of the more comprehensive system of offense elements and defenses as analyzed in this project.

of practical reasoning. Acts performed by those who selected their action-plans through such distorted processes
cannot be attributed to the actors as competent practical reasoners for reasons that are not addressed by the
failure-of-proof defenses or by the traditional excusing
conditions of ignorance or coercion.

The NGRI defense complements the conceptual framework for the structure of offenses advanced in Chapter 4 by
providing a *sui generis* general defense for those whose acts
cannot be attributed to them as competent practical reasoners
because their cognitive impairment prevented them from selecting an action-plan through the processes that are ordinarily available to competent practical reasoners. This defense is a specific excuse because it exculpates the defendant
from liability for a specific act due to the presence of an
excusing condition regarding that act.

The disability that gives rise to the NGRI defense must
take the form of substantial impairment of the capacities
for cognitive focusing, reasoning, concept formation, reality relatedness, or other cognitive operations necessary for
selecting action-plans through effective practical reasoning.
Disorder of cognitive process, as opposed to belief content, is an excusing condition that is unique to the NGRI
defense, and it constitutes the only currently articulated
conception of a volitional defect that is applicable to the
NGRI defense.

Many writers propose a set of jury instructions embody-
ing their interpretation of the correct theoretical foundations of the NGRI defense. Statutory formulations, however, should state the exculpatory grounds for the defense
as clearly and precisely as possible, whereas jury instructions should communicate the nature and justification of
the defense as effectively as possible to the average juror.
Thus, formulating appropriate jury instructions requires
not only an accurate interpretation of the function and justification of the defense, but also an understanding of the
linguistic and psychological processes of communication

that affect the jury's comprehension of the instructions.[60] Such an exercise in applied communication extends well beyond the scope of this book.

I will only provide a concise statement of the defense, therefore, leaving the appropriate jury instructions to those who are more qualified to develop them. I assume, however, that satisfactory jury instructions would explain the central terms and concepts. I assume also that the formulation given next is for an affirmative specific excuse that is part of a comprehensive penal code that includes a structure of offense elements similar to that of the MPC.

> A person is not responsible for criminal conduct if he performed that conduct while suffering major distortion of his cognitive capacities that substantially impaired his ability to decide whether or not to perform that conduct through the process of practical reasoning that is ordinarily available to an adult who does not suffer major cognitive disorder. This requirement is met if and only if the defendant decided to perform the conduct constituting the objective elements of the offense while suffering gross disturbance of his capacity for concept formation, comprehension, reasoning, reality relatedness, or other cognitive processes, and this disorder substantially impaired his ability to engage in the ordinary process of practical reasoning regarding that conduct.

This formulation does not employ phrases such as "mental disease," "disease of the mind," or "mental illness" because these phrases serve no essential purpose in the defense, and they often serve to blur the central issues. On this account, substantial impairment in the defendant's capacity for practical reasoning regarding the offense is the excusing condi-

---

60   *See, for example*, A. Elwork, B.D. Sales, and J.J. Alfini, Making Jury Instructions Understandable (Charlottesville, VA: Michie Co., 1982). The authors review evidence supporting the contention that juries often do not understand either the instructions they receive regarding the substantive law or the nature of their tasks as juries. They also provide a methodology for reformulating jury instructions in a manner comprehensible to juries.

tion, and gross disturbance of cognitive processes such as concept formation or reasoning is the disability.

Most defendants who qualify under this standard will be psychotic because we have developed a conception of psychosis that depends heavily on major cognitive disorder.[61] This formulation might also exculpate some defendants, however, who are not usually classified as psychotic. The seriously retarded individual, for example, who pulls fire alarms or sets fires because he likes to watch the fire-engines may lack the capacities of concept formation, comprehension, or reasoning required to function as a minimally competent practical reasoner. He may not comprehend simple concepts such as "wrong" or "illegal", and he might lack the capacity to reason from his action to slightly removed consequences such as the possibility that fire-fighters could be injured at the fire or in the process of responding to the alarm.

Consider an individual who has suffered severe memory impairment through neurological illness or injury. His capacity for cognitive storage and recall is so severely impaired that he cannot engage in a conversation because he cannot remember a question long enough to answer it, and he cannot engage in a simple process of reasoning because he cannot remember one or two premises long enough to draw the conclusion. He is unable to make very simple decisions because he is unable to remember what he was trying to decide. Such an individual would be unable to engage in even the most simple process of practical reasoning.

Finally, recall that an individual in the post-ictal state following a seizure might suffer both clouded consciousness and delusional thought processes.[62] This defendant might qualify under both the automatism and NGRI defenses as proposed in this book because he lacks access to complete consciousness and suffers major impairment of his ability to reason from his wants and beliefs to an action-plan. On the

61 *See supra*, chapter 6.4.
62 *See supra*, chapter 5.3.

account presented here, these two defenses are independent but not mutually exclusive.

Chapters 1–4 have presented an action theory interpretation of the MPC's structure of offense elements that explicates the nature of the requirements addressing the psychological processes of the defendant and the relationships among them. In addition, Chapters 5 and 6 have argued that this conceptual framework helps clarify the ongoing difficulties regarding the automatism and NGRI defenses. Chapter 7 will argue that this framework not only provides a coherent integration of these offense elements and defenses, but also conforms to an intuitively plausible and morally defensible conception of personal responsibility.

Chapter 7

Moral foundations

The first six chapters advance an interpretation of the provisions in the MPC system of offenses and defenses that directly address the psychological states and processes of the defendant. On this account, the MPC voluntary act and culpability requirements limit criminal liability to acts performed in such a way as to allow attribution of the offense to the actor as a practical reasoner. This analysis provides a consistent interpretation of the voluntary act and culpability requirements and of the relationship between the two. These chapters also interpret the automatism and NGRI defenses in a manner that integrates these defenses into the larger system with the structure of offense elements at its core. This analysis enables one to understand the automatism defense as a failure-of-proof defense addressing the voluntary act requirement, and the NGRI defense as a *sui generis* specific excuse that applies to defendants whose psychological dysfunction prevents them from performing their offenses as competent practical reasoners.

A satisfactory system of criminal offenses and defenses should be not only conceptually consistent but also morally defensible. Chapter 7 argues that the analysis advanced in the first six chapters provides a morally defensible account of the significance of the defendant's psychological states and processes for criminal liability. This chapter does not attempt to construct or defend a complete theory of moral responsibility. Rather, it contends only that the system of offenses and defenses presented in the first six chapters is consistent with common intuitions regarding the necessary conditions of moral and legal accountability.

Contemporary American criminal law has not been designed as an integrated system intended to embody an ideal moral theory. Rather, it has developed over an extended period from roots in English and American common law. As such, it reflects a wide variety of political and practical forces that have influenced its development. Although it would be unrealistic to expect such a legal system to constitute a fully formulated social morality, it is not unreasonable to demand that the standards according to which the criminal law distributes punishment withstand moral scrutiny. This chapter argues that the MPC's provisions that directly address the psychological states, processes, and dysfunction of the defendant constitute a generally morally defensible approach to these issues.

The argument proceeds in the following manner. Section 7.1 sets the context of the discussion in recent philosophical debate regarding free will. Sections 7.2 and 7.3 advance a conception of free will as psychological capacity, and argue that this is the conception of free will that we need and intuitively apply for moral and legal purposes. Section 7.4 demonstrates that the MPC offense elements and defenses discussed in the first six chapters are consistent with this conception of free will as well as with other intuitive conditions of responsibility. Finally, Section 7.5 summarizes and concludes this chapter as the culmination of the entire work.

7.1 CONTEXT

The first six chapters argued that the voluntary act and culpability requirements as well as the automatism and NGRI defenses exculpate defendants due to distortion of their psychological states or processes that preclude attribution of the offense to the defendant as a competent practical reasoner. These provisions do not exhaust the category of exculpating and mitigating factors. Justification and provocation, for example, raise additional legal and moral concerns about the acceptability of the conduct or the blameworthiness of the defendant.

The exculpatory provisions discussed in the first six chapters address cases that many people might describe intuitively as ones in which the defendant did not mean to do what he did; in some of these cases, an observer might say that the behavior constituting the offense was not really the defendant's act at all. Certain instances of the failure-of-proof defense regarding the voluntary act requirement involve behavior that literally cannot be attributed to the defendant as an act. For example, the hypothetical case in Chapter 6 of Diane, who struck the victim with her car while she was paralyzed from a stroke, involved no act. Most of the other cases discussed, however, were ones in which the defendants acted, but the offenses were not appropriately attributable to the defendants as competent practical reasoners because the actors lacked the capacities that would allow them to direct their behavior in the ordinary manner through the process of practical reasoning. These are cases of which many people would intuitively say that the defendants did the forbidden acts, but they did not mean to do them, or that they did not do them voluntarily or of their own free will.

The debate regarding the NGRI defense, for example, has historically involved discussion of free will. In *People v. Wolff,* the court identified free will as the central premise of our social order and upheld the *M'Naghten* test as consistent with the role of free will in society.[1] In contrast, the court in *Parsons v. State*[2] declared *M'Naghten* inadequate as an NGRI standard because it failed to accommodate the importance of free will. In *Parsons,* the court established the irresistible impulse test as the volitional standard needed to supplement the cognitive *M'Naghten* test. The *Parsons* court considered this volitional standard necessary to address the significance of those forms of mental illness that exculpated defendants by "overmas-

---

1 People v. Wolff, 394 P.2d 959, 971 (Cal. Sup. Crt. 1964).
2 Parsons v. State, 2 So. 854 (Ala. Sup. Crt. 1887).

tering" their will or by subverting their will and destroying their free agency by the "duress of the disease."[3] The California Supreme Court, which had upheld *M'Naghten* in *Wolff* as consistent with the premise of free will, replaced *M'Naghten* with the MPC standard in *People v. Drew* because the court considered the MPC test to be more compatible with the idea of free will that is central to the criminal law and the NGRI defense.[4]

The commentators, like the courts, have differed about the appropriate relationship between free will and the NGRI defense. Herbert Fingarette dismisses "metaphysical" concepts such as free will, determinism, choice, and compulsion as irrelevant to the criminal law. He contends that such terms are used with different meanings in metaphysical and legal discourse in that metaphysicians are interested in causal necessitation whereas courts are concerned with responsibility. He concludes that legal discussions of such metaphysical concepts cloud the true jurisprudential issues.[5] Donald Hermann, in contrast, identifies free will as a prerequisite of the moral justification of punishment. He contends that punishment is justified only if the defendant could have done otherwise in some categorical sense that includes both freedom of action and freedom of choice.[6]

In summary, the courts' opinions sometimes discuss the NGRI defense in terms of free will, but the exact nature and significance of the concept is not clarified. Hermann also treats free will as an important moral presupposition to justified punishment, but his conception of free will is not entirely clear either. Fingarette defines free will and determinism as incompatible metaphysical concepts and declares them irrelevant to the law. Free will and the NGRI defense

---

3 *Id.* at 866.
4 People v. Drew, 22 Cal. 3d 333, 346, 583 P. 2d 1318, 1324, 149 Cal. Rptr. 275, 281 (1978).
5 H. Fingarette, The Meaning of Criminal Insanity 69–84 (Berkeley: Univ. of Calif. Press, 1972).
6 D. Hermann, The Insanity Defense 76–94 (Springfield, IL: C.C. Thomas, 1983).

continue to be discussed in relation to one another, but neither free will, the NGRI defense, nor the relationship between the two is well understood.

The significance of the free will debate for criminal liability depends partially on the manner in which one frames the concepts and issues involved in the philosophical dispute regarding free will. Fingarette's conclusion that free will is irrelevant to the criminal law is partially a product of his understanding of free will as incompatible with determinism and causal necessitation. Recent philosophical discussion, however, has included various compatibilist notions of free will that interpret that concept in terms other than freedom from causal antecedents.

Bernard Williams has recently discussed the kind of human free will that we need for ethical purposes. He advocates a "reconciling project" directed at integrating three sorts of considerations: (1) determinism (or some similar pattern of naturalistic explanation), (2) psychological items such as choice, decision and rational action, and (3) ethical notions such as blame and responsibility.[7] Harry Frankfurt has identified two criteria that a satisfactory conception of free will must meet; it must (1) explain why free will is desirable, and (2) differentiate humans from other animals.[8]

The reconciling project suggested by Williams seeks a conception of free will that addresses important ethical concerns. This set of concerns includes the moral justification of legal punishment and the moral principles underlying exculpation. If we approach the problem of free will with a primary interest in understanding the notion of free will that we need and intuitively apply for moral and legal purposes, Frankfurt's criteria seem reasonable because we usually limit the

---

7   Williams, *How Free Does the Will Need to be?*, The Lindley Lecture (Lawrence, Kan.: Univ. of Kansas, 1985). The discussion of free will in this chapter draws on arguments presented in Schopp, *Free Will as Psychological Capacity and the Justification of Consequences*, 21 Philosophical Forum 324 (1990).
8   Frankfurt, *Freedom of the Will and the Concept of a Person*, in Free Will 93 (G. Watson, ed., New York: Oxford Univ. Press, 1982).

range of agents subject to ethical evaluation to some subset of relatively mature and intact human beings. This conception of free will may or may not satisfy the traditional metaphysical disputes. I take no position regarding that question here because this project addresses the moral defensibility of the system of offense elements and defenses discussed in the first six chapters.

Frankfurt endorses a conception of free will that treats the relationships between the person's desires and volitions as central to both free will and responsibility. Many arguments regarding personal responsibility rest on the widely accepted principle of alternative possibilities (PAP), which holds that an individual should not be held responsible for his behavior unless he could have done otherwise. Frankfurt, however, challenges the traditional PAP and advances a revised PAP: "A person is not morally responsible for what he has done if he did it only because he could not have done otherwise."[9] This revised PAP shifts our attention away from the issue of causal determination and toward the relationship between the act and the actor's reasons for performing that act. Frankfurt contends that a person exercises free will when he conforms his will (the desire by which he is moved to act) to his second-order volition (the second-order desire regarding which first-order desire he wants to move him to act). For Frankfurt, a person's will is free when the desire that motivates him to action corresponds to that which he wants to motivate him to action.[10]

Gary Watson argues that Frankfurt's conception of a second-order volition is inadequate for the task. Watson introduces a Platonic distinction between desires and values, and he contends that a free agent is one who can translate values into action.[11] Both writers address free will (or free action) in terms of the relationship between the action and certain mental events. Roughly, an actor acts of his own free

---

9 Frankfurt, *Alternative Possibilities and Moral Responsibility*, 23 The Journal of Philosophy 829 (1969).
10 Frankfurt, *supra* note 8, at 90.
11 Watson, *Free Agency*, in G. Watson, *supra* note 8, at 96.

will when his actions correspond with his values (Watson) or when his activating desire corresponds with his second-order volitions (Frankfurt). For the sake of convenience, I will refer to this position as the "correspondence thesis." Consider the significance of the following hypothetical situation for this thesis.

Imagine a case in which a clergyman leaves a church with donations collected at the sunday services. While getting into a car, he drops a bag containing $500 in cash and drives away. There is only one witness, and that person takes the money. In addition, imagine each of the following four persons in that role:

> W is concerned purely with his first-order desires. Although he has the capacities necessary to understand norms and to reflect upon and evaluate his own desires and behavior, he simply disregards these issues. He does not form second-order desires or values, but rather acts for the satisfaction of his first-order desires.[12]

> D recognizes honesty as an important value and wants to be an honest person. He believes that theft is illegal and immoral but he gives in to temptation and then, having stolen the money, he reduces his discomfort by telling himself that he has not really stolen because he needs the money more than the church does and will put it to better use.

> E is identical to D with a single exception. Unlike D, E is unable to rationalize[13] his action, and thus he continues to suffer guilt and anxiety.

12 As I understand Frankfurt, W would fit his concept of a wanton. *See supra* note 8, at 86–89.
13 It is important to distinguish the ordinary from the clinical meanings of "rationalize." In the ordinary sense, to rationalize is "to render conformable to reason; to explain on a rational basis" [II Oxford English Dictionary (compact ed., Oxford: Oxford Univ. Press, 1971)]. Clinically, rationalization is a process of "making a thing appear reasonable, when otherwise its irrationality would be evident. It is said that a person 'covers up,' justifies, rationalizes an act or an idea that is unreasonable." L.E. Hinsie and R.J. Campbell, Psychiatric Dictionary 645 (4th ed., New York: Oxford Univ. Press, 1970). The term is used here in its second, clinical sense. Notice that this clinical sense

F recognizes honesty as an important value and wants to be an honest person. His most overriding value, however, requires that he follow whatever he believes to be God's will. F is a paranoid schizophrenic who suffers from markedly impaired reality testing and delusional thought processes. He periodically hears an hallucinatory voice telling him to perform various acts. He interprets these experiences as direct instructions from God and as proof that he embodies the second coming of Jesus Christ. He understands his immediate circumstances and the presence of the words "in God we trust" on the money as a divine message, instructing him to take the money and use it to publish pamphlets containing his own version of God's word. He follows these "instructions" while maintaining his commitment to honesty. He notices no conflict between his decision to take the money and his belief that theft is always wrong, and he experiences no dissonance regarding these two positions.

As I understand the correspondence thesis, W did not act of his own free will because he has no values or second-order volitions for his will to correspond to. D and E did not act of their own free will because their actions were not consistent with their values and second-order volitions. F acted of his own free will because his action was consistent with his dominant value and second-order volition, which require that he conform to what he believes to be God's will. Yet these conclusions seem to contradict common moral intuitions. Intuitively, I believe that most of us would see W as a common criminal who understood what he was doing, who acted of his own free will, and who should be held accountable for it. In contrast, F would not usually be held responsible for his act. His psychopathology would be sufficient to support the insanity defense, and most observers would absolve him of moral responsibility. Finally, D and E most resemble most of us in those situations in which we give in

of the term does not refer to rationalization as a form of severe psychopathology but rather as a common process through which many people avoid confronting uncomfortable aspects of their lives. In contrast, the term is used in its ordinary sense in chapter 4's discussion of practical reasoning.

to temptation and perform some act that we believe to be wrong. Frequently, we would even acknowledge (at least in moments of relative detachment) that we have acted wrongly of our own free will and should be held responsible.

The correspondence thesis does not claim that a person is responsible for his actions if and only if he acts on free will. Traditionally, however, we usually consider free will to be an important condition of responsibility, yet in these cases the correspondence thesis seems to yield an inverse relationship between free will and usual ascriptions of responsibility. An advocate of the correspondence thesis might argue that the case of F is misleading because it is assumed that values or second-order volitions lead to our activating motives through unimpaired rational process. As far as I can tell, this is not a requirement of the correspondence thesis. If it is, then it is reasonable to ask what relationship is posited between this requirement and correspondence, because there seems to be no reason to assume that the two will coincide.

The cases of W, D, E, and F create some tension with commonly considered moral intuitions. Yet, the correspondence thesis contains a valuable insight insofar as it directs our attention towards the relationship between acts and mental events. Section 7.2 will develop an alternative conception of free will that builds upon this insight. This formulation concentrates on the cognitive processes by which the actor directs and evaluates his own behavior, and it is partially rooted in the nature of normative institutions.

7.2 FREE WILL AS PSYCHOLOGICAL CAPACITY

7.2.1 Consequences and normative institutions. By a normative institution, I mean a social system that endorses and applies a relatively comprehensive and coherent set of standards regulating some sphere of human behavior. Such institutions are usually intended to provide a statement of values, standards, and limits as well as to guide behavior according to these norms. The institution guides behavior by communicating the standards to those who are subject to them and by evaluating behavior that falls within its scope as well as by the distribution of consequences. These consequences may be tangible (for example, reward and punishment) or symbolic (for example, praise and blame or approval and disapproval). Whether tangible or symbolic, these consequences are intended at least partially as behavior guiding devices.

Some examples of common normative institutions as the term is used here are the criminal justice system, professional organizations or licensing boards that enforce codes of professional ethics, and religious or social subcultures that endorse and apply standards or rules for individual behavior that are formed on some relatively well systematized religious or moral theory. Criminal justice systems that apply penal codes such as the MPC or similar systems of state criminal statutes are paradigmatic normative institutions. Questions regarding free will often arise when individuals have committed offenses against a normative institution, but the fairness of holding them responsible, and thus subject to the consequences, is in doubt.

One mainstream psychological theory has identified three modalities by which consequences such as those administered by normative institutions can affect human behavior. The first is the direct reinforcement process in which the person (S) performs act (A) and experiences consequences (C) that increase or decrease S's tendency to do A. This appears to be the dominant process of behavior-shaping in cognitively unsophisticated beings such as nonhuman species and seriously impaired humans. This modality plays a relatively minor role, however, for unimpaired adults. The second is vicarious reinforcement, in which S sees T perform A and experience C, which alters S's tendency to do A. This process, which requires more cognitive sophistication than direct reinforcement, has been shown to be effective with young children. The third modality is the cognitively self-mediated one in which S performs or considers performing

227

A, symbolically applies C, and hence alters his tendency to repeat or perform A.[14] In this third modality, the actor directs his behavior in light of the consequences that he expects to follow certain acts. Thus, his behavior can be influenced by consequences he has never experienced or seen experienced.

There are also three types of reinforcement functions that are involved in the three modalities. The modalities refer to the manner in which the reinforcing events are experienced: directly, vicariously, or only through mental representation such as memory or imagination. The reinforcement functions are the processes by which the reinforcing events affect behavior. The informative function refers to the processes by which consequences provide the subject with information regarding what actions will elicit certain sorts of consequences as well as more abstract information such as what sort of actions are approved or disapproved. The motivational function refers to the capacity of humans (and possibly other cognitively advanced beings) to be motivated by anticipated consequences that they are able to symbolically represent. Finally, the automatic reinforcement function is defined largely by the absence of sophisticated symbolic processing. It refers to the process that occurs when an animal's tendency to perform A is altered through the experience of C shortly after A in the absence of any apparent capacity for significant symbolic representation or comprehension.[15]

When environmental stimuli affect behavior through the direct modality (predominant in lower animals and seriously impaired humans), all three functions may be operative to some degree. When behavior is directed through the vicarious or cognitively self-mediated modalities, the informative and motivational functions are dominant.[16]

14 A. Bandura, Social Learning Theory 95–158 (Englewood Cliffs, NJ: Prentice Hall, 1977). Note that "reinforcement" is used in this chapter, as it is by Bandura (p. 21), in its broad sense in which it refers to the process of regulating behavior through consequences without any implicit suggestion that this always occurs automatically; that is, without cognitive mediation.
15 *Id*. at 17–22.
16 *Id*. at 17–22, 96–158.

In summary, external events shape the behavior of un-impaired adults primarily through the vicarious and self-mediated modalities. In these modalities, the external events influence the individual's behavior primarily by providing information regarding the likely consequences of behavior and, thus, by motivating the actor to perform certain actions and to avoid others. When the interaction between environmental events and the person takes place primarily through the cognitively self-mediated modality, we can develop models of self-regulatory capacities through which the actor can direct his behavior in light of anticipated consequences.

Sections 7.2 and 7.3 contend that these cognitive self-regulatory capacities can be interpreted in such a manner as to provide the conception of free will that we need and intuitively apply in legal and moral judgments. This interpretation integrates familiar psychological and philosophical concepts in order to present a conception of free will as a psychological capacity that is consistent with current psychological theory, common moral intuitions, and Frankfurt's criteria. According to this conception, an individual's will is free if and only if he possesses certain psychological capacities that allow him to interact with the environment, and possibly be determined by it, in a manner that is unique to those who are usually considered moral agents. It is intended to be particularly germane to normative institutions that impose consequences for behavior, and to be neutral as to determinism.[17]

A satisfactory conception of free will as a psychological capacity should provide an interesting theoretical account of that capacity, and it should show that such a capacity does the legal and moral work that we usually expect of a conception of free will. Section 7.2 pursues the first of these two requirements, and Section 7.3 addresses the second.

17 For the purpose of this chapter, I will accept Watson's description of determinism as "the view, roughly, that every event and state of affairs is 'causally necessitated' by preceding events and states of affairs." G. Watson, *supra* note 8, at 2.

7.2.2 Psychological explanation. In his 1983 work on the nature of psychological explanation, Robert Cummins describes two types of explanatory theories: state transition theories and property analysis.[18] State transition theories explain changes in a system through the method of causal subsumption. They are concerned with identifying a set of causal laws that apply to a given system in such a manner that any particular state change (event) in that system can be subsumed under causal law.[19] Such theories explain events and event types, but they only specify dispositions of the system, rather than explaining them.

Property theories explain the properties of the system by addressing the question, "In virtue of what does the system have this property?"[20] Properties are explained by analyzing them into a set of components and the pattern of organization among these components. When the property is a capacity, the appropriate analysis is a functional one in which the capacity is broken down into less problematic capacities and their program of organization. Functional analysis of a capacity is of explanatory relevance if it analyzes the capacity into components that are less sophisticated than the analyzed capacity, different in kind from it, and organized in a relatively complex manner.

State transition theories and property analysis can interact in an important way. When an event occurs in a system, there is a state change that can be explained by a state transition theory that specifies dispositions of the system and a causal law under which the state change can be subsumed. Then the dispositions that were specified by the state transition account can be explained by functional analysis. The state change is fully explained when the event is subsumed under causal law, and the disposition is explained through analysis.

Human actions can be seen as state changes in a system

18 R. Cummins, The Nature of Psychological Explanation 1–51 (Cambridge, MA: MIT Press, 1983).
19 *Id.* at 9–14.
20 *Id.* at 15.

(the human being who acts). When the action is an intentional one, we often explain it as the product of the interaction between environmental conditions and the actor's beliefs, desires and intentions. For example, we might be surprised to see Jill jogging at six A.M. because we know that she hates to get out of bed in the morning. If told, however, that Jill is worried about her health because she has a family history of heart disease and her older sister recently suffered a heart attack, that she believes that jogging will improve her health, and that she can run only in the morning because she works too late to run in the evening, we would accept this as a reasonable explanation of her behavior.

Recall the discussion of reasons as causes in Chapter 4.3.2. Jill's learning about her sister's heart attack serves as a triggering cause for Jill's behavior in that it explains why Jill started to jog when she did. It does not, however, explain why Jill chose to jog rather than to lift weights or chant a mantra. In order to explain why Jill chose the particular activity of jogging, we would cite her reasons for jogging as the structuring cause of her decision to engage in this particular activity rather than some alternative.

On Dretske's account, Jill's wants and beliefs constitute a structuring cause for her acts because their representational content provides reasons that rationalize those acts as means to satisfy those wants. Her reasons for acting supply the internal link between the present conditions and previous experiences in which she satisfied similar desires in similar circumstances. The three modalities described (direct, vicarious, and cognitively self-mediated reinforcement) can be understood as three different sets of processes by which the actor associates past success with current circumstances and thus forms reasons for actions that provide structuring causes for her acts.[21]

In those cases in which environmental events affect the actor's behavior through the cognitively mediated self-regulatory mode, the explanation of the manner in which

21 *See supra,* chapter 4.3.2.

the actor's reasons for acting produced her acts invokes a complex set of cognitive capacities that can be analyzed into more simple components and a pattern of organization. We might explain Jill's decision to begin jogging today by citing her older sister's heart attack. In order to explain how the sister's heart attack caused Jill to run, we might cite Jill's fear of a similar attack, her belief that running will decrease the probability of such an event, and the consequent relief that she experiences when she reminds herself that her running alters the probability in this manner. This explanation would assume that Jill's beliefs about possible future heart attacks can alter her present behavior, but it would not explain how this process of cognitive self-regulation works. A complete explanation of behavior directed by the self-regulatory process would include the causal explanation of the specific act and the explanation through analysis of the self-regulatory capacity.

This chapter contends that the complex set of psychological capacities that combine to form the self-regulatory capacity can be explained in a manner that provides a conception of free will that is theoretically interesting, consistent with the framework advanced in Chapter 4, and important for legal and moral concerns. If free will is seen as a psychological capacity, corresponding roughly to the self-regulatory capacity, then according to Cummins, the appropriate form of theoretical explanation would be functional analysis and the appropriate question to address would be: "In virtue of what does this person have the capacity of free will?" A satisfactory explanation would take the form of a relatively complex organization of relatively simple and better understood psychological capacities. The next section will sketch such an analysis.

7.2.3 The self-regulatory capacity. The self-regulatory capacity can be analyzed at the first level into three component processes, each of which is stated in terms of relatively common psychological capacities. The first is standard comprehension or setting. The individual develops a set of criteria of ac-

232

ceptability for his own behavior. As the phrase suggests, the individual may comprehend and accept previously existing standards from some external source, or he may develop his own criteria of acceptability, usually by combining and modifying existing standards from various sources. The second component process is that of self-evaluation and self-instruction during which the individual analyzes his own behavior in terms of the standards and directs himself in light of the standards and the evaluation. The third component is self-reinforcement or the self-directed application of consequences, usually in the form of positive or negative appraisals of one's own performance. Frequently, the self-evaluation and self-reinforcing functions are carried out in the same cognitive act of self-appraisal.[22]

As an example of this process, consider the case of G who encounters the lost money situation described previously as encountered by W, D, E, and F. G realizes that the money would benefit him greatly and that the chances of his being caught are extremely slight. Hence the external circumstances promote his taking it. He has adopted a set of standards, however, that label theft as evidence that the thief is a weak, incompetent person who is unable to succeed on his own (standard setting). He considers taking the money, but identifies this act as theft and tells himself that he will return it because he is not an incompetent weakling and only such a person would take it (self-evaluation and self-instruction). By making this appraisal, he adds an aversive aspect to the prospect of taking it (self-reinforcement). He delivers the money to the church and confirms his evaluation of himself as honest and self-sufficient (self-evaluation and self-

22 Bandura, *supra* note 14, at 128–58; Mischel and Mischel, *A Cognitive Social Learning Approach to Morality and Self-Regulation,* in Moral Development and Behavior 84–107 (T. Lickona, ed., New York: Holt, Rinehart & Winston, 1976). The account of the self-regulatory capacity presented in this chapter is drawn primarily from Bandura's 1977 book (cited at note 14). Bandura has presented a somewhat updated but essentially unchanged account of self-regulation as part of a more comprehensive theory in a more recent work. *See,* A. Bandura, Social Foundations of Thought and Action 335–89 (1986).

reinforcement). In a slight variation of this process, his self-reinforcement might take the form of anticipated external consequences rather than self-evaluative labeling; for example, he might remind himself that if he did get caught stealing from a church, the police and courts would have no mercy and he would never be able to do business in the town again.

Each of the three first-level components can be analyzed further into subcomponents. Standard acquisition can occur through several familiar processes of learning. Empirical research has demonstrated that children will adopt and apply standards of behavior through an interaction of several processes including: direct teaching, modeling of standards by others, being treated according to those standards by adults, and observing conflicting standards of peers.[23]

As a person's ability to symbolically represent events and standards improves, the process of standard comprehension and setting becomes less directly dependent on other people. The individual develops the ability to symbolically represent standards as relatively abstract properties or principles, and he learns to apply these criteria to his own behavior, both prospectively and retrospectively. The young child, for example, must be told by his mother not to take his sister's toys. Later, he will remind himself (frequently by speaking aloud) that he should not take his sister's toys, and as he learns more general concepts, he might broaden that standard to the general category of stealing. Finally, as an adult, he will hold himself to an abstract standard of honesty that applies to a wide variety of situations.

The process of self-evaluation can be broken down into a variety of component evaluations. Whether standards are adopted from others, or constructed by the individual, an adult living in a complex environment actually maintains a

---

23 Aronfreed, *Moral Development from the Standpoint of a General Psychological Theory*, in Lickona, *id.* at 58–59; Bandura, *supra* note 14, at 133–37.

variety of standards for different situations and types of behavior. He must evaluate the situational conditions to determine which set of standards is appropriate; then he must evaluate each possible act in light of the conditions and standards. Finally, he evaluates the standards themselves in order to determine whether they should be altered.

F, for example, endorses a standard that condemns theft categorically and values honesty highly. He did not comprehend the inconsistency between this standard and his action, however, because his delusional belief that he was acting on direct orders from God prevented him from thinking of this act as one that was subject to moral review. In effect, God's orders served as a trump card over all other standards. An observer might think that if F believes that God is all good and that God has just ordered him to steal, then F can not believe that stealing is always wrong. One aspect of F's thought disorder, however, is that F, like Mary and Bill in Chapter 6, holds blatantly inconsistent beliefs without experiencing dissonance. This is one reason that he is unable to perform the various cognitive operations involved in the self-regulatory process.

Two types of self-reinforcement can be identified. First, self-mediated reinforcement can involve the anticipation of external consequences. Some instances of "weakness of will" can be interpreted as cases in which a person acts for immediate reward rather than to maximize the long-term consequences. Jill, for example, might stay in bed because that seems so pleasant now, while the feared heart attack is remote. The individual who possesses the capacities necessary to anticipate and symbolically represent future external consequences of the act he is considering is able to direct his own behavior in light of environmental consequences he has not yet experienced and in some cases may never experience. Second, in addition to anticipating external contingencies, the self-reinforcement process allows the person to generate his own consequences in the form of self-evaluative labeling, which may augment or override external conditions. These two types of self-reinforcement are exemplified by the second and first variations, respectively, of the case of G described earlier.

As described previously, automatic reinforcement can be effective with beings who are very unsophisticated cognitively. The more cognitively advanced the subject, the more heavily reinforcement works through the informational and motivational functions. Beings who learn primarily through the vicarious and self-mediated modalities must represent stimuli symbolically and perform cognitive transformations on those representations.

The terms "stimulus transformation" or "cognitive transformation" refer to cognitive operations that alter the interpretation or effective impact of a stimulus condition.[24] For example, ten dollars may be a reinforcing stimulus for a particular person in that he would usually perform a particular act for that sum, and having been so rewarded, he would be likely to perform the act again under similar circumstances in the future. If he discovered that others were receiving thirty dollars for the same task, however, he might interpret the ten dollar fee as an insult, and by virtue of that interpretation, the ten dollar sum would be transformed from a reinforcing stimulus to an aversive one. That is, the ten dollar sum, in conjunction with his knowledge that others were receiving thirty dollars and his interpretation of the discrepancy as an insult, would decrease rather than increase his willingness to perform that task under the same conditions in the future. Cognitive representation and transformation are involved in virtually all aspects of the self-regulatory process.

The self-regulatory process is not merely cognitive. The motivational force of the symbolic representations of standards and events is partially a function of the externally mediated consequences and emotional responses associated with them. Standards are typically taught by care givers or

---

24 Bandura, *supra* note 14, at 129, 160–73; Mischel and Mischel, *supra* note 22, at 93–94.

power figures who tend to communicate approval or disapproval along with the cognitive content of the standards. Interactions during which the standards are learned involve positive and negative consequences that are delivered in response to, and along with, acts and statements relevant to the standards. Positive and negative consequences and the accompanying emotional correlates become associated with acts as well as with statements and judgments regarding behavioral standards. Once the cognitive content of these standards has become associated with the externally mediated consequences and the emotional correlates, the processes of self-evaluation and self-reinforcement can be almost inseparable because self-evaluation immediately elicits the associated affective responses.

When the individual evaluates his act (retrospectively or prospectively) in light of conditions or standards, his evaluation of the act and of himself as actor cue expectations of consequences and associated emotional responses that serve as one form of self-mediated reinforcement. For example, when G (in the case described earlier) considers taking the money, and interprets such an act as evidence of weakness, he may experience the emotional aspects of shame and embarrassment that have previously been associated with similar episodes. By returning the money, he eliminates these feelings and experiences the emotional correlates of pride and self-satisfaction as he appraises himself positively.

The important point here is that the self-regulatory process is not an isolated process, entirely distinct from emotional experience and externally mediated conditioning and teaching. Rather, it is a process in which external conditioning, cognitive processes, and emotional responses are integrated. It is the capacity to symbolically represent events and standards as well as to perform cognitive manipulations on these representations that enables the individual who is relatively sophisticated cognitively to interact with significant environmental determinants of his behavior in a manner that is not available to cognitively less developed beings. Relatively advanced cognitive capacities are necessary in the self-regulatory process in order to allow the person to interpret external conditions and contingencies, store abstract standards, interpret situations in light of those standards, anticipate the results of actions and the likely consequences, associate positive or negative responses with cognitive representations, and employ cognitive representations as effective reinforcements.

In summary, the self-regulatory capacity is a complex one that can be analyzed into three component capacities: standard comprehension and setting, self-evaluation and instruction, and self-reinforcement. Each of these can in turn be analyzed into less complex and relatively well understood functions. The complex interaction of these relatively simple functions marks the self-regulatory capacity as a complex human capacity that enables the human being to interact with environmental behavior determinants through the cognitively self-mediated modality that is a fundamentally different process than is available to those who are limited to direct or vicarious conditioning.

Specific instances of directing behavior through consequences can be conceptualized as falling along a continuum from the directly externally conditioned to the predominantly self-regulated. As one moves from the direct to the self-regulated poles, the required level of capacity for symbolic representation and transformation increases. Hence, the most self-regulated point on this continuum at which a given individual can function is limited by his cognitive capacities. Some researchers claim that cognitive capacities develop in discreet invariable stages, whereas others argue that this development is more heavily affected by social learning factors. Nevertheless, it is generally agreed that cognitive immaturity or impairment can limit an individual's ability to learn through consequences to a relatively elementary level such as direct conditioning or simple vicarious learning.[25]

25 Kohlberg, *Moral Stages and Moralization: The Cognitive-Developmental Approach*, in Lickona, *supra* note 22, at 31–53; Mischel and Mischel, *supra* note 22, at 84–107.

7.2.4 Free will as self-regulatory capacity and the justification of consequences. Human social systems often attempt to direct the behavior of their members according to a normative institution through the application of consequences. This practice raises important questions regarding justification, particularly when punishment is involved. Many writers argue that individuals can justly be punished only if they possess certain minimal capacities. H.L.A. Hart refers to these capacities as "capacity-responsibility," and argues that an individual must be responsible in this sense in order to justly be held accountable because it is only in this case that the individual has a fair opportunity to conform his behavior to the law.[26] Capacity-responsibility consists of the ability to control one's conduct and the cognitive abilities of understanding and reasoning.[27] When capacity-responsibility is absent, many would say that the individual should not be held accountable because he did not act of his own free will. We may mean by this that the actor was not free to act according to his will, or that his will was not free.

These two interpretations of "he did not act of his own free will" can be understood as corresponding to the components of capacity-responsibility. If the actor is free of external constraints and internal disability, and thus has the ability to physically control his own conduct, then he is free to act according to his will. This corresponds to the conditional understanding of "could have done otherwise" often required by compatibilists.

If in addition to this capacity, he also possesses the ability to engage in psychological processes, including understanding and reasoning, required to choose his action in light of the norms, the situation, and the likely consequences of his choice, then his will was free in the sense that he was able to form his will in light of the normative institution and likely consequences without having to directly experience those consequences. In this sense, to say that an individual's will

26 H.L.A. Hart, Punishment and Responsibility 17–24, 215–30 (Oxford: Oxford Univ. Press, 1968).
27 *Id.* at 227.

is free does not mean that it is free of causal determination or that it is consistent with values or second-order volitions. Rather, it means that his cognitive capacities are free of impairment, and therefore he is able to participate in a normative institution, and be partially determined by it, in a manner unique to the unimpaired human adult. This uniquely human manner of participating in a cooperative social system is a product of the psychological capacities that allow the unimpaired person to direct his behavior in light of the institution's standards and consequences through the cognitively mediated self-regulatory process without actually having experienced the consequences.

In short, on this conception of free will, a person's will is free when the psychological abilities that constitute the cognitively mediated self-regulated capacity are free of impairment, and hence the person is capable of directing his behavior in light of the applicable norms, circumstances, and anticipated consequences through the processes of cognitive self-regulation that are available to the unimpaired adult. Ordinarily these capacities will develop gradually through childhood and remain relatively stable through the adult years. Marked fluctuations are possible, however, if an individual suffers periods of acute impairment. One who ordinarily possesses the cognitive self-regulatory capacities of the average adult, for example, might suffer an acute period of psychotic disorganization during which his capacity to reason is markedly impaired. That person's will would have been free until the onset of the psychotic episode and again after recovery. The will would not have been free, however, during the period of disorganization.

This conception of free will meets Frankfurt's requirements. It distinguishes humans from animals because it requires capacities possessed only by unimpaired adult humans. Although cognitive capacities play a central role in this conception of free will, it is not one that could be embodied in an artificial device such as a computer or a robot. As described here, the cognitively mediated self-regulating capacity is not divorced from the physical and emotional processes that are associated with various activities. Rather, it is a process by which a person can employ his cognitive capacities to regulate his responses to his felt needs, desires, fears, and so on. As far as we know, only unimpaired adult humans combine the physical and emotional needs and sensations of sentient beings with the cognitive capacities required for cognitively mediated self-regulation. Some day we might discover another species that shares our cognitive capacities, or we might develop a robot that shares the physical and emotional sensations of sentient beings. It is not obvious, however, that notions such as free will and responsibility would still be considered uniquely appropriate to human beings under those circumstances.

Free will, as understood here, is desirable because it allows one to direct one's behavior in such a manner as to elicit preferred consequences and avoid unwanted ones, as well as to direct one's life according to a conception of the kind of person one wants to be. Hart contends that the purpose of the law is to direct behavior while maintaining a choosing system in which each individual has the maximum opportunity to control his own life through the exercise of rational choice.[28] A system that directly applies consequences that are sufficiently tangible, intense, consistent, and immediate could probably alter the behavior of almost any animal through the direct conditioning modality. Learning by this process, however, follows the actual experience of the consequences.

Responsible individuals (those with the requisite cognitive capacities) have an opportunity to direct their behavior through the cognitively mediated process described here. Hence, they maintain the maximum opportunity to direct their lives through the exercise of rational choice, according to their own conception of the kind of person they want to be, and without actually experiencing the consequences that they chose to avoid.

This conception of free will as the ability to direct one's

28   *Id.* at 40–50.

actions through the cognitively mediated self-regulatory process is neutral as to determinism. If the libertarians are correct, and there is some sense in which we are all prime movers who cause our behavior by our choices without our choices being caused by some prior events, the manner in which we make those choices would still be important. The ability to make those choices through the self-regulatory process would allow us to pursue our own conception of the good, as well as to avoid offense against the normative institution and the resulting consequences.[29]

If determinism is true, presumably our choices serve as causal factors in the determination of our behavior. Furthermore, our choices are partially determined by the consequences of past behavior and by the anticipation of the likely consequences of the behavior under consideration. An individual with free will would be determined in a fundamentally different manner than one who did not have free will. The behavior of the individual with free will would be determined largely by the anticipation of expected future consequences through the vicarious and self-regulated modalities with relatively little need to directly experience undesirable consequences, because the anticipation of them would serve as a causal factor.

In contrast to the person who possesses the capacities that constitute free will, the individual without free will would be less able to direct his life in light of anticipated consequences, and thus more dependent on the actual experience of those consequences (in proportion to the severity of cognitive impairment). In addition, the individual with free will would be in a position to direct his life in a manner consistent with his own standards regarding the kind of person he wants to be. The process of self-evaluation and self-reinforcement through self-evaluative labeling in light of the standards the individual has accepted requires comprehension of the standards, accurate categorization of acts or po-

---

29 *See supra*, chapter 4.3 regarding the discussion of personal agency and state and event causation.

tential acts in light of those standards, and effective reasoning from standards to action-plans likely to provide necessary or sufficient conditions to meet those standards. The individual whose will is not free, in the sense that his self-regulatory capacities are impaired, is less able to pursue realization of his own standards, in proportion to the severity of that impairment.

If determinism is true, it would be possible in principle to explain any particular act (as a state change) through subsumption under causal law. It would still be possible, however, to explain the capacity of free-will (as conceptualized here) according to the method of analysis in the manner pursued here. As long as free will is viewed as a psychological capacity, it can be explained through analysis regardless of whether each individual act is subsumed under causal law.

7.3 MORAL AND LEGAL APPLICATIONS

A review of the examples of W, D, E, and F by this conception of free will yields conclusions that are consistent with commonly endorsed moral judgments. All four were free of constraint and physical disability, and thus were free to act according to their wills. W, D, and E possessed the capacities that constitute free will, and thus would all be held accountable for their actions.

F's delusional disorder sufficiently impaired his cognitive capacities as to render his will unfree. F would not be exculpated merely because he held an unusual belief about God's will. F, as described earlier, demonstrates significant impairment of his abilities to accurately perceive reality, reason from general standards to specific acts, and comprehend the contradiction in his own belief that theft is categorically wrong, but his decision to take the money is right. This substantial cognitive dysfunction prevents him from effectively directing his behavior through the exercise of unimpaired self-regulation in light of the applicable standards and conditions. Therefore, we would not hold him accountable, although we might subject him to compulsory treatment or monitoring.

According to the conception of free will advanced in this chapter, F's will was not free because his cognitive impairment prevented him from directing his behavior through the cognitively mediated self-reinforcement process in light of the applicable norms and the circumstances that he actually encountered. The hallucinatory voice, his belief that he is Jesus Christ, and his impaired reasoning processes all prevented him from accurately evaluating his own behavior by the standard of honesty he endorsed. Whether he thought that God would protect him from legal sanctions or that he, as Jesus Christ, must suffer these sanctions to atone for the sins of mankind, his cognitive disorder distorted the usual behavior guiding effect of the anticipated legal conviction and punishment. Similarly, his decision to take the money while holding that theft is wrong did not give rise to any feelings of guilt or shame that might have served as self-generated sources of reinforcement because his thought disorder prevented him from recognizing the conflict between his standard proscribing theft and his act as an instance of theft.

We all interpret reality through our own needs and biases, but F's hallucinations, delusions, and impaired thought processes distort his judgments in a fundamentally different manner. The unimpaired adult experiences dissonance if he interprets reality in a manner that conflicts with observable external events or requires that he accept clearly inconsistent beliefs. F's cognitive disorder removes these limits on the degree to which his internal needs or biases influence his interpretations of events. Thus, his ability to direct his behavior through the process of cognitive self-regulation in light of the norms and circumstances is markedly impaired.

The conception of free will that one needs for legal and moral purposes must explicate the grounds on which some people are held accountable for their actions and others are not. When free will is conceived of as a set of psychological capacities, the actors who are appropriately held accountable are those who possess the capacities that enable them to direct their own actions according to applicable norms, the likely consequences, and their own conceptions of the kind of persons they want to be. The analysis of the cognitively mediated self-regulatory capacities advanced in this chapter suggests that this ability of moral agents to direct their own lives can be analyzed fruitfully in terms of the cognitive processes that these agents have available for standard setting, self-evaluation, and self-reinforcement.

The individual who lacks the minimal comprehension and reasoning of the unimpaired adult cannot direct his own behavior, or participate in a social system according to normative institutions, in the same manner that moral agents can. Admittedly, this conception of free will does not provide a "bright line" criterion for determining how much impairment is sufficient to render one's will unfree. There will still be borderline cases. This conception does explain, however, why a markedly impaired individual such as F should be exculpated, and how his capacity for self-direction is inadequate.

Furthermore, this conception of free will suggests a procedure for evaluating the significance of other types of disorders for free will. If, for example, Anne suffers a severe memory impairment, we can determine whether this renders her will unfree by evaluating the impact of this impairment on her ability to perform the cognitive operations involved in the self-regulatory process. If the memory impairment is so severe, for example, that she is unable to simultaneously recall the act, the standard, and the likely consequences, we might conclude that she is unable to perform the required cognitive operations and, thus, that she lacks free will.

This position can also accommodate several other difficult situations that are frequently interpreted in terms of free will. Consider the bank clerk who is ordered to hand over the money or be shot. Given the situation as it confronts him, if he decides through unimpaired reasoning to hand over the money in order to avoid being shot, then he is free to act according to his will (that is, free of physical constraint or disability) and his will is free (that is, he is able to form his will through unimpaired rational process). We would not subject him to sanctions for his decision because the option he chose was justifiable, not because he did not choose it of his own free will. If he had chosen the same course of action when threatened with being called nasty names rather than with being shot, we might well hold him liable because his will was free, and his choice was not justified.

On this conception of free will as the unimpaired capacity for cognitively mediated self-regulation, emotional factors are relevant to free will in at least three different ways. First, intense fear may defeat the actor's ability to act on his will. If, for example, the bank clerk described here decides to hand over the money, step on the alarm bell, or take any other particular action, but is literally paralyzed by fear and thus unable to act on that decision, then he is unable to act on his will. That is, his will is free because his ability to make behavioral decisions through the cognitively self-mediated process is unimpaired, but the paralyzing effect of the fear prevents him from translating that decision into action.

Alternately, mood disorder can include psychotic disturbance of cognitive processes that renders the will unfree; that is, the psychotically disturbed victim of a major mood disorder can suffer cognitive distortions of the type that defeats the capacity for unimpaired cognitively mediated self-regulation.[30] Z from Chapter 2.1.2 exemplifies this pattern. In these cases, emotional factors render the will unfree precisely because those factors produce cognitive dysfunction that precludes effective exercise of the cognitively mediated self-regulatory process.

Finally, emotional factors may render it unusually difficult for the actor to exercise the self-regulatory capacity. The actor may experience, for example, strong anger or fear that produces a strong want to act contrary to the standards of the applicable normative institution. George and Harvey from Chapter 6.6.2 exemplify this pattern. When free will is under-

30 *See supra,* chapter 6.6.2 for a discussion of major mood disorder with
    and without psychotic dysfunction.

stood as a psychological capacity, however, this type of emotional factor is relevant to free will, but it does not defeat an ascription of free will. George and Harvey retain the capacities that constitute free will, although circumstances may render it very difficult for them to exercise these capacities in the manner demanded by the normative institution. It would be appropriate, therefore, to consider them less blameworthy for failing to exercise those capacities. To say that it would have been difficult for an actor to exercise certain capacities under the circumstances, however, is not to say that he lacked the capacities.

In short, when free will is conceived of as psychological capacity, emotional factors can support the contention that the actor did not act of his own free will in either of two ways. First, those factors might produce impairment in the capacities that constitute free will, in which case the actor's will was not free of impairment. Second, those factors might render the actor literally unable to act on his decision, in which case he was not free to act on his will.

It is important to notice here that to say that an individual acted of his own free will (according to this conception of free will) is *not* to say that he acted voluntarily. Recall Feinberg's broad conception of voluntariness and his analysis of voluntariness reducing factors including coercion, mistake, and impairment.[31] According to the conception of free will advanced in this chapter, impairment is the only one of these three voluntariness reducers that is directly related to free will. Hence, if one accepts Feinberg's analysis of voluntariness, free will is a necessary but not a sufficient condition of voluntariness. Cognitive impairment sufficient to support the conclusion that the actor's will is not free also reduces voluntariness, according to Feinberg's theory. It remains possible, however, that an act may be a product of the actor's free will, yet not be fully voluntary due to the effects of

---

31 *See supra*, chapter 1.1 for a brief description of Feinberg's account of voluntariness. For a complete account, *see, generally,* J. Feinberg, Harm to Self (New York: Oxford Univ. Press, 1986).

coercion or mistake. The bank teller who rationally decided to hand over the money to avoid being shot is an example of one who acted of his own free will but did not act voluntarily in Feinberg's sense.

Admittedly, this conception interprets "constraint" and "free to act on his will" very narrowly. Under it, one would be constrained and thus not free to act according to his will only if, having made a decision to act, he was physically unable to translate that decision into action by virtue of external or internal factors such as physical restraint or paralysis due to illness or terror. Some would prefer to construe these terms more broadly in order to say that people under duress (such as the bank teller described earlier) were not free to act according to their will. I adopt this narrow conception because it facilitates the process of drawing distinctions between situations in which the actor is physically unable to act and those in which it is unreasonable to expect him to. It seems likely that we will obfuscate rather than clarify our moral notions by trying to include too many morally relevant considerations under the rubric of free will.

This conception is consistent with the common practice of attributing different moral significance to threats than to offers. Imagine two bank clerks, the first of whom is threatened with being shot if he does not open the vault, and the second is offered half the contents if he does. Presuming that neither is panicked nor paralyzed by fear, I believe we would usually excuse the first, but not the second, for opening the vault. However, the difference is not a matter of free will; both acted according to their wills and both wills were free. The first could not have been expected to do otherwise by our usual standards, whereas the second would have been. This difference reflects our usual practice of including coercion, but not inducement, in the category of voluntariness reducers. That is, the key issue in these cases is voluntariness in the broad sense rather than freedom of the will.

Three other types of behavior that are often presented as relevant to free will are addiction, compulsive behavior, and phobias. These are particularly difficult to address because the manner in which these behaviors are thought to effect freedom of the will is not clear. They often seem to be presented as conditions in which the individual literally could not have done other than he did, regardless of how hard he had tried. If this is the case, and if he did as he did only because he was unable to do otherwise, the situation is analogous to paralysis and the actor was not free to act on his will.[32] If these conditions are seen as sources of cognitive impairment that prevented the actor from exercising normal cognitive capacities in his choice, then his will was not free. Finally, if these conditions merely provided a strong desire to act in a given way, then the individual was free to act according to his will and his will was free. We might acknowledge these conditions, however, as mitigating circumstances to be considered when applying sanctions because such conditions might make it unusually difficult for an individual to conform to the applicable norms. In this way, these conditions may have significance similar to the substantial affective component of the behavior attributed to George and Harvey in Chapter 6.

Some will find this analysis of these conditions wanting because desires that are unusually strong or that arise from unusual sources are frequently seen as defeating an ascription of free will. Suppose, for example, that a particular desire is the product of an addiction or hypnosis, or that it has been induced by an evil neurosurgeon. Assume that such desires are not accompanied by impairment of cognitive processes or of the capacity to physically control behavior. The net result is that the individual experiences a desire, the etiology of which he may not be aware, and that he may wish he did not have. It is not clear to me in what morally significant way

32 In this case, the process thought to be at work remains mysterious unless one thinks that these conditions involve some sort of physical causal process that overrides the decision-making process. This interpretation seems highly unlikely. The third alternative seems to be the most accurate account of the actual effect of these processes.

such a desire would differ from many of those we experience every day (and presumably have developed in a more mundane manner).

Suppose I experience a strong desire to punch my opponent in the nose whenever I lose a tennis match. Suppose further that unbeknownst to me, this desire is a product of early interactions with my very competitive siblings. We may assume that I consider this desire to be an unreasonable one and that I am puzzled and embarrassed by it. Should I indulge this desire, we would not usually think that I had not acted of my own free will, or that I should not be held responsible for my behavior. Yet, this desire is one that was inculcated in me by others in a way that I did not understand and do not remember, very much as is the case in the less mundane examples listed earlier.

When hypothetical cases of desires arising from exotic origins are shorn of implicit assumptions about the actor's inability to direct his behavior regarding these desires, it is not clear why the source of the desires would have moral significance. According to the position advanced in this chapter, the important factor concerning desires for matters of free will and responsibility is not the source of the desires, but rather the resources the actor has available for managing them.

In summary, I am advancing a conception of free will that follows the lead of Frankfurt and Watson insofar as it turns on the relationship between the will and certain mental states or capacities. The critical aspect of this relationship, however, is the availability of unimpaired cognitive capacities that are used in the formulation of the will, rather than the final correspondence of the will with higher-order volitions or values. According to this conception, a person's will is free if and only if the cognitive processes that allow him to form his will in light of the situation, the norms and the probable consequences of his act are free of impairment, and thus he is able to interact with his environment through the cognitively mediated self-regulatory process.

This process requires the unimpaired adult's capacities

for comprehension, reasoning, and abstract-concept formation. The precise set of capacities necessary to constitute free will would be determined by further evaluation of the requirements of effective self-regulation as described here. There would remain, of course, hard cases in which it would be very difficult to determine whether the individual possessed sufficient capacities. The question to be addressed in these cases, however, would remain the same. Does this person's impairment substantially limit his ability to perform the cognitive operations required to direct this aspect of his behavior through the cognitively mediated self-regulatory process?

A person is free to act according to his will if he is free of any unusual constraint or disability (narrowly construed) that prevents him from acting on his will. The individual whose will is free and who acts as he does because it is his will, acts of his own free will and is therefore able to participate in a normative institution in a manner unique to moral agents. If, in addition, he acts in the absence of any other voluntariness reducers (that is, coercion or mistake), he acts voluntarily and he is appropriately held accountable for his actions.[33]

7.4 THE ACTION THEORY ANALYSIS, FREE WILL, AND THE MPC

7.4.1 The action theory analysis. According to the analysis presented in Chapter 4, acts are appropriately attributed to actors as practical reasoners when those actors act on action-plans that they select through an intact process of practical reasoning. During this process, the actors reason from their wants and their beliefs about which acts are likely to fulfill those wants to decisions to perform those acts. This practical

---

33 Accountability does not imply liability because the individual who acts of his own free will and voluntarily may also act in a manner that is justified.

reasoning takes place as part of a larger associative process of deliberation in which the actors become aware of and consider the likely effects of possible acts on their broader array of wants, selecting action-plans in light of these comprehensive networks.

On this account, the processes of practical reasoning and deliberation allow the actors to select action-plans that they consider more likely than any available alternative plan to satisfy their comprehensive sets of wants in light of the circumstances. These processes require at least intact consciousness and the cognitive capacities of perception, comprehension, and reasoning. Actors who possess these capacities at the level of the unimpaired adult have the ability of the ordinary practical reasoner to direct their actions in a manner intended to fulfill their wants in light of the norms, circumstances, and probable consequences of their actions.

7.4.2 The MPC defenses. The provisions of the MPC identified in the first six chapters as those that exculpate actors because their offenses are not attributable to them as practical reasoners fall into two categories. The first contains the failure-of-proof defense regarding the voluntary act requirement and the NGRI defense. These defenses apply to cases in which the conduct constituting the objective elements of the offense charged is not attributable to the defendant as a competent practical reasoner due to some distortion in the cognitive processes by which the actor's wants and beliefs produced these acts. I shall argue here that these are cases in which the actors lack the capacity to direct their behavior through the cognitive self-regulatory capacity, and thus do not act of their own free will as that concept is interpreted in Chapter 7.

The failure-of-proof defense regarding the culpability requirement constitutes the second category. These are cases in which the actors' wants and beliefs cause their behavior through unimpaired cognitive capacities that allow them to direct their behavior through the cognitive self-regulatory process. These actors act of their own free will, but their action-plans do not bear the required relation to the conduct constituting the objective elements of their offenses. Consequently, these actors' acts are appropriately attributable to them as competent practical reasoners, but the offenses are not. That is, the acts that are attributable to the actors as competent practical reasoners do not constitute the offenses in question, although they might fulfill the requirements for some lesser offense.

Returning to the first category, consider the failure-of-proof defense regarding the voluntary act requirement. Extreme cases such as paralysis or seizure involve no act. Recall Diane from Chapter 6.3 who struck a victim with her car as a result of an unanticipated stroke she suffered while driving. Diane performed no act because her physical impairment prevented her from translating her wants and beliefs into action; her wants and beliefs did not produce her movement.

In other cases, the actors' wants and beliefs might produce movement without serving as reasons for action. The variation of the John-killing-James example in Chapter 4 in which John's anger and desire to kill James caused his heart attack and fall, which in turn caused James's death, is a case of this type. John's wants and beliefs caused his movement, but they did not do so as reasons for action but rather as a triggering cause for John's heart attack. Thus, the movement that caused James's death did not include an act. In cases such as these in which the defendants' internal disability or external constraint prevent them from acting on action-plans, the movement does not constitute an act and can not be attributed to the actors as practical reasoners. These actors do not act of their own free will because they are not free to act on their wills. They do not act at all in Goldman's terms. Although they do act in the minimal sense of bodily movement required by the MPC conception of an act, these acts do not fulfill the MPC's voluntary act requirement.

Most cases involving the automatism defense, such as conduct performed in the post-ictal state following a seizure, prevent attribution of that conduct to the actor as a voluntary act in a more subtle manner. These actors' wants and beliefs produce their behavior, but not in the characteristic manner that wants and beliefs usually serve as reasons for action. The actors lack access to important aspects of their own standing wants, beliefs, and values, resulting in serious impairment in the associative process of deliberation. The actors' wants, beliefs, and intentions do not elicit awareness of relevant standing wants and beliefs regarding likely consequences, norms, or the kind of person they want to be. Clouded consciousness prevents these actors from selecting their actions through the ordinary processes of practical reasoning and deliberation because action-plans are made and acted upon without awareness of their likely significance for the actors' comprehensive network of wants. In this way, clouded consciousness undermines attribution of these acts to the actors as practical reasoners.

These actors' wills are not free because their capacity for cognitive self-regulation is impaired. Two important components of this capacity are self-evaluation and self-reinforcement. These actors cannot effectively self-evaluate, however, because that process requires access to the relevant norms, including the norms comprised of one's own standards and values.

Self-reinforcement can take the form of self-evaluative labeling or of anticipation of external consequences. These processes require awareness of the norms for use in self-evaluation and reasonable expectations regarding the probable consequences of acts. Inability to consider these factors regarding contemplated acts prevents prospective self-evaluation and self-reinforcement, which are important aspects of the self-regulatory capacity. Thus, when free will is understood as the ability to direct one's actions through the self-regulatory capacity, such defects in consciousness constitute impairment of free will and prevent attribution of the acts to the actors as practical reasoners.

The failure-of-proof defense regarding the culpability requirement exculpates for reasons that involve free will in a different manner. In some cases, the mistake that negates the culpability element might be the result of a pathological process that also grounds the NGRI defense. Consider, however, a pure mistake defense in which the defendant does not suffer any major distortion of psychological process. Suppose an actor's role in a play calls for him to hit another performer with a "trick-bottle" that is designed to shatter on impact, causing the "victim" no harm. Each night before the performance, the prop-man places the trick-bottle in the appropriate place, the actor picks it up and hits the victim on cue, the victim falls to the floor, the curtain closes, and the victim gets up without injury. One night, however, the prop-man places the wrong bottle on the stage, and the actor unknowingly hits his victim with an ordinary bottle, causing serious injury.

This case involves no disorder of psychological process, and the act clearly fulfills the objective elements of the crime of assault because the actor caused bodily injury to another human being.[34] The applicable defense for this actor would be the failure-of-proof defense regarding the culpability element; the actor's honest and reasonable mistake of fact precluded him from committing the objective offense elements purposefully, knowingly, or recklessly. This actor possessed the capacities to engage in the processes of practical reasoning and deliberation. Thus, the act is attributable to the actor as a competent practical reasoner. Similarly, there was no impairment of the cognitive self-regulatory capacity, so the actor's will was free and he was free to act on his will.

Although the actor's act is attributable to him as a competent practical reasoner, his mistake regarding a material element of the offense prevented him from reasoning to an action-plan in a manner that justifies attributing the *offense* to him as a practical reasoner. That is, the offense is defined in such a way as to require both a certain type of act and a

---

34 American Law Institute, Model Penal Code and Commentaries sec. 211.1 (official draft and revised comments, 1985). Assault occurs when the defendant causes bodily injury purposefully, knowingly, or recklessly. Causing bodily injury fulfills the objective offense requirements, whereas the three culpability levels listed fulfill culpability requirement.

mental state that fulfills the culpability requirement. Criminal liability for that offense requires both that the act be attributable to the actor as a practical reasoner and that the actor fulfill the culpability element. Whereas the failure-of-proof defense regarding the voluntary act requirement exculpates the actor because the act cannot be attributed to him as a practical reasoner, the failure-of-proof defense regarding the culpability element exculpates despite the fact that the act can be attributed to the actor as a practical reasoner. This defense exculpates because the act that can be so attributed to the actor does not constitute the offense as defined in the code.

The mistake or ignorance that negates the required culpability element involves belief content rather than distortion of cognitive process. Thus, it exculpates without preventing attribution of the act to the actor as a practical reasoner and without impairment that would provide grounds for saying that the actor did not act of his own free will. It is important to distinguish impairment of cognitive *process*, which undermines practical reasoning, deliberation, and free will, from defective belief *content*, which leaves those processes intact but prevents the defendant from fulfilling other offense elements. Substantial disturbance of cognitive process distorts cognitive self-regulation, impairing free will and preventing attribution of the *act* to the actor as a competent practical reasoner. Defective belief content, in contrast, prevents attribution of the *offense* to the actor as a practical reasoner despite the fact that he acted of his own free will.

Although the failure-of-proof defense regarding the voluntary act requirement exculpates some actors who suffer impairments that prevent them from acting of their own free will, it does not address all such cases. The NGRI defense exculpates some defendants who suffer distortion of cognitive process that impairs practical reasoning, deliberation, and free will, but does not do so in a manner that involves the voluntary act requirement. Pure cases of the NGRI defense do not include delusional belief content that might ground a failure-of-proof defense regarding the culpability

256

element. Mary and Bill from Chapter 6, Z from Chapter 2, and F from Chapter 7 all fall into this category. All four of these actors suffered delusional thought disorder, but their false belief content was not such that if true it would have provided legal justification for their act or prevented the actor from fulfilling an offense element.

Recall Mary, who entertained no mistake regarding either a material element of the offense or legal justification. She knew that she was purposefully killing an innocent human being and that she had no reason to think that she was in imminent danger. In addition, she attempted no less drastic method of protecting herself from the danger she perceived. Finally, she experienced no disturbance of consciousness. Neither failure-of-proof defense applies to Mary, yet she is clearly psychotic and at least an intuitively plausible candidate for exculpation.

As interpreted in Chapter 6, Mary's acts were not attributable to her as a competent practical reasoner because her distorted cognitive processes prevented her from selecting an action-plan through the processes that are available to a competent practical reasoner. She was unable to reason effectively from her comprehensive network of wants, beliefs, and values, including her wants to be a good person, please God, and avoid unpleasant consequences, to a course of action likely to fulfill those wants.

Mary's inability to recognize the contradictions in her own beliefs or the conflicts between her intended actions and her wants also prevented her from effectively engaging in the cognitive self-regulatory process that constitutes free will. Her inability to reason clearly from norm to specific act prevented her from accurately evaluating her decisions according to her own norms. For example, she wanted to be a good person and believed that killing innocent persons was inconsistent with being good, but she did not comprehend the significance of these beliefs for her own decision to kill her innocent victim. Hence, she did not accurately evaluate her decision in light of her own norms. In addition, her inability to accurately categorize her actions or predict external responses to them prevented her from effectively engaging in self-reinforcement, either with self-evaluative labeling or by anticipating external consequences. When she decided to kill her victim, the idea that this act would be contrary to her own criteria of the kind of person she wanted to be or that others would arrest or confine her never occurred to her. Thus, these factors did not affect her decision.

In short, the impairment that precluded attribution of Mary's act to her as a competent practical reasoner also prevented her from acting of her own free will. The NGRI defense, like the failure-of-proof defense regarding the voluntary act requirement, exculpates actors who suffer distortion of cognitive process that impairs practical reasoning, deliberation, and free will.

This review of these three MPC defenses that directly address the psychological states and processes of the defendant reveals two different patterns of exculpation. The failure-of-proof defense regarding the voluntary act requirement and the NGRI defense address cases in which the defendants do not act of their own free will. A few of these defendants, including Diane from Chapter 6.3, suffer from seizures or paralysis that prevent them from acting on their wills. Other defendants are free to act on their wills, but their wills are not free of impairment because they suffer from clouded consciousness or other forms of psychopathology that distort the cognitive processes by which the actors' wants and beliefs produce their acts. The failure-of-proof defense regarding the voluntary act requirement exculpates when clouded consciousness allows access to only a limited and nonrepresentative sample of wants and beliefs. The NGRI defense applies to cases in which the defendants have access to their wants and beliefs but suffer distortion in the cognitive processes by which they form beliefs and reason to action-plans.

Impairment of cognitive process undermines practical reasoning, deliberation, and cognitive self-regulation. Intact practical reasoners are those who have the capacity to direct their behavior through the process of practical reasoning at the level of the unimpaired adult. On the conception of free will as psychological capacity presented in this chapter, the individual with free will possesses the capacities necessary to engage in the process of practical reasoning that the un-impaired adult can engage in. Distorted cognitive processes that undermine free will prevent the actor from engaging in effective practical reasoning and preclude attribution of the act to the actor as a competent practical reasoner. On this account, free will is a necessary condition for attribution of an act to an actor as a competent practical reasoner. On ordinary moral intuitions, free will is a necessary condition for moral responsibility. Thus, impairment that renders the will unfree would preclude both attribution of the act to the actor as a competent practical reasoner and moral respon-sibility. In these cases, the MPC and this conception of free will correspond to ordinary moral intuitions.

In contrast, defenses involving mistaken belief content do not impugn free will or preclude the attribution of the act to the actor as a competent practical reasoner. In these cases, the actor directs his behavior as a competent practical rea-soner and acts of his own free will, but the conduct consti-tuting the objective elements of the offense does not stand in the relation to the action-plan that is required by the of-fense definition. Thus, the *act* is attributable to the actor as a practical reasoner, but the *offense* is not. These defenses will correspond to ordinary moral intuitions if, but only if, the offense definition reflects ordinary intuitions about the level of culpability necessary to ground liability for the act that constitutes the objective elements.

Defenses that address belief content exculpate defendants who acted in circumstances that would lead many observers to say intuitively that the defendants acted of their own free will, but they did not know what they were doing, or they did not mean to do *that*. In such cases the observer would not mean that the defendants did not mean to do the acts they performed or did not mean to do that act; rather, the observer would mean that the defendants were not aware of the circumstances and, hence, did not realize their acts would have the consequences they had. In terms of the framework presented in Chapter 4, these acts were weakly intentional; the defendants intentionally performed some acts on their act-trees, but did not anticipate that these acts would generate the acts constituting the objective elements of offenses. The actor in the play who hits his colleague with the wrong bottle exemplifies this pattern.

In summary, these two types of defenses exculpate defendants for fundamentally different reasons. The first excuses the actor who lacked the capacity to function as a competent practical reasoner at the time of the offense and, if free will is understood as psychological capacity, who did not act of his own free will. The second does not impugn the actor's status as a practical reasoner who possesses free will. Rather, it exculpates the defendant whose act did not constitute the offense in question. Although these two defenses exculpate for different reasons, they share the common feature of identifying cases that appeal to common moral intuitions regarding blameworthiness. Thus, as interpreted in this book, these provisions of the MPC are roughly consistent with common moral intuitions.

7.5 CONCLUSIONS

This book advances an interpretation of several MPC provisions that directly address the psychological states and processes of the defendant. The first chapter identifies the culpability and voluntary act requirements as the provisions establishing offense elements that directly involve these states and processes, and it argues that neither of these requirements nor the relationship between them is clear. The next two chapters review the current law regarding the NGRI and automatism defenses and contend that both reflect the lack of clarity identified in Chapter 1. That is, the courts have not developed satisfactory formulations of either defense, and this lack of an adequate practical approach reflects, at least partially, the lack of a clear foundation in the structure of offense elements.

Chapter 4 advances a conceptual framework, based in philosophical action theory, that interprets the MPC structure of offenses as intended to limit criminal liability to offenses that can be accurately attributed to the defendant as a practical reasoner. It contends that such an attribution is appropriate only when the actor's wants and beliefs produce acts by serving as reasons for acting in an intact process of practical reasoning. Such reasons provide structuring causes that explain why the actor performed that particular act. Chapter 5 and 6 argue that this framework enables one to clarify the status and rationales of the automatism and NGRI defenses as a failure-of-proof defense regarding the voluntary act requirement and as a *sui generis* specific excuse, respectively.

Finally, Chapter 7 contends that this interpretation is consistent with common moral intuitions in that it exculpates those whom many observers would intuitively say did not act of their own free will, did not know what they were doing, or did not mean to do what they did. Insofar as the MPC accurately represents the dominant themes of modern American criminal law, this analysis demonstrates that if this legal system is interpreted in the manner advanced here, it can provide a reasonable approximation of common moral intuitions regarding the conditions under which a person should be exculpated due to disruption of psychological states or processes. In addition, it suggests that the foundation of both moral and legal responsibility for criminal offenses involves a notion of a person as a competent practical reasoner who has the ability to select action-plans by using a set of cognitive capacities that constitutes the conception of free will that we need and intuitively apply for moral and legal purposes.

Index

actuation hypothesis, 10–11, 12, 13–14
actus reus, 1, 9n24
addiction, 248–9
affect, 150–1, 172; *see also* mood disorders
affective aspects of personality: in insanity defense, 32–3, 34–5
affirmative defenses, 155, 157–8n38; impaired consciousness and, 156
agent causation, 114
American Bar Association (ABA), 37, 51
American Law Institute, 1, 2
American Law Institute Model Penal Code; *see* Model Penal Code (MPC)
American Psychiatric Association (APA), 37, 51
anticipated acts, 92, 93, 94, 95, 98, 128
assault, 255n34
associations: loosening of, in schizophrenia, 185, 186
associative learning, 123–4, 142–3
associative process, 189, 190, 191, 194–5; deliberation as, 203
attribution of offense to actor as practical reasoner, 155–6, 158, 176, 190–201, 203, 210, 218, 219, 220, 261, free will and, 251–60
automatic reinforcement function, 228
automatism, 3, 22, 70; as failure-of-proof defense, 26, 72–3, 74, 75, 84; problematic cases of, 149–58; as problematic defense, 71–85, 108
automatism defense, 27, 191, 195, 216, 217, 218; action theory analysis of, 136–49; action theory applied to, 132–59; current

approaches to, 132–6; exculpates due to distortion of psychological states and processes, 219; free will and, 253–4; inadequacy of, 24–6, 131, 260; *mens rea* in, 23–4; status and rationale of, 261

basic act(s), 87, 89–90, 91, 93, 96, 98, 99, 105, 106, 107, 128–9, 131, 136, 144; in action-plans, 92; in automatism defense, 149; decision to perform, 146; epistemic criteria for, 115–16n43, 118; epistemic indicator of, 111–13; inherently intentional, 104–5, 112–13, 118
basic act-token(s), 91, 93
behavior: guided by normative institutions, 226–9; relationship with movement and action, 145n18; theory of, 120–8
belief content, 178–9, 181–2, 188, 194, 214; defenses of, 259–60; false, 199, 201, 256–7, 259
belief-desire sets: acts and, 110–11; causation by, 111–12, 113, 115–16, 119, 120, 125–6, 129
belief process, 179–81
beliefs, 91, 100, 101, 104, 105, 107, 108, 109–10, 114, 119–20, 131, 190; access to, 145, 146–7, 149, 150–1, 154, 191, 193, 195, 254, 258; causing action, 123f, 122–5, 127–8, 136–7, 138, 143, 146, 148, 151–2, 157, 191, 252–4, 261; contradictory/inconsistent, 179–80, 196, 235, 243, 244, 257; epistemically justified, 182–4; in intentional action, 119; occurrent, 143, 144; in practical reasoning, 117–18; reasoning from, 188–9, 193, 195, 216, 251, 257; in repre-

Index

free will, 26, 114n41, 261; and action theory analysis, 251–2; criteria for concept of, 222–4; impaired, 256, 258; moral and legal applications of, 243–51; and MPC defenses, 252–60; and normative institutions, 227; philosophical debate regarding, 219–26; as psychological capacity, 226–43, 246–7, 258–9, 260; as self-regulatory capacity, 239–43
Fulcher v. State, 73–4
functional analysis, 230, 232
functional impairment, 133, 155n29, 213; in epilepsy, 152–3; and insanity defense, 165, 168, 169, 170; in psychopathology, 175–6

general defense(s), 2, 3, 4, 22, 24, 130, 214; automatism as, 25, 132; insanity as, 40, 57–61; lack of voluntariness as, 156, 157, 158; *mens rea* in, 23, 24; need for, 194
generation: and causation, 88
generational relations, 88–9
Goldman, Alvin, 86, 87, 96, 104, 105, 106, 108, 109–10, 111–14, 115, 116–18, 119–20, 121, 128, 143, 145n18, 253
Goldstein, J., 53
Gross, Hyman, 100–1

hallucinations, 152, 170, 197; in insanity defense, 176, 179; in mood disorders, 205; in schizophrenia, 185
Hare, Richard, 189, 190
Harman, Gilbert, 189–90
Hart, H.L.A., 8–9, 14, 105, 108, 144, 156, 192, 239, 241
Hermann, Donald, 221

Hinckley verdict, 31, 50
homicide; *see* criminal homicide
Husak, Douglas, 62–3, 165, 167, 173
hypnosis, 4, 153–4, 155n29, 249
hypoglycemia, 80–1, 83, 155n29

icon, 198
idiosyncratic interpretations, 187, 196
ignorance, 3, 51, 57, 59–60, 98, 165, 194, 212, 214; in automatism defense, 133; exculpatory force of, 20, 25, 57–8, 59, 76–80; in insanity defense, 33–4, 37–8, 181, 201; regarding physical characteristics of consequences of act, 210–11; and voluntariness, 6, 8, 103–4; of wrongfulness, 171, 172, 211
ignorance clauses, 76–7, 78–9, 80, 166, 172; as excusing conditions, 60–1; in insanity defense, 176–7, 178
ignorance defense, 130, 148–9, 198
ignorance standards/tests, 28, 174; *M'Naghten* test as, 53–5, 56, 194n45
immaturity, 18–19, 62, 157
impaired consciousness, 133, 145, 148, 191; as affirmative defense, 156; in automatism defense, 71, 74, 195
impairment, 6, 103–4, 247
inability to appreciate criminality of act, 28, 30–1
inability to conform conduct to law, 28, 30, 36, 59–60, 64, 69–70, 164
inability to control one's conduct, 211–12; in insanity defense, 165, 166, 167, 173

269

inconsistency, 190, 193, 195, 196, 199
infancy, 19, 20–1, 22, 62, 193
inference, 115, 116–17, 119, 129; practical, 138–40, 192–3, 198, 199
information: access to, 137, 145; encoding/categorizing, 198–9
information processing model, 198, 199
information storage and retrieval, 141–2, 143, 146
informative function (reinforcement), 228
insane automatism, 75, 79, 81, 83, 133, 153n26, 155n29
insanity (NGRI) defense, 3, 22, 27–70, 134, 152, 157, 193; action theory analysis, 160–217; analysis of, 168–9, 171–4; as application of standard excusing conditions, 57–61; automatism as, 25, 72, 73–4, 132, 133; in British courts, 82–3; changes in, 31–42; classification issues in, 201–13; cognitive process distortion in, 203; exculpates due to distortion of psychological states/processes, 219; as excuse, 17, 18–19, 20–1; as failure-of-proof defense, 51–7, 66, 68–70, 166; free will and, 220–2, 252, 255, 256–8; hard cases, 199–200; lack of clarity in, 24–6, 131, 260; *mens rea* in, 23–4; mood disorders in, 204–10; and practical reasoning, 194–5; psychopathology and, 176–88, 219; restricting scope of, 32, 50–1; search for satisfactory standard in, 27–51, 68–70, 84, 164, 174–6; specific excuse/status offense, 68–70, 210–13; state-

ment of, 215; as status excuse, 61, 62–8; status of, 51–68, 261; structure of, 167–71; as *sui generis* specific excuse, 212, 218; tests in, 27–51, 201–2
intent, 1, 10, 39–40, 42; lack of, in automatism defense, 72, 73; role of, 51
intentional acts, 92–3, 94, 95, 96, 99, 104–5, 106, 109, 128–9; belief-desire in, 111–12, 115–16, 119, 125–6, 129; epistemic criteria for, 116n43, 118; generated by basic acts, 118; reasons in, 114–15, 120; weakly intentional, 104, 131, 260
intentionality: in causal theories, 111
intentions (of actor), 91, 100, 101–2
intuitive implication, 193, 195
involuntary acts/behavior, 103n24, 105, 108, 149; in hypnosis, 153, 154
irresistible impulse test, 165, 220–1
irresistible impulses, 28, 37

Jones v. State, 73
judicial process, 83
jury(ies), 36, 37, 44, 174–5, 199–200, 201
jury instructions, 214–15
justification, 57, 58, 194, 208, 219–20, 257; of consequences, 239–43; reasonable mistake regarding, 130
justification defense, 14, 16–17, 177
justificatory function, 169, 170–2, 173, 174, 175
juvenile court, 19, 21, 62
juveniles, 21; *see also* children; infancy

Kadish, Sanford, 23
Katz, J., 53

55–6, 59; volitional clause, 59–
60, 61; voluntariness in, 156;
see also culpability requirement; voluntary act
requirement
Model Penal Code (MPC) defenses: and free will, 252–60
Model Penal Code (MPC) standard, 200, 201
mood disorders, 204–10, 246
Moore, Michael, 19–22, 23, 65–6,
68, 109–20, 174, 192, 203–4,
213n59
moral accountability, 219
moral agent, 229, 245, 251; as
practical reasoner, 120
moral applications: of concept of
free will, 243–51
moral foundations, 218–61
moral intuitions, 45, 49, 218–19,
225, 226, 229, 243, 261; and
free will, 259, 260; of jury,
175
moral mistakes, 44, 46–50; avoiding, 36, 37, 38, 42, 43, 49, 50,
51, 164, 167
moral responsibility, 107, 261; free
will requisite for, 259
moral standard(s), 43, 44–50, 51
moral theory, 172, 173
morality: reason-giving explanations in, 112, 119, 127
Morse, Steven, 68–9, 174, 213n59
motivational function (reinforcement), 228
movement: behavior as cause of,
120–2; beliefs as cause of,
123f; causes of, 191; inability
to control, 166; relationship
with behavior and action,
145n18; *see also* bodily
movement
MPC: *see* Model Penal Code
(MPC)

nature of act, 176, 178; appreciation of, 40–2, 47, 49, 52, 53,
54, 58–9, 64, 76, 133
necessity (defense), 16–17
negligence, 1, 2, 7, 10, 11, 13–14,
107
negligently [culpability level], 95,
99, 100, 106; and automatism
defense, 134
nonexculpatory defenses, 14, 16,
21, 67, 211, 213
nonexculpatory exemptions from
punishment, 211
nonculpable mistakes, 177, 194
normative institutions, 239, 242,
246, 247, 251; ability to participate in, 240; consequences
and, 226–9; defined, 226–7
not guilty by reason of insanity
(NGRI); *see* insanity defense
(NGRI)

objective justification, 183
offense elements, 1–2, 4–14, 24,
27, 84, 134, 260; action theory
analysis of, 94–108; and actor
as practical reasoner, 190–1;
burden of proving, 56, 68,
155–6; conceptual structure for
analysis of, 25, 85, 86–131 (*see
also* structure of offense elements); culpability level, 52;
and excuses, 17; fulfilling,
256; implicit notions of personal responsibility in, 175;
insanity defense and, 27, 29,
40, 69, 84; psychopathology in
prevention of acting with
mens rea in, 53; relationship of
action plans to, 253, 259; role
of psychological processes
and impairment in, 7–8, 21–2,
26; satisfaction of, and defen-

Index

Proposition 8 (Calif.), 38–42
provocation, 219–20
psychological capacity(ies): complex organization of, 232–8; free will as, 226–43, 246–7, 258–9, 260
psychological dysfunction/impairment, 211–12; in criminal liability and exculpation, 24–6, 193; in criminal offenses/defenses, 21–2; exculpatory force of, 28, 31, 33–4, 54–5, 57, 60, 62, 66; and failure-of-proof claim, 40
psychological explanation, 230–2
psychological processes, 3, 4, 217, 258, 260–1; authoring actions through, 114; and defenses, 16–17, 84; disorder of, 194; exculpation due to distortion of, 219; and free will, 239–40; and mistake defense, 255–7; and moral/legal accountability, 218–19; and offense elements, 7–8; relationship between act and, 100, 105, 107; relationship with bodily movements, 6–7; role of, in criminal offenses/defenses, 21–2, 24; and voluntary act/culpability requirements, 12–13, 14, 15, 16, 24
psychological states, 3, 4, 258, 260–1; exculpation due to distortion of, 219; and moral/legal accountability, 218–19
psychopathology, 3, 152, 212–13; affective, 205–10; cognitive, 202–3; and criminal liability/practical reasoning, 190–201; culpability and voluntary act requirements in, 8, 107; and excusing clauses in insanity defense, 33–5; and free will,

258; functional impairment in, 165, 175–6; and insanity defense, 30, 33–4, 40, 171, 176–88; and practical reasoning, 188–201; in problematic defenses, 85; unrelated to crime, 67–8
psychosis, 170, 171; hallucinations in, 197; insanity defense, 176, 216
psychotic depressives, 205–7
public health model, 158
public policy considerations, 16; in automatism defense, 158; status excuses and, 66–7
punishment, 207, 208–9, 210, 219, 239; moral justification of, 221, 222–3; suspension of, 209
purpose, 102, 103, 104
purposeful action, 2, 7, 12–13, 14
purposely [culpability level], 52, 95, 96, 100–2, 106; and automatism defense, 134, 135–7

quality of act: appreciation of, 40–2, 47, 49, 53, 54–5, 58–9, 64, 76, 133; insanity defense, 176, 178

R. v. Charlson, 76
R. v. Clarke, 77
R. v. Kemp, 76, 77
R. v. Sullivan, 76, 78, 79, 81
rationality, 64–5, 222
rationalization, 110, 111, 113, 115, 125, 126, 127–8, 129, 144; practical reasoning in, 118; term, 224–5n13; wants/beliefs in, 119, 120
Rawls, John, 45
reality relatedness, 185, 187, 188, 211, 214; impaired, 196–7, 199
reality sense, 187
reality testing, 187, 196–7

274